AN INTRODUCTION TO

PROGRAMMING IN C

A BOOK ON C

AL KELLEY

IRA POHL

The Benjamin/Cummings Publishing Company, Inc.
Menlo Park, California. Reading, Massachusetts
London. Amsterdam. Don Mills, Ontario. Sydney

D0377758

Sponsoring Editor: Alan Apt
Cover Designer: Nancy Benedict
Book Designer: Marilyn Langfeld
Copy Editor: Carol Dondrea
Production Manager: Laura Argento
Composition: Graphic Typesetting Service

UNIX is a registered trademark of Bell Laboratories

Library of Congress Cataloging in Publication Data

Kelley, Al.
    An introduction to programming in C.

    Includes index.
    1. C. (Computer program language)   I. Pohl, Ira.
II. Title.
QA76.73.C15K44   1984   001.64′24   84-9357
ISBN 0–8053–6860–4

  BCDEFGHIJ-AL-8 987654

The Benjamin/Cummings Publishing Company, Inc.
2727 Sand Hill Road
Menlo Park, California 94025

The Benjamin/Cummings Series in
Structured Programming

G. Booch
Software Engineering with Ada (1983)

D. M. Etter
Structured FORTRAN 77 for Engineers and Scientists (1983)

D. M. Etter
Problem Solving with Structured FORTRAN 77 (1984)

D. M. Etter
WATFIV: Structured Program and Problem Solving (1984)

P. Linz
Programming Concepts and Problem Solving: An Introduction to Computer Science Using Pascal (1983)

W. Savitch
Pascal Programming: An Introduction to the Art and Science of Programming (1984)

R. Sebesta
Structured Assembly Language Programming for the VAX II (1984)

R. Sebesta
Structured Assembly Language Programming for the PDP-11 (1984)

M. Sobell
A Practical Guide to the UNIX System (1984)

M. Sobell
A Practical Guide to UNIX System V (1985)

TO OUR PARENTS

PREFACE

A book on C must convey an appreciation for both the elegant simplicity and the power of this general purpose programming language. By presenting interactive running programs from many application areas, this book provides an introduction to programming in the C language. C is comprehensively presented in a step by step manner including such new features as enumeration types and structure assignment. Dozens of example programs are available to illustrate each important language feature, and many tables summarize key information and provide easy access for later reference. Each chapter ends with a summary and exercises. The summary reviews key elements presented in the chapter, and the exercises augment and extend the text.

This book assumes a general purpose use of the C language and will be useful to students and professionals. For student use, it is intended as a first or second programming book. However, it can be readily used in conjunction with courses on topics such as: operating systems, software design, comparative programming languages, graphics, data structures, database systems, numerical analysis, programming methodology, and scientific applications. Applications from each of these domains are suitable to C and all features of C needed to code such applications are explained. It is appropriate for a data structures course because advanced data structuring features such as enumeration types, unions, self-referential structures, and ragged arrays are discussed. For operating systems courses concerned with UNIX, the book explores the UNIX file structure and systems routines that enable the C programmer to add to existing UNIX libraries and understand the C code underlying UNIX. For applications programming and scientific programming there is discussion of how to write sample function libraries. Statistics, root finding, sorting, text manipulation, file handling, and game playing are all represented with working code.

Complete C Language. Computer professionals will have access to a complete treatment of the language including enumeration types, list processing in C, and the C/UNIX interface. An overview of the language is presented in Chapter 1. After reading this chapter, the professional will already be able to write C code. Chapters are self-contained so that the knowledgeable reader can skip to particular sections as needed. The professional system programmer needing to use C to work within a UNIX environment is given a thorough introduction to this topic in Chapter 11.

Interactive Environment. This book is written entirely with the modern interactive environment in mind. Experimentation is encouraged throughout. Screen and terminal input/output is taken as the norm and its attendant concerns are explained. Thus the book is useful to users of small home and business computers as well as to users of large interactive systems. The assumption is that the reader will have access to an interactive system. Our reference system is UC Berkeley 4.2 UNIX and its C compiler and system, but the book can be used with any existing C system. The text describes how to test your local system for machine and system dependent properties.

Working Code. Our approach to describing the language is to use examples, explanation, and syntax. Working code is employed throughout. Small but useful examples are used to describe important technical points. Small because small is comprehensible. Useful because programming is based on a hierarchy of building blocks and ultimately is pragmatic. The programs described can be made use of in actual systems. The authors' philosophy is that one should enjoy and experiment.

Flexible Organization. This book is constructed to be very flexible in its use. In Chapter 1 a specially developed technique, program dissection, is introduced for explaining new language features. Chapter 1 is in two parts. The first part explains the crucial programming techniques needed for interactive terminal input/output, material which must be understood by all. The second part of Chapter 1 goes on to survey the entire language and will be comprehensible to experienced programmers familiar with comparable features from other languages. This second part should be postponed in a first programming course.

Chapter 2 describes the lexical level of the language and syntactic rules which are selectively employed to illustrate C language constructs. The instructor may decide to teach BNF notation as described in Chapter 2 or may omit it without any loss of continuity. The book uses BNF style syntactic descriptions so that the student can learn this standard form of programming language description. In addition, language components are thoroughly described by example and ordinary explanation.

New Features include Enumeration Types. Chapters 3 through 9 cover the language feature by feature. Many advanced topics are discussed but may be omitted on first reading without loss of comprehension. For example, enumeration types and structure assignment while available on many current systems are not universally available. Machine dependent features such as word size considerations and floating point representation are discussed. However, these details need not concern the beginner. Exercises frequently discuss how to test these considerations on a local system different from our reference system.

Recursion and List Processing. Chapter 8 has an illuminating discussion of recursion, often a mystifying topic to the beginner. Discussion of its relative merits in comparison to iteration is made. Chapter 10 describes basic list processing techniques. Knowledge of these techniques is necessary in advanced programming and data structure courses.

UNIX Connection. Chapter 11 makes the UNIX connection. It explains how to do file processing and provides the language constructs necessary to do systems programming. It discusses at length the various standard library input/output functions. These advanced topics can be used selectively according to the needs of the audience. They make the basis for an excellent second course in programming practice, or as an auxiliary text to advanced computer science courses which employ C as their implementation language.

Tables, Summaries, and Exercises. Throughout the book there are many tables and lists which succinctly summarize key ideas. These tables aid and test language comprehension. For example, C is very rich in operators and allows almost any useful combination of operator mix. It is crucial to understand the order of evaluation and association of each of these operators separately and in combination. These points are illustrated in tables throughout the text. As a reference work, the tables and code are easily looked up. The exercises test elementary features of the language and discuss advanced and system dependent features. Many exercises are problem solving oriented, others strictly test the syntactic or semantic understanding of C. Some problems include tutorial discussion that would be tangential to the text but may have special interest to different readers. The exercises offer the instructor all levels of questions, so as to allow assignments suitable to the audience.

ACKNOWLEDGMENTS

Our special thanks go to Robert Field, University of California, Santa Cruz, who acted as the chief technical reviewer for this book. We found his expertise and suggestions extremely valuable. We also would like to thank the following reviewers who provided helpful suggestions: Randolph Bentson, Colorado State University, Ft. Collins; Timothy Budd, University of Arizona, Tucson; Nick Burgoyne, University of California, Santa Cruz; Jeff Donnelly, University of Illinois, Urbana; Carole Kelley, University of California, Santa Cruz; Tilly Shaw, University of California, Santa Cruz; Matt Stallmann, University of Denver. In addition we would like to thank our sponsoring editor Alan Apt for his enthusiasm, support, and encouragement; and Laura Argento for her careful attention to the production of this book on C.

Al Kelley   Ira Pohl
University of California, Santa Cruz

CONTENTS

0. STARTING FROM ZERO ══════════ 1

  0.1 WHY C?   1
  0.2 EXERCISE   3

1. AN OVERVIEW OF C ══════════ 4

  1.1 PROGRAMMING AND
       PREPARATION   4
  1.2 PROGRAM OUTPUT   6
  1.3 VARIABLES, EXPRESSIONS, AND
       ASSIGNMENT   8
  1.4 THE USE OF #define AND
       #include   11
  1.5 THE USE OF printf() AND
       scanf()   14
  1.6 FLOW OF CONTROL   17
  1.7 THE USE OF getchar() AND
       putchar()   24
  1.8 FUNCTIONS   28
  1.9 ARRAYS, STRINGS, AND
       POINTERS   33
  1.10 FILES   44
  1.11 AN EXAMPLE: RANDOM NUMBERS AND
       A BEST POSSIBLE ALGORITHM   47
  1.12 SUMMARY   52
  1.13 EXERCISES   53

2. SYNTAX AND THE LEXICAL LEVEL ══ 56

2.1	CHARACTERS AND TOKENS	56
2.2	SYNTAX RULES	58
2.3	IDENTIFIERS	60
2.4	KEYWORDS	61
2.5	OPERATORS AND SEPARATORS	61
2.6	STRINGS	62
2.7	COMMENTS	62
2.8	CONSTANTS	63
2.9	SUMMARY	64
2.10	EXERCISES	65

3. DECLARATIONS, EXPRESSIONS, ASSIGNMENT, DATA TYPES ══ 66

3.1	DECLARATIONS	66
3.2	FUNDAMENTAL DATA TYPES	67
3.3	EXPRESSIONS, STATEMENTS, AND ASSIGNMENT	68
3.4	THE DATA TYPE int	70
3.5	ARITHMETIC OPERATORS WITH int DATA	72
3.6	INCREMENT AND DECREMENT OPERATORS WITH int DATA	75
3.7	THE INTEGRAL TYPES short, long, AND unsigned	77
3.8	THE FLOATING TYPES	78
3.9	MATHEMATICAL FUNCTIONS	82
3.10	THE DATA TYPE char	83
3.11	ASSIGNMENT OPERATORS	85
3.12	CONVERSIONS AND CASTS	86
3.13	CONSTANTS	88
3.14	HEXADECIMAL AND OCTAL CONSTANTS	89
3.15	ORDER OF EVALUATION	92
3.16	SUMMARY	93
3.17	EXERCISES	94

4. FLOW OF CONTROL ══════════════ 99

4.1 RELATIONAL, EQUALITY, AND
     LOGICAL OPERATORS   99
4.2 RELATIONAL OPERATORS AND
     EXPRESSIONS   100
4.3 EQUALITY OPERATORS AND
     EXPRESSIONS   103
4.4 LOGICAL OPERATORS AND
     EXPRESSIONS   104
4.5 THE COMPOUND STATEMENT   108
4.6 THE EMPTY STATEMENT   109
4.7 THE if AND THE if-else
     STATEMENTS   109
4.8 THE while STATEMENT   114
4.9 THE for STATEMENT   116
4.10 AN EXAMPLE: BOOLEAN
     VARIABLES   118
4.11 THE COMMA OPERATOR   119
4.12 THE do STATEMENT   120
4.13 AN EXAMPLE: FIBONACCI
     NUMBERS   122
4.14 AN EXAMPLE: PRIME NUMBERS   124
4.15 SUMMARY   125
4.16 EXERCISES   126

5. FUNCTIONS ══════════════ 136

5.1 FUNCTION DEFINITION   136
5.2 THE return STATEMENT   138
5.3 INVOCATION AND CALL BY
     VALUE   142
5.4 THE TYPE SPECIFIER void   144
5.5 AN EXAMPLE: ELEMENTARY
     STATISTICS   145
5.6 SCOPE RULES   147
5.7 PARALLEL AND NESTED
     BLOCKS   149

5.8   THE STORAGE CLASS auto   149
5.9   THE STORAGE CLASS extern   150
5.10 THE STORAGE CLASS register   152
5.11 THE STORAGE CLASS static   153
5.12 STATIC EXTERNAL VARIABLES   154
5.13 SUMMARY   155
5.14 EXERCISES   156

6. BRANCHING STATEMENTS, BITWISE
   EXPRESSIONS, AND enum ══════════════ 162

6.1   THE goto STATEMENT   162
6.2   THE break AND continue
      STATEMENTS   163
6.3   THE switch STATEMENT   165
6.4   THE CONDITIONAL OPERATOR   166
6.5   BITWISE OPERATORS AND
      EXPRESSIONS   167
6.6   MASKS   171
6.7   PACKING AND UNPACKING   172
6.8   ENUMERATION TYPES   174
6.9   AN EXAMPLE: THE GAME OF PAPER,
      ROCK, SCISSORS   177
6.10 SUMMARY   182
6.11 EXERCISES   183

7. POINTERS, ARRAYS, AND STRINGS ═══════ 188

7.1   POINTERS   188
7.2   POINTER PARAMETERS IN
      FUNCTIONS   191
7.3   ONE-DIMENSIONAL ARRAYS   193
7.4   THE RELATIONSHIP OF POINTERS TO
      ARRAYS   195
7.5   ARRAYS AS FUNCTION
      ARGUMENTS   197
7.6   AN EXAMPLE: BUBBLE SORT   198

7.7 AN EXAMPLE: MERGE AND MERGE
SORT 199
7.8 STRINGS 203
7.9 AN EXAMPLE: WORD COUNT 209
7.10 MULTI-DIMENSIONAL ARRAYS 209
7.11 ARRAYS OF POINTERS 212
7.12 ARGUMENTS TO main() 215
7.13 RAGGED ARRAYS 216
7.14 SUMMARY 218
7.15 EXERCISES 219

8. RECURSION, FUNCTIONS AS ARGUMENTS, AND THE PREPROCESSOR

8. RECURSION, FUNCTIONS AS ARGUMENTS,
AND THE PREPROCESSOR ═════ 225

8.1 RECURSION 225
8.2 AN EXAMPLE: QUICKSORT 229
8.3 AN EXAMPLE: FINDING THE Kth RANK
ORDER ELEMENT 232
8.4 FUNCTIONS AS ARGUMENTS 233
8.5 AN EXAMPLE: USING BISECTION TO
FIND THE ROOT OF A FUNCTION 235
8.6 THE PREPROCESSOR 238
8.7 AN EXAMPLE: THE USE OF
qsort() 244
8.8 SUMMARY 245
8.9 EXERCISES 246

9. STRUCTURES, UNIONS, AND typedef

9. STRUCTURES, UNIONS, AND typedef ═══ 253

9.1 THE USE OF typedef 253
9.2 STRUCTURES 255
9.3 ACCESSING A MEMBER 257
9.4 STRUCTURES AND FUNCTIONS 259
9.5 OPERATOR PRECEDENCE AND
ASSOCIATIVITY:
A FINAL LOOK 262
9.6 AN EXAMPLE: COMPLEX
ARITHMETIC 263

9.7 AN EXAMPLE: STUDENT
RECORDS   265
9.8 UNIONS   268
9.9 FIELDS   269
9.10 INITIALIZATION OF
STRUCTURES   272
9.11 AN EXAMPLE: PLAYING POKER   272
9.12 SUMMARY   275
9.13 EXERCISES   275

10. STRUCTURES AND LIST PROCESSING ══ 280

10.1 SELF-REFERENTIAL
STRUCTURES   280
10.2 LINEAR LINKED LISTS   282
10.3 LIST OPERATIONS   283
10.4 SOME LIST PROCESSING
FUNCTIONS   287
10.5 STACKS   291
10.6 AN EXAMPLE: POLISH NOTATION AND
STACK EVALUATION   293
10.7 BINARY TREES   296
10.8 GENERAL LINKED LISTS   299
10.9 SUMMARY   303
10.10 EXERCISES   304

11. INPUT/OUTPUT AND THE UNIX ENVIRONMENT ══════ 309

11.1 THE OUTPUT FUNCTION
printf ()   309
11.2 THE INPUT FUNCTION scanf ()   314
11.3 RELATED FUNCTIONS fprintf (),
sprintf (), fscanf (), AND
sscanf ()   317
11.4 FILES   317
11.5 THE MACROS IN ctype.h   323

11.6 AN EXAMPLE: CRUNCH A C
      PROGRAM   324
11.7 FILE DESCRIPTOR INPUT/
      OUTPUT   327
11.8 REDIRECTION AND PIPING IN
      UNIX   331
11.9 AN EXAMPLE: PRINTING A TABLE OF
      CONTENTS   332
11.10 THE cc COMPILER   337
11.11 THE C VERIFIER lint   340
11.12 THE C PRETTY PRINT COMMAND
      cb   341
11.13 THE make COMMAND   342
11.14 THE FUTURE OF C: SOME FINAL
      COMMENTS   343
11.15 SUMMARY   344
11.16 EXERCISES   346

APPENDIX: ASCII CHARACTER CODES   349

INDEX TO SELECTED PROGRAMS
    AND FUNCTIONS   351

INDEX   355

0
Starting from Zero

Zero is the natural starting point for C. C counts from 0. C uses 0 to mean false and not 0 to mean true. C array subscripts have 0 as a lower bound. C strings use 0 as an end-of-string sentinel. C pointers use 0 to designate a null value. This book will initiate you into these mysteries, and the pleasures of programming in C.

C is a programming language designed by Dennis Ritchie of Bell Laboratories and implemented there on a PDP-11 in 1972. It was designed to be the systems language for the UNIX[1] operating system. Ken Thompson, the developer of UNIX, used both assembler and a language named B to produce initial versions of UNIX in 1970. C was invented to overcome the limitations of B.

B was a programming language based on BCPL, a language developed by Martin Richards in 1967 as a typeless systems programming language. Its basic data type was the machine word, and it made heavy use of pointers and address arithmetic. This is contrary to the spirit of structured programming, which is characterized by the use of strongly typed languages such as the ALGOL-like languages. C evolved from B and BCPL and incorporated typing.

C is a mature general-purpose language that has developed from these roots. Its definition as of 1978 appears in the appendix, "C Reference Manual," in the book *The C Programming Language* by Brian W. Kernighan and Dennis M. Ritchie (Englewood Cliffs, NJ: Prentice-Hall, 1978). The most recent recommended language standard appears in the June 1983 Bell Laboratories' document entitled *The C Programming Language—Reference Manual* by Dennis M. Ritchie. The C language as described herein follows this recommended standard. Included are some extended features of the language such as enumeration types.

0.1 WHY C?

C is a small language. And small is beautiful in programming. C has fewer keywords than Pascal, where they are known as reserved words, yet it is arguably the more powerful language. C gets its power by carefully including the right control structures

---

[1]UNIX is a registered trademark of Bell Laboratories.

and data types, and allowing their uses to be nearly unrestricted where meaningfully used. The language is readily learned as a consequence of its functional minimality.

C is the native language of UNIX, and UNIX is the most important interactive operating system. Languages do not gain popularity on their own merits. It is the system environment that is the hidden secret of a language's success. For example, C does not need to have embedded input/output constructs or complicated interrupt handlers, but instead relies on library routines for these functions.

C is portable. C is portable by virtue of being small and by initially being defined on a small machine, a PDP-11. The semantics are frequently left as implementation dependent where a foolish consistency would require very elaborate and difficult translation. The code is readily tailored to a new host machine. A C compiler can be coded in less than 10000 lines of C code and booted over to a new system in a few person-months. Also, the system utilities and preprocessor allow the programmer to isolate possible machine dependencies outside of the main code. This makes for easy redefinition from one to another C system.

C is terse. C has a very powerful set of operators. Many of these indicate the personal taste of its designers and what was available on its original environment. The increment operator ++ has a direct analogue in PDP-11 machine language. Indirection and address arithmetic can be combined within expressions to accomplish in one statement or expression what would require many statements in another language. For some this is elegant, for others obscure. Software productivity studies show that programmers can produce, on average, a small amount of working code a day. A language that is terse explicitly magnifies the underlying productivity of its programmer.

C is modular. C supports one style of routine, the external function, which calls parameters by value. It does not allow function nesting. C does allow limited forms of privacy by using the storage class static within files. These features, along with the typical UNIX environment, readily support user-defined libraries of functions and modular programming.

C is not without criticism. It is not as strongly typed as other recent programming languages. It allows the compiler to reorder evaluation within expressions and parameter lists. It has no automatic array bounds checking. It makes multiple use of such symbols as * and =. For example, a common programming mistake is using the operator = in place of the operator ==.

Nevertheless, it is an elegant language. It places no straitjacket on the programmer's access to the machine. The imperfections it has are easier to live with than a perfected restrictiveness. C is appealing in its puzzlelike character and in its unfettered nature. A C programmer strives for functional modularity and effective minimalism. A C programmer welcomes experimentation and interaction. Indeed, experimentation and interaction are the hallmarks of this book. It is our view that C is the best commonly available interactive programming language on micros and mainframes. Language, system, and machine form a dynamic entity that is best understood by experiment. As a start, we provide a traditional first program, obscurely written to stimulate the readers' curiosity.

```
/*** a traditional first program - obscurely written ***/

main()
{
    union {
        char    what[16];
        int     cipher[4];
    } mystery, *p;

    p = &mystery;
    p -> cipher[0]  =  0x6c6c6568;
    p -> cipher[1]  =  0x77202c6f;
    p -> cipher[2]  =  0x646c726f;
    p -> cipher[3]  =  0x0000000a;
    printf("%s", p -> what);
}
```

0.2 EXERCISE

1. Run the traditional first program. Be aware that the program is system dependent. It was designed to work on a VAX, and typically, it will run correctly on any 32-bit machine that uses the ASCII character set. A total understanding of this program does not come until Chapter 9. Of course, an equivalent program can be written in a completely nonmysterious way suitable for any machine.

1
An Overview
of C

This chapter gives an overview of the C programming language. A series of programs is presented, and the elements of each program are carefully explained. Experimentation and interaction are emphasized throughout the text. An interactive programming environment allows one to experiment readily on the screen, and this accelerates the learning process immensely. In this chapter an emphasis is placed on how to make use of the basic input/output functions of C. The first hurdle in learning any language is getting information into and out of a machine.

This first chapter is designed to meet the needs of both experienced programmers and beginners. All the material in this chapter up to and including the section on functions should be read by everyone. If a reader has had experience with arrays and pointers in some other language, then he or she can read the remaining sections of this chapter to get a more complete overview of C. Others can come back to the material when they feel they are ready. Everyone should read this chapter with the sense that technical details and further explanations will come in later chapters.

1.1 PROGRAMMING AND PREPARATION

Programming is the activity of communicating algorithms to computers. An algorithm is a computational procedure whose steps are completely specified. We are used to giving instructions in English and having other people carry out these directions. The programming process is analogous, except that computers have no tolerance for ambiguity and must have all steps specified in tedious detail. Computers require that these instructions be written out in a very precise language.

The problem-solving process starts with a problem specification and concludes with a correct program.

The problem-solving process

1. Specify the problem.
2. Find an algorithm for its solution.
3. Code the algorithm in C.
4. Test the solution.

A computer is a digital electronic machine capable of storing information and acting on instructions. Functionally, the machine has three main components: memory, processor, and input/output peripherals. The high-speed memory is capable of storing information and instructions. The processor is capable of interpreting instructions taken from memory. Input/output devices take information from agents external to the machine and provide information to those agents. Input devices are typically terminal keyboards, disk drives, and tape drives. Output devices are typically terminal screens, printers, disk drives, and tape drives.

Resident on the machine is a collection of special programs called the *operating system*, which we will assume throughout this text is UNIX. An operating system is much like a traffic cop, directing the flow of routines and processes. Among the many software packages of UNIX are the C compiler and various text editors. The principal text editor on our system is called *vi*. We assume that the reader is able to make use of some text editor to create files containing C code. These are called source files, and they are compiled on our system with the *cc* command, which invokes the C compiler. Because the *cc* command invokes the compiler, the name of the command is also the name of the compiler. Thus "C compiler" and "*cc* compiler" are used interchangeably. Roughly speaking, a compiler translates source code to object code, which is executable. On our system this compiled code is automatically created in the file *a.out*.

STEPS TO BE FOLLOWED IN WRITING AND RUNNING A C PROGRAM

1. Create a text file with its name ending in *.c* and type a C program into it; for example

   vi example.c

   vi is the name of a UNIX text editor; a knowledge of editor commands to insert and modify text is necessary to make use of an editor.

2. Compile the program using the *cc* compiler; for example

   cc example.c

   If there are no errors in the code, this automatically creates the executable file *a.out* and the program is ready to be executed; if there are errors, then the process must start again at step 1. Errors that occur at this stage are called syntax errors or compile-time errors. A program called *lint* can be used to find syntax errors and to make other checks:

   lint example.c

3. Execute the program. This is done with the command

   a.out

   If the program compiled successfully, it will start to execute. Typically, if the program has no run-time errors, it will complete execution and a system prompt will reappear on the screen; if for some reason the program needs to be changed, the process must start again at step 1.

Different kinds of errors can occur in a program. Syntax errors are caught by the compiler; other errors manifest themselves only when the program is executed. The second kind of error is called a *run-time* error. As an example of this, if an attempt to divide by zero is encoded into a program, it will exhibit a run-time error. In the exercises at the end of this chapter specific examples are given of both compile-time and run-time errors.

1.2 PROGRAM OUTPUT

Programs must communicate to be useful. Our first example is a program that prints on the screen the phrase "from sea to shining C." The complete program is

```
main()
{
    printf("from sea to shining C\n");
}
```

Using a text editor, this is typed into a file ending in *.c*. The choice of a file name should be mnemonic. Let us suppose the program has been written in the file *sea.c*. The command

    cc sea.c

invokes the *cc* compiler. If there are no errors in the code, it creates the executable file *a.out*. Now the command

    a.out

executes the program and prints on the screen

    from sea to shining C

The default name for the compiled target code is *a.out*. If you now compile another program, it will overwrite the file *a.out* and create new executable code. Therefore, if you wish to save the executable code in *a.out* you must move (rename) the file. Typically, if the source code is in a file such as *sea.c*, then the corresponding executable code in *a.out* is moved to *sea*. The command that does this is

    mv a.out sea

Many UNIX commands have options, and these are usually flagged with a minus sign. The *cc* command has many options, one of which is −*o*. The effect of this option is to redirect the output of the compiler to the file immediately following the −*o*. Thus

    cc −o sea sea.c

will compile *sea.c* and put the executable code directly into *sea*. Now the command

    sea

prints on the screen

```
from sea to shining C
```

DISSECTION OF THE *sea* PROGRAM

`main()`

>   Every program has a function named `main` where execution begins; the paren-
>   theses following `main` indicate to the compiler that it is a function.

`{`

>   Braces surround the body of a function; braces are also used to group statements
>   together.

`printf()`

>   The C system contains a standard library with functions that can be used in
>   programs; this is a function from the standard library that prints on the screen.

`"from sea to shining C\n"`

>   A string constant in C is a series of characters surrounded by double quotes.
>   This string is an argument to the function `printf()` and it controls what is to
>   be printed. The two characters `\n` at the end of the string (read "backslash n")
>   represent a single character called *newline*; it is a nonprinting character, and its
>   effect is to advance the cursor on the screen to a new line.

`}`

>   This right brace matches the left brace above and ends the function `main()`.

The function `printf()` acts to print continuously across the screen. It moves to a new
line when a newline character is read. The screen is a two-dimensional display that
prints from left to right and top to bottom. To be readable, output must appear properly
spaced on the screen.

We can rewrite our first program as follows.

```
main()
{
    printf("from sea ");
    printf("to shining ");
    printf("C");
    printf("\n");
}
```

While it is different from the first version, it will produce the same output. Each time
`printf()` is called, printing starts at the position where the previous call to `printf()`
left off. We can use newline characters to print our phrase on three lines.

```
main()
{
    printf("from sea\n");
    printf("to shining\n");
    printf("C\n");
}
```

When executed, this program will print

```
from sea
to shining
C
```

Let us write one further variation on this program, one that will box the phrase in a rectangle of asterisks. It will show how each character, including blanks and newline characters, is significant, and when it is run it will give some sense of the screen proportions.

```
main()
{
    printf("\n\n");
    printf("        *********************\n");
    printf("        *   from sea        *\n");
    printf("        *   to shining      *\n");
    printf("        *   C               *\n");
    printf("        *********************\n");
    printf("\n\n");
}
```

1.3 VARIABLES, EXPRESSIONS, AND ASSIGNMENT

We will write a program to convert the distance of a marathon in miles and yards to kilometers. In English units a marathon is defined to be 26 miles and 385 yards. These numbers are integers. To convert miles to kilometers, we multiply by the conversion factor 1.609, a real number. Machines represent integers differently from reals. To convert yards to miles, we divide by 1760.0, and as we shall see, it is essential to represent this number as a real, rather than as an integer.

Our conversion program will use variables capable of storing integer values and real values. In C all variables must be declared, or named, at the beginning of the program. A variable name, also called an identifier, consists of a sequence of letters, digits, and underbars, but may not start with a digit. Identifiers should be chosen to reflect their use in the program. In this way they serve as documentation, making the program more readable.

```
/*** the distance of a marathon in kilometers ***/

main()
{
        int     miles, yards;
        float   kilometers;

        miles = 26;
        yards = 385;
        kilometers = 1.609 * (miles + yards / 1760.0);
        printf("\na marathon is  %f  kilometers\n\n", kilometers);
}
```

The output of the program is

```
a marathon is  42.185970  kilometers
```

DISSECTION OF THE *marathon* PROGRAM

```
/*** the distance of a marathon in kilometers ***/
```

Anything written between the characters /* and */ is a comment and is ignored by the compiler. All programs in this book that start with a comment of this style are listed in an appendix.

```
int     miles, yards;
```

This is a declaration. int is a keyword and is one of the fundamental types of the language; it informs the compiler that the variables following it are of type int and are to take on integer values. Thus, the variables miles and yards in this program are of type int.

```
float   kilometers;
```

This is a declaration. float is a keyword and is one of the fundamental types of the language; it informs the compiler that the variables following it are of type float and are to take on real values. Thus, the variable kilometers in this program is of type float. Variables of type double are also used to store real values; a variable of type double typically can represent a number with more decimal points (precision) than one of type float.

```
miles = 26;
yards = 385;
```

These are assignment statements. Statements in C end with a semicolon. The equal sign is an assignment operator. The two numbers 26 and 385 are integer constants in the program. The value 26 is assigned to the variable miles, and the value 385 is assigned to the variable yards.

```
kilometers = 1.609 * (miles + yards / 1760.0);
```

This is an assignment statement. The value of the expression on the right side of the equal sign is assigned to the variable `kilometers`. The operators `*`, `+`, and `/` stand for multiplication, addition, and division, respectively. Operations inside parentheses are performed first. Since division has higher precedence than addition (see Chapter 3), the value of the subexpression

```
yards / 1760.0
```

is calculated first; that value is added to the value of the variable `miles` to produce a value that is then multiplied by `1.609`. This final value is assigned to the variable `kilometers`.

```
printf("\na marathon is   %f  kilometers\n\n", kilometers);
```

This is a statement that invokes, or calls, the `printf()` function. The function `printf()` can have a variable number of arguments. The first argument is always a string, called the control string. The control string in this example is

```
"\na marathon is   %f  kilometers\n\n"
```

It is the first argument to the function `printf()`. Inside this string is the conversion specification, or format, `%f`. The formats in a control string, if any, are matched with the remaining arguments in the `printf()` function. In this case, `%f` is matched with the argument `kilometers`; this tells the machine that the value of the variable `kilometers` is to be printed as a floating point number and inserted into the print stream at the place where the format `%f` occurs.

Certain identifiers, called keywords, are reserved and cannot be used by the programmer as names of variables. For example, `int`, `float`, and `double` are keywords. A table of keywords is given in Chapter 2. Other names are known to the C system and normally would not be redefined by the programmer. The name `printf` is an example. Since `printf` is the name of a function in the standard library, it usually is not used as the name of a variable.

A decimal point in a number indicates that it is a floating point constant, rather than an integer constant. Thus the numbers `37` and `37.0` would be treated differently in a program. Although there are two floating types, `float` and `double`, and variables can be declared to be of either type, floating constants are automatically of type `double`.

Expressions typically are found on the right side of assignment operators and as arguments to functions. The simplest expressions are just constants such as `385`, `26`, `1.609`, and `1760.0`, all used in the previous program. Just the name of a variable can be considered an expression, and meaningful combinations of operators such as `+` and `*` with variables and constants are also expressions. The evaluation of expressions can involve conversion rules. This is an important point. The division of two integers results in an integer value, and any remainder is discarded. Thus, `7/3` has the `int` value 2. But the expression `7.0/3` is a `double` divided by an `int`, and when the

expression is evaluated, 3 is converted to a double and 7.0/3 has the value 2.333 . . . .
Suppose the statement in the previous program

```
kilometers = 1.609 * (miles + yards / 1760.0);
```

is changed to

```
kilometers = 1.609 * (miles + yards / 1760);
```

Since the variable yards is of type int and has value 385, the expression

```
yards / 1760
```

has the int value 0. Since this is not what is wanted, the constant 1760.0 was used instead.

1.4 THE USE OF #define AND #include

The *cc* compiler has built into it a preprocessor. If the lines

```
#define    LIMIT    100
#define    PI       3.14159
```

occur in a file that is being compiled, the preprocessor first changes all occurrences of the identifier LIMIT to 100 and all occurrences of the identifier PI to 3.14159, except in quoted strings. A #define line can occur anywhere in a program, but it must start in column 1. It has an effect only on lines in the file that follow it. Normally, all #define lines are placed at the beginning of the file. By convention, all identifiers that are to be changed by the preprocessor are written in capital letters. The contents of quoted strings are never changed by the preprocessor. For example, in the statement

```
printf("\nPI = %f", PI);
```

only the second PI will be changed by the above #define commands to the preprocessor. The use of symbolic constants in a program makes it more readable. More importantly, if a constant has been defined symbolically by means of the #define facility and used throughout a program, it is easy to change the constant later, if necessary. For example, in physics the letter *c* is often used to designate the speed of light, which is approximately 299792.4562 km/sec. If we write

```
#define   C   299792.4562
```

and then use C throughout thousands of lines of code to symbolically represent the constant 299792.4562, it will be easy to change the code when a new physical experiment produces a better value for the speed of light. All the code is updated by simply changing the constant in the #define line.

The following program illustrates the use of the #define facility.

```
/*** measuring the pacific sea ***/

#define   AREA                         179680425
#define   SQ_MILES_PER_SQ_KILOMETER    0.3861021585424458
#define   SQ_FEET_PER_SQ_MILE          (5280 * 5280)
#define   SQ_INCHES_PER_SQ_FOOT        144
#define   ACRES_PER_SQ_MILE            640

main()
{
    int       pacific_sea = AREA;      /*  in sq kilometers  */
    double    acres, sq_miles, sq_feet, sq_inches;

    printf("\nthe pacific sea covers an area");
    printf(" of  %d  square kilometers", pacific_sea);
    sq_miles = SQ_MILES_PER_SQ_KILOMETER * pacific_sea;
    sq_feet = SQ_FEET_PER_SQ_MILE * sq_miles;
    sq_inches = SQ_INCHES_PER_SQ_FOOT * sq_feet;
    acres = ACRES_PER_SQ_MILE * sq_miles;
    printf("\n\nin other units of measure this is:\n");
    printf("\n%22.7e  acres", acres);
    printf("\n%22.7e  square miles", sq_miles);
    printf("\n%22.7e  square feet", sq_feet);
    printf("\n%22.7e  square inches\n\n", sq_inches);
}
```

This program makes conversions to various units of measure and prints the results. The output of this program is

```
the pacific sea covers an area of 179680425 square kilometers

in other units of measure this is:

        4.4400000e+10  acres
        6.9375000e+07  square miles
        1.9340640e+15  square feet
        2.7850522e+17  square inches
```

The new programming ideas are described in the following dissection.

DISSECTION OF THE *pacific_sea* PROGRAM

```
#define   AREA                         179680425
```

The #define beginning in column 1 is a command to the preprocessor. The preprocessor will replace all occurrences of the identifier AREA by 179680425 in the rest of this file. It is a convention to use capital letters for identifiers that will be changed by the preprocessor; if at some future time a new map is made and a new figure for the area of the Pacific is computed, only this line need be changed to update the program.

```
#define     SQ_MILES_PER_SQ_KILOMETER     0.3861021585424458
```

The floating constant 0.3861021585424458 is a conversion factor. The use of a symbolic name for the constant makes the program more readable.

```
#define     SQ_FEET_PER_SQ_MILE          (5280 * 5280)
```

The preprocessor changes occurrences of the first sequence of characters into the second. If a reader of this program knows that there are 5280 feet in a mile, then that reader will quickly recognize that this line of code is correct; instead of (5280 * 5280) we could have written 27878400. Notice that although the parentheses are not necessary, they do no harm either; symbolic expressions sometimes need parentheses for technical reasons (see Chapter 8).

```
int       pacific_sea = AREA;     /*  in sq kilometers  */
```

When the code is compiled, the preprocessor first changes AREA to 179680425; the compiler then interprets this line as a declaration of the identifier pacific_sea as a variable of type int and initializes it to have the value 179680425. Sometimes there are advantages to initializing a variable, but here we could just as well have written

```
int       pacific_sea;
double    acres, sq_miles, sq_feet, sq_inches;

pacific_sea = AREA;
```

The initialization has been replaced by an assignment statement.

```
double    acres, sq_miles, sq_feet, sq_inches;
```

The variables acres, etc. are defined to be of type double. float and double are the two floating types; they are both used to store real values. Typically a float will store 6 significant digits and a double will store 16 significant digits. Since the program prints out 8-digit numbers, the variables are declared to be of type double rather than float.

```
printf("\n%22.7e  acres", acres);
```

This statement causes the line

```
4.4400000e+10   acres
```

to be printed; this number is written in scientific notation and is interpreted to mean 4.44×10^{10}. Numbers written this way are also said to be written in an e-format. The conversion specification %e causes the system to print a floating expression in an e-format with default spacing; a format of the form %M.Ne where M and N are positive integers causes the system to print a floating expression in an e-format in *M* spaces total with *N* digits to the right of the decimal point (see Chapter 11).

In a program, a line such as

```
#include "my_file"
```

is also a command to the preprocessor. A #include line can occur anywhere in a file, but it must start in column 1. The quotes surrounding the name of the file are necessary. The effect of the line is to include in the code at that point a copy of the contents of the file *my_file*. Typically the #include lines are written at the beginning of a program. An included file can contain #define lines and other #include lines. Such a file is often considered a "header" file, and by convention such files end in *.h*.

To illustrate how the #include facility works, suppose we create a file called *pacific.h* and put the following lines in it.

```
#define  AREA                      179680425
#define  SQ_MILES_PER_SQ_KILOMETER  0.386021585424458
#define  SQ_FEET_PER_SQ_MILE        (5280 * 5280)
#define  SQ_INCHES_PER_SQ_FOOT      144
#define  ACRES_PER_SQ_MILE          640
```

We can now rewrite the *pacific_sea* program as follows:

```
#include  "pacific.h"

main()
{
      .   .   .   .   .
```

1.5 THE USE OF printf() AND scanf()

The function printf() is used for output. Similarly, the function scanf() is used for input. Technically, these functions are not part of the C language, but rather are part of the C system. They exist in a standard library and are available for use wherever a C system resides. The f in printf() and scanf() stands for "formatted." Both functions have a parameter list consisting of two parts:

control_string   and   *argument_list*

where *control_string* is a string and may contain conversion specifications, or formats. A conversion specification begins with a % character and ends with a conversion character. For example, in the format %d the letter d is the conversion character. As we have already seen, this format is used to print the value of an expression as a decimal integer. To print the letters ABC on the screen, we could use the statement

```
printf("ABC");
```

Another way to do this is with the statement

```
printf("%s","ABC");
```

The format %s causes the argument "ABC" to be printed in the format of a string. Yet another way to do this is with the statement

```
printf("%c%c%c",'A','B','C');
```

Single quotes are used to designate character constants. Thus 'A' is the character constant corresponding to the capital letter A. The format %c prints the value of an expression as a character. Notice that a constant by itself is considered an expression. In addition to character constants, the C language provides variables of data type char, which can be used to manipulate character values. For example, the declaration

```
char    c1,c2,c3;
```

tells the compiler that the variables c1, c2, and c3 are of type char, and the code

```
c1 = 'A';
c2 = 'B';
c3 = 'C';
printf("%c%c%c", c1, c2, c3);
```

will once again print the letters ABC on the screen. Notice that a variable name by itself is considered an expression.

printf ()	
Conversion character	*How the corresponding argument is printed*
c	as a character
d	as a decimal integer
e	as a floating point number in scientific notation
f	as a floating point number
g	in the e-format or f-format, whichever is shorter
s	as a string

When an argument is printed, the place where it is printed is called its *field* and the number of characters in its field is called its *field width*. The field width can be specified in a format as an integer occurring between the % and the conversion character. Thus the statement

```
printf("\n%3c%5c%7c",'A','B','C');
```

will print

```
    A    B      C
```

The function scanf() is analogous to the function printf(), but is used for input rather than output. Its first argument is a control string with formats corresponding to the various ways the characters in the input stream can be interpreted as values for the different variable types. The argument list is made up of *addresses* of variables. The symbol & represents the address operator. For example, the statement

```
scanf("%d", &x);
```

contains the format %d, which causes scanf() to interpret the input characters as a decimal integer and to put the value at the address of x. When the keyboard is used to input values into a program, a sequence of characters is typed, and a sequence of characters is received by the program. This sequence is called the "input stream." If 1337 is typed, the person typing it may think of it as a decimal integer, but the program receives it as a sequence of characters. The scanf() function can be used to convert strings of decimal digits into integer values and to store them in the appropriate place.

scanf()	
Conversion character	*What characters in the input stream are converted to*
c	to a character
d	to a decimal integer
f	to a floating point number (float)
lf	to a floating point number (double)
s	to a string

The details concerning printf() and scanf() are found in Chapter 11. Here we want to present only enough information to get data into and out of the machine in a minimally acceptable way. The following program reads in three characters and some numbers, and then prints them out.

```
main()
{
        char    c1, c2, c3;
        int     k;
        float   x;
        double  y;

        printf("\n%s\n%s\n%s\n%s",
                "input the following:   three characters,",
                "                        an int,",
                "                        a float,",
                "                        and a double:   ");
        scanf("%c%c%c%d%f%lf", &c1, &c2, &c3, &k, &x, &y);
        printf("\nhere is the data that you typed in:\n");
        printf("%3c%3c%3c%5d%17e%17e\n\n", c1, c2, c3, k, x, y);
}
```

If we compile the program and run it and type in ABC   3   55   77.1, then this is what appears on the screen.

```
input the following:  three characters,
                       an int,
                       a float,
                       and a double:  ABC  3   55   77.1
here is the data that you typed in:
   A  B  C    3     5.500000e+01     7.710000e+01
```

When reading in numbers, scanf() will skip white space (blanks, newlines, and tabs), but when reading in a character, it will not. Thus, the program will not run correctly with the input AB C   3   55   77.1. The third character read in is a blank, which is a perfectly good character; scanf() then attempts to read C as a decimal integer, which causes difficulties.

One of the differences between printf() and scanf() involves the format %f. With printf(), this format can be used to print the value of an argument of either type float or type double. In contrast, when scanf() is used to read in a number and to place it at the address of a variable, the format %f is used if the variable is of type float and the format %lf is used if the variable is of type double. The letter l in this context stands for "long," and "long float" can be considered a synonym for double.

Another difference between the two functions is that printf() does not return a value, but scanf() does. It returns the number of successful conversions accomplished as an int. Although in the last program no use was made of the value returned by scanf(), in the next section we will see how the returned value is typically used.

1.6 FLOW OF CONTROL

Statements in a program are normally executed one at a time in sequence. When a machine is executing a particular statement, we think of that statement at that moment as being under machine "control." Most programs require alteration of the normal sequential flow of control. The while and for statements provide looping mechanisms, and the if and if-else statements take action based typically on the evaluation of a logical expression.

The following program illustrates the use of a while statement.

```
main()
{
    int   i = 1, sum = 0;

    while (i <= 5) {
        sum += i;
        ++i;
    }
    printf("\nsum  =   %d\n\n", sum);
}
```

First i is initialized to 1 and sum is initialized to 0. The code

```
while (i <= 5) {
    sum += i;
    ++i;
}
```

is a while statement, or while loop. The symbols <= represent the operator "less than or equal to." A test is made to see if i is less than or equal to 5. If it is, the group of statements enclosed by the braces { and } is executed and then control passes back to the beginning of the while loop and the process starts over again. The while loop is executed repeatedly until the test fails, that is, until i is not less than or equal to 5. At that point control passes to the statement immediately following the while statement, in this case the printf() statement. The statement

```
sum += i;
```

increments the stored value of sum by the value of i. An equivalent statement is

```
sum = sum + i;
```

The variable sum is assigned the old value of sum plus the value of i. The symbols ++ represent the increment operator. The statement

```
++i;
```

increments the stored value of i by 1. A hand simulation of the program shows that the while loop is executed five times, with i taking on the values 1, 2, 3, 4, 5, successively. When control passes beyond the while statement, the value of i is 6, and the value of sum is

$$1 + 2 + 3 + 4 + 5$$

or 15, and that is the integer printed by the printf() statement.

A group of statements surrounded by braces constitutes a *compound statement*. Syntactically, a compound statement is itself a statement; a compound statement can be used anywhere that a statement can be used. A while statement is of the form

```
while (expression)
    statement
```

where *statement* is either a simple statement or a compound statement. In C any nonzero value is considered to represent *true* and the value zero is considered to represent *false*. When the while statement is executed, *expression* is evaluated. If it is nonzero (*true*), then *statement* is executed and control passes back to the beginning of the while loop. This process continues until *expression* has value zero (*false*). At this point, control passes on to the next statement. A logical expression such as i <= 5 has int value 1 (*true*) if i is less than or equal to 5, and has int value 0 (*false*) otherwise.

Another looping construct is the for statement. It has the form

```
for (expression1; expression2; expression3)
    statement
```

If all three expressions are present, then this is equivalent to

```
expression1;
while (expression2) {
        statement
        expression3;
}
```

Typically *expression1* performs an initial assignment, *expression2* performs a test, and *expression3* increments a stored value. Note that *expression3* is the last thing done in the body of the loop. The for loop is repeatedly executed as long as *expression2* is nonzero (*true*). As an example, let us rewrite the last program to make use of a for loop instead of a while loop.

```
main()
{
        int    i, sum = 0;

        for (i = 1; i <= 5; ++i)
            sum += i;
        printf("\nsum   =   %d\n\n", sum);
}
```

We use a for loop in the next program to compute the sum of floating numbers. Moreover, we print out the count, the item, and the running total as the program proceeds.

```
/*** computing sums ***/

main()
{
        int       i;
        double    x, sum = 0.0;

        printf("\n%12s%12s%15s\n", "count", "item", "running sum");
        for (i = 1; scanf("%lf", &x) == 1; ++i)
            printf("\n%12d%12.1f%15.3f", i, x, sum += x);
        printf("\n\n");
}
```

Suppose that this program is compiled and the executable code is put into the file *sum*. If we then create a file called *data* with the following numbers in it

```
2.2   -30.673   77.11111   -1.09   1.1335577e+2
```

and then give the UNIX command

sum < data

the following is what appears on the screen:

count	item	running sum
1	2.2	2.200
2	-30.7	-28.473
3	77.1	48.638
4	-1.1	47.548
5	113.4	160.904

DISSECTION OF THE *sum* PROGRAM

```
printf("\n%12s%12s%15s\n", "count", "item", "running sum");
```

This statement prints headings; the field widths in the formats are chosen to put headings over columns.

```
for (i = 1; scanf("%lf", &x) == 1; ++i)
    printf("\n%12d%12.1f%15.3f", i, x, sum += x);
```

The body of this for loop is executed as long as the expression

```
scanf("%lf", &x) == 1
```

is nonzero (*true*). The function scanf() returns an int value, which is the number of successful conversions accomplished; as long as it is able to read in a number, convert it to a double, and place it at the address of x, the value 1 will be returned. The symbols == represent the equals operator. If the value returned by scanf() equals 1, then the expression is nonzero (*true*), otherwise it is zero (*false*). When an end-of-file mark is read, then typically scanf() returns the value −1. Thus, the loop terminates when the end-of-file mark is read or an attempt is made to read something other than a number. The field widths in the printf() statement correspond to the field widths in the previous printf() statement.

```
sum += x;
```

The value of sum is incremented by the value of x and the value of the expression as a whole is the new value of sum. Thus, a running total is accumulated in the variable sum; this assignment statement is equivalent to

```
sum = sum + x;
```

Here we think of the new value of sum being assigned the old value of sum plus the value of x. A construct of the form

variable op= expression

where *op* is an operator such as +, −, *, / is equivalent to

variable = variable op (expression)

The symbol $<$ in the UNIX command

  sum $<$ data

causes the input to be taken from the file *data* rather than from the keyboard. The program will read numbers from the file until a character other than a white space character or a decimal digit is encountered or until the end-of-file mark is reached. The symbolic name EOF is typically used in C programs to designate a value associated with an end-of-file mark. Typically, an EOF value can be entered at the keyboard by typing a control-d immediately following a carriage return. However, this is system dependent and you may need to type something different to effect an EOF.

The if statement and if-else statement are two constructs commonly used to affect flow of control. An if statement is of the form

  if (*expression*)
    statement

If *expression* is nonzero (*true*), then *statement* is executed; otherwise it is skipped. Consider as an example the code

```
b = 1;
if (a == 3)
     b = 5;
printf("%d", b);
```

A test is made to see if the value of a is 3. If it is, then b is assigned the value 5 and control passes to the printf() statement. Since the value of b is 5, this value is printed. If, however, the value of a is not 3, then the statement

```
b = 5;
```

is skipped and control passes directly to the printf() statement. Since the value of b is 1, that is what is printed. A compound statement can be used in place of a simple statement to control several actions.

```
if (a ==  3) {
     b = 5;
     c = 7;
}
```

Here, if a has value 3, then two assignment statements are executed; if a does not have value 3, then the two statements are skipped.

An if-else statement is of the form

  if (*expression*)
    statement1
  else
    statement2

It is important to recognize that the whole construct, even though it contains statements, is itself a single statement. Suppose it is followed by *next_statement*.

```
if (expression)
     statement1
else
     statement2
next_statement
```

If *expression* is nonzero (*true*), then *statement1* is executed, *statement2* is skipped, and control passes to *next_statement*. If *expression* is zero (*false*), then *statement1* is skipped, *statement2* is executed, and control passes to *next_statement*. For example, the code

```
if (i == 11) {
     a = 3;
     b = 5;
     c = 7;
}
else {
     a = 11;
     b = -5;
     c = -7;
}
printf("%d", a + b + c);
```

will cause 15 to be printed if i has value 11, and will cause −1 to be printed otherwise.

The following program makes use of if statements to find the minimum and maximum values in a file of integers.

```
main()
{
     int   min, max, x;

     scanf("%d", &x);
     min = max = x;
     while (scanf("%d", &x) == 1) {
          if (min > x)
               min = x;
          if (max < x)
               max = x;
     }
     printf("\nthe minimum value is   %d\n", min);
     printf("\nthe maximum value is   %d\n", max);
}
```

Every time a new value of x is obtained from the input stream, a test is made to see if the current value of min is greater than x. If it is, then min is reset to this value. A similar action is taken with respect to the variable max. The code that does this is in the body of the while loop. Since the value of min is always less than or equal to the value of max, a slight improvement in the code can be made by rewriting the code as

```
while (scanf ("%d" , &x)  == 1)
     if (min > x)
          min = x;
     else if (max < x)
          max = x;
```

The compound statement consisting of two if statements has been changed to a single
if-else statement, where the statement part of the else part is another if statement.
Since a single statement is under control of the while loop, braces are no longer
needed. When the expression min > x is true, the expression max < x has to be false,
and there is no need to test for the condition. The next program incorporates this
change and also handles the case of no input in a more robust fashion. It is designed
to process a file of real numbers, and it prints running data as the program proceeds.

```
/*** compute minimum, maximum, sum, and average ***/

main()
{
     int      i;
     double   x, min, max, sum, avg;

     if (scanf ("%lf", &x) != 1)
          printf ("\nno data entered\n\n");
     else{
          printf ("\nrunning data: \n%5s%12s%12s%12s%12s%12s\n",
                  "count", "item",
                  "minimum", "maximum", "sum", "average");
          min = max = sum = avg = x;
          printf ("\n%5d%12.1f%12.1f%12.1f%12.3f%12.3f",
                  1, x, min, max, sum, avg);
          for (i = 2; scanf ("%lf", &x) == 1; ++i) {
               if (min > x)
                    min = x;
               else if (max < x)
                    max = x;
               sum += x;
               avg = sum / i;
               printf ("\n%5d%12.1f%12.1f%12.1f%12.3f%12.3f",
                       i, x, min, max, sum, avg);
          }
          printf ("\n\n");
     }
}
```

Suppose that we compile this program and put the executable code in the file *minmax*
and put the numbers

```
2   3   1   -44.4   0.0111e1
```

into the file *data*. If we then give the UNIX command

minmax < data

the following appears on the screen:

```
running data:
count          item      minimum     maximum        sum      average

 1            2.0         2.0         2.0        2.000       2.000
 2            3.0         2.0         3.0        5.000       2.500
 3            1.0         1.0         3.0        6.000       2.000
 4          -44.4       -44.4         3.0      -38.400      -9.600
 5            0.1       -44.4         3.0      -38.289      -7.658
```

1.7 THE USE OF `getchar()` AND `putchar()`

The system provides `getchar()` and `putchar()` to deal with the input and output of characters. In the next program `getchar()` gets a character from the input stream and assigns it to the variable c. Then `putchar()` is used to print the character twice on the screen.

```
main()
{
    char    c;

    while (1) {
        c = getchar();
        putchar(c);
        putchar(c);
    }
}
```

The variable c is declared to be of type `char`, one of the fundamental types of C. Variables of this type can take on character values. Because 1 is nonzero, as an expression it is always *true*. Thus the construct

```
while (1) {
    .  .   .    .    .
}
```

is an infinite loop. The only way to stop this program is with an interrupt, which typically is effected by typing a control-c.

What you see on your screen when the above program is executed depends on how your operating system is configured. Typically, when a character is typed on the keyboard, that character is echoed on the screen, but the operating system waits until a line of characters ending with a carriage return is typed before it processes the input. When a carriage return is typed, all the characters on the line are passed to the machine at once. If we run the program and the type

abc *<CR>*

where <CR> represents a carriage return, the program will print on the screen on a new line

        aabbcc

This line is being printed by the program. The carriage return caused a newline character to be passed to the machine, so two newline characters are printed as well. Some operating systems process a character as soon as it is typed on the keyboard. The UNIX operating system usually processes a line at a time, but it can be set differently. The UNIX command

    stty cbreak

will cause the system to process each character as soon as it is typed. Suppose this is done and the program is executed again. Now if the letter a is typed, the letters

        aaa

appear on the screen. The first a is the echo of the character that was typed, the next two are printed by the program. If abc is typed, then

        aaabbbccc

appears on the screen. The UNIX command

    stty −cbreak

will reset the operating system so that it processes a line at a time.
    A more robust way to write the above program is as follows:

```
#include   <stdio.h>

main()
{
    int   c;

    while ((c = getchar()) != EOF) {
        putchar(c);
        putchar(c);
    }
}
```

The first line of the program is a command to the preprocessor to include the header file <stdio.h>. The angle brackets around stdio.h tell the system to look for the file in the "usual place." The location of this place is system dependent. On our system, an equivalent command would have been

```
#include   "/usr/include/stdio.h"
```

Other systems may have the file in some other place. In any case the file *stdio.h* is a standard header file supplied with the C system, and the file is typically included in programs that make use of certain standard input/output constructs. One line of this header file is

```
#define   EOF   (−1)
```

The identifier EOF is mnemonic for "end-of-file." What is actually used as an end-of-file mark is system dependent. Although the int value −1 is often used, different systems can have different values. By including the file *stdio.h* and using to the symbolic constant EOF, we have made the program portable. This means that the source file can be moved to a different system and run with no changes. Portable code is often desired.

Notice that the variable c has been declared in the program as an int rather than a char. Whatever is used to mark the end of a file, it cannot be a value that represents a character. Since c is an int, it can hold all possible character values as well as the special value EOF. It is valid to think of a char as a very short integer type, and int as a more general integer type that is capable of representing all possible values of a char and more.

The expression

```
(c = getchar()) != EOF
```

is composed of two parts. The subexpression

```
c = getchar()
```

gets a value from the keyboard and assigns it to the variable c and the value of the subexpression takes on that value as well. The symbols != represent the "not equal" operator. As long as the value of the subexpression c = getchar() is not equal to EOF, the body of the while loop is executed. Typically, an EOF value can be entered at the keyboard by typing a control-d immediately following a carriage return. This is system dependent. The parentheses around the subexpression c = getchar() are necessary. Suppose that we had typed

```
c = getchar() != EOF
```

Because of operator precedence (see Chapters 3 and 4), this is equivalent to

```
c = (getchar() != EOF)
```

which is semantically correct, but not what we want.

Constants of type char are written 'a', 'b', 'c', etc. A program that prints the line

```
she sells sea shells by the seashore
```

on the screen can be written as follows:

```
main()
{
    putchar('s');
    putchar('h');
    putchar('e');
    putchar(' ');
         .    .    .    .
    putchar('e');
    putchar('\n');
}
```

This is a tedious way to accomplish the task; the use of a printf () statement would be much easier. Notice that '\n' represents the constant character newline. Escape sequences such as \n for newline and \t for tab are used to represent certain hard-to-get-at character constants.

Characters have an underlying integer valued representation that, on most C systems, is the numeric value of their 7-bit ASCII representation (see Chapter 3). For example, the constant char 'a' has value 97. If one thinks of characters as small integers, then doing arithmetic on characters makes sense. Since the values of the letters in both the lowercase and uppercase alphabet occur in order, the expression 'a' + 1 has the value 'b', the expression 'b' + 1 has the value 'c', and the expression 'z' - 'A' has value 25. Moreover, 'A' - 'a' has a value that is the same as 'B' - 'b', which is the same as 'C' - 'c', etc. Because of this, if the variable c has the value of a lowercase letter, then the expression c + 'A' - 'a' has the value of the corresponding uppercase letter. These ideas are incorporated into the next program, which capitalizes all lowercase letters and doubles the newline characters.

```
/*** capitalize lowercase letters and double space ***/

#include   <stdio.h>

main()
{
    int    c;

    while ((c = getchar()) != EOF)
        if ('a' <= c && c <= 'z')
            putchar(c + 'A' - 'a');
        else if (c == '\n') {
            putchar('\n');
            putchar('\n');
        }
        else
            putchar(c);
}
```

DISSECTION OF THE *capitalize* PROGRAM

while ((c = getchar()) != EOF)

The function getchar() gets a character and assigns it to the variable c. As long as the value of c is not EOF, the body of the while loop is executed.

if ('a' <= c && c <= 'z')
    putchar(c + 'A' - 'a');

Because of operator precedence (see Chapter 4), the expressions

'a' <= c && c <= 'z'   and   ('a' <= c) && (c <= 'z')

are equivalent. The symbols <= represent the operator "less than or equal to"; the subexpression 'a' <= c tests to see if the value 'a' is less than or equal to the value of c, and the subexpression c <= 'z' tests to see if the value of c is less than or equal to the value 'z'. The symbols && represent the operator "logical and"; if both subexpressions are *true*, then the expression

```
'a' <= c && c <= 'z'
```

is *true*, otherwise it is *false*. Thus, the expression is *true* if and only if c is a lowercase letter; if the expression is *true*, then the statement

```
putchar(c + 'A' - 'a');
```

is executed, causing the corresponding uppercase letter to be printed.

```
else if (c == '\n') {
    putchar('\n');
    putchar('\n');
}
```

The symbols == represent the operator "equals". If c is not a lowercase letter, a test is made to see if it is equal to a newline character; if it is, two newline characters are printed.

```
else
    putchar(c);
```

If the value of c is not a lowercase letter and it is not a newline character, then the character corresponding to the value c is printed. An else is always associated with the immediately preceding if.

This program can be compiled and run with input from the keyboard. Another alternative is to redirect the input so that the program capitalizes the lowercase letters obtained from an already existing text file. Suppose the executable program is in *a.out* and we want to use a file called *infile* as input. The UNIX command

a.out < *infile*

will do this.

1.8 FUNCTIONS

The heart and soul of C programming is the function. A function represents a piece of code that is a building block in the problem solving process. All functions are on the same external level; they cannot be nested one inside another. A program consists of one or more functions in one or more files. Precisely one of the functions is a main() function, where execution of the program begins. Other functions are called from within main() and from within each other.

To illustrate the use of functions, we set for ourselves the following task:

1. First print information about the program (this list).

2. Read in a value for the `int` variable n.

3. Read in n real numbers of type `double`.

4. Process the data to compute the minimum and maximum values.

Here is a program that does this.

```
main()
{
    int       i, n;
    double    min, max, x, minimum(), maximum();

    info();
    printf("\n\ninput  n :   ");
    scanf("%d", &n);
    printf("\n\ninput  %d  real numbers:   ", n);
    scanf("%lf", &x);
    min = max = x;
    for (i = 2; i <= n; ++i) {
        scanf("%lf", &x);
        min = minimum(min, x);
        max = maximum(max, x);
    }
    printf("\n\nmin value  =  %f\nmax value  =  %f\n\n", min, max);
}

info()
{
    printf("\n%s\n%s\n%s",
        "info: this program reads in an int value for n",
        "     and then processes  n   real numbers to find",
        "     the minimum and maximum values.");
}

double minimum(x, y)
double    x, y;
{
    if (x < y)
        return(x);
    else
        return(y);
}
```

```
double maximum(x, y)
double   x, y;
{
     if (x > y)
          return (x);
     else
          return (y);
}
```

Suppose that this code is all in one file, say *process.c*. The command

  cc − o process process.c

will compile the file and put the executable output into the file *process*. To test the program we give the command

  process

and type in 5 followed by the line

```
737.7799  −11.2e+3  −777  .001  3.14159
```

This is what appears on the screen.

```
info:  this program reads in an int value for n
       and then processes  n  real numbers to find
       the minimum and maximum values.

input  n :   5

input  5  real numbers:  737.7799  −11.2e+3  −777  .001  3.14159

min value  =  −11200.000000
max value  =  737.779900
```

It is also possible for this program to take its input from a file. To do this, we create a file, say *data*, where the first entry is the count of the remaining real numbers in the file. Then the command

  process < data

will cause the input to the program to be taken from the file *data*.

DISSECTION OF THE *process* PROGRAM

```
double   min, max, x, minimum(), maximum();
```

This declares the variables min, max, and x to be of type double, and it declares the functions minimum() and maximum() to return values of type double. If the functions were not declared here, then by default the compiler would consider them to be functions that return a value of type int.

```
info();
```

This statement invokes the function `info()`; the function contains a single `printf()` statement, which prints information about the program.

```
scanf("%lf", &x);
min = max = x;
```

The first real number is read in and its value is placed in the variable x; then `min` and `max` are both assigned that value. Because of the associativity of the assignment operator (see Chapter 3), an equivalent statement is

```
min = (max = x);
```

```
for (i = 2; i <= n; ++i) {
    scanf("%lf", &x);
    min = minimum(min, x);
    max = maximum(max, x);
}
```

Each time through the loop, a new value is read in for x; the current values of min and x are passed as arguments to the function `minimum()`, and the smaller of the two values is returned and assigned to `min`. The current values of `max` and x are passed as arguments to the function `maximum()`, and the larger of the two values is returned and assigned to `max`. In C, arguments to functions are *always* passed "by value"; this means that a copy of each argument is made, and it is these copies that are processed by the function. The effect of this is that the original arguments to a function are *not changed* in the calling environment.

```
info()
{
    .   .   .   .   .
}
```

This code defines the function `info()`. The header for a function definition occurs before the left brace {. The body of a function definition consists of the statements between the braces { and }. The code in the body of this function is a single `printf()` statement.

```
double minimum(x, y)
double   x, y;
{
    if (x < y)
        return (x);
    else
        return (y);
}
```

This code defines the function `minimum()`. The first two lines are the header for the function; the body of the function consists of everything between the braces. The first keyword `double` in the header tells the compiler that this function is to return a value of type `double`. The identifiers x and y are formal parameters of the function; the parameter list consists of all the identifiers separated by commas within the parentheses (and). Identifiers in a parameter list are declared following the right parenthesis; thus x and y are declared to be formal parameters of type double by the line

```
double  x, y;
```

Although the identifiers x and y are used here as well as in the function main(), there is no relationship between them. Parameters in a function can be thought of as place holders. When values are passed as arguments to a function, the body of the function describes what is to be done with those values; the body of this function consists of a single if-else statement which in turn contains two return statements. A return statement is of the form

```
return;          or          return expression;
```

A return statement causes control to be passed back to the calling environment. If an expression follows the keyword return, then the value of the expression is passed back as well. It is customary to put the expression in parentheses so that it can be seen more clearly.

```
double maximum(x, y)
double   x, y;
{
     .   .   .   .   .
}
```

This code defines the function maximum().

Now suppose we put the function main() in the file *process.c*; put the function info() in the file *info.c*; put the function minimum() in the file *minimum.c*; and put the function maximum() in the file *maximum.c*. Then the UNIX command

   cc − o process process.c info.c minimum.c maximum.c

will cause the *cc* compiler to place an executable program into the file *process*. Also, since *cc* is invoked to work on more than one file, corresponding *.o* files are created. Thus, the files *process.o*, *info.o*, *minimum.o*, and *maximum.o* are created. These files contain object code that can be thought of as being close to executable. Suppose that the source code of one of the functions has to be changed; say, *info.c* is modified. Then the command

   cc − o process process.o info.c minimum.o maximum.o

will recompile the program. The use of *.o* files where possible, instead of *.c* files, will speed the work of the compiler. In Chapter 11 we explain how to use the command *make*. It keeps track of which source files are dependent on others and provides for an efficient recompilation of a program. This facility is very useful when developing a program consisting of many source files. The *.o* files are extensively used by *make*.

1.9 ARRAYS, STRINGS, AND POINTERS

This section and the ones that follow continue to give an overview of C. However, the concepts and examples presented are somewhat more advanced. The experienced programmer will have no trouble following the presentation, but anyone without experience with arrays and pointers in some other language may find the reading difficult. *Any reader who finds the material obtuse should turn to Chapter 2 and proceed from there*. Even the reader who understands the material that follows needs to know many details not found in Chapter 1. The material gives only the flavor of the language, not all the details.

An array name is itself a pointer, and a string is just an array of characters. Because of this, the concepts of arrays, strings, and pointers are intimately tied together. A pointer is just an address of something in memory. Unlike most languages, C provides for pointer arithmetic. Moreover, because pointer expressions of great utility are possible, pointer arithmetic is one of the strong points of the language. However, until all the nuances are absorbed, the beginner may experience some difficulty with the use of pointers. This section definitely does not present those nuances, but rather just gives the flavor of how the code looks and presents explanations that indicate why the various C constructs might be useful.

Arrays

Arrays are used when many variables all of the same type are desired. For example, the declaration

```
int  x[3];
```

allocates three variables of type int that can be referenced as x[0], x[1], and x[2]. The index, or subscript, of an array always starts at 0. The following program reads in five scores, computes their sum, sorts them and prints them out in order, and finally prints the sum of the scores and the class average.

```
#define  CLASS_SIZE  5

main()
{
    int    i, j, score[CLASS_SIZE], sum = 0, temp;

    printf("\ninput  %d  scores:  ", CLASS_SIZE);
    for (i = 0; i < CLASS_SIZE; ++i) {
        scanf("%d", &score[i]);
        sum += score[i];
    }
    /*  bubble sort the scores  */
    for (i = 0; i < CLASS_SIZE - 1; ++i)
        for (j = CLASS_SIZE - 1; i < j; --j)
            if (score[j-1] < score[j]) {      /*  out of order?  */
                temp = score[j-1];
                score[j-1] = score[j];
                score[j] = temp;
            }
    printf("\n\nthe ordered scores are:\n");
    for (i = 0; i < CLASS_SIZE; ++i)
        printf("\n    score[%d]  =%7d", i, score[i]);
    printf("\n\n%23d%s\n%23.1f%s\n\n",
        sum, "  is the sum of all the scores",
        (double) sum / (double) CLASS_SIZE,
        "  is the class average");
}
```

If the program is executed, the prompt

```
input  5  scores:
```

will appear on the screen. If the integers 68, 43, 97, 51, 77 are then entered, we will see on the screen

```
input  5  scores: 68 43 97 51 77

the ordered scores are:

    score[0]  =    97
    score[1]  =    77
    score[2]  =    68
    score[3]  =    51
    score[4]  =    43

    336  is the sum of all the scores
    67.2  is the class average
```

A bubble sort is used in the program to sort the scores. This construction is typically done with nested `for` loops, with a test being made in the body of the inner loop to check on the order of a pair of elements. If the elements being compared are out of order, their values are interchanged. This interchange is accomplished by the code

```
temp = score[i];
score[i] = score[j];
score[j] = temp;
```

In the first statement the variable `temp` is used to temporarily store the value of `score[i]`. In the next statement the stored value in memory of `score[i]` is being overwritten with the value of `score[j]`. In the last statement the value of `score[j]` is being overwritten with the original value of `score[i]`, which is now in `temp`. Hand simulation of the program with the given data will show the reader why this bubble sort construct of two nested `for` loops achieves an array with sorted elements. The name "bubble sort" comes from the fact that at each step of the outer loop, the desired value among those left to be worked over is "bubbled" into position. Although bubble sorts are easy to code, they are relatively inefficient. Other sorting techniques execute much faster. This is of no concern when sorting a small number of items infrequently, but if the number of items is large or the code is repeatedly used, then efficiency is, indeed, an important consideration. The expression

```
(double) sum / (double) CLASS_SIZE
```

which occurs as an argument in the final `printf()` statement makes use of a cast operator. The effect of

```
(double) sum          and          (double) CLASS_SIZE
```

is to cast, or convert, the `int` value of `sum` to a `double` and the `int` value of the symbolic constant `CLASS_SIZE` to a `double`, respectively. Because the cast operator has higher precedence than the division operator (see Chapter 3), the casts are done before division occurs. If no casts were used, then integer division would occur and any fractional part would be discarded.

Strings

A string is just an array of characters. The following program illustrates an interactive use of strings.

```
/*** have a nice day ***/

#define    LINESIZE    100

main ()
{
        char    c, line [LINESIZE];
        int     i;

        printf ("\nhi!  what is your name?   ");
        for (i = 0; (c = getchar()) != '\n'; ++i)
            line[i] = c;
        line[i] = '\0';
        printf ("\nnice to meet you ");
        for (i = 0; line[i] != '\0'; ++i)
            putchar (line[i]);
        printf (".\nyour name spelled backwards is ");
        while (i != 0)
            putchar (line[--i]);
        printf (".\n\nhave a nice day!\n\n");
}
```

When this program is executed, the line

```
hi! what is your name?
```

is printed. This is called a "prompt," because it prompts the user to respond. Without such a message, the user might not know that the program expected input. If the user now replies with the name Alice B. Carole, the following appears on the screen:

```
hi! what is your name? Alice B. Carole

nice to meet you Alice B. Carole.
your name spelled backwards is eloraC .B ecilA.

have a nice day!
```

DISSECTION OF THE *nice_day* PROGRAM

```
#define    LINESIZE    100
```

This will set the maximum size of the character array named line. We are making the assumption that the user of this program will not type in more than 100 characters.

```
char    c, line [LINESIZE];
int     i;
```

c is a variable of type char; line is an array of type char with LINESIZE elements; i is an int.

```
printf ("\nhi!  what is your name?   ");
```

This is a prompt to the user; the program now expects a name to be typed in followed by a carriage return.

```
for (i = 0; (c = getchar()) != '\n'; ++i)
    line[i] = c;
```

The variable i is assigned the value 0. getchar() gets a character and assigns it to c, and a test is made to see if it is a newline character; if it is not, the value of c is assigned to the array element line[i] and i is incremented; the for loop is repeatedly executed until a newline character is received.

```
line[i] = '\0';
```

After the for loop is finished, the null character \0 is assigned to the element line[i]; by convention all strings end with a null character. Functions that process strings, such as printf(), use the null character \0 as an end-of-string sentinel; we now can think of the array line in memory as

A	l	i	c	e		B	.		C	a	r	o	l	e	\0	...		...
0	1	2	3	4	5	6	7	8	9	10	11	12	13	14	15	16		99

```
printf("\nnice to meet you ");
```

The following line is printed:

```
nice to meet you
```

```
for (i = 0; line[i] != '\0'; ++i)
    putchar(line[i]);
```

The elements of the array line, starting with line[0], are printed until the end-of-string sentinel \0 is encountered.

```
printf(".\nyour name spelled backwards is ");
```

A period is printed at the end of the current line followed by a newline character followed by . . . .

```
while (i != 0)
    putchar(line[--i]);
```

At the start of this while loop the value of i is 15 (assuming that "Alice B. Carole" followed by a carriage return has been typed in). The expression --i first decrements the stored value of i by 1 and then assigns this new value to the expression. The effect of this loop is to print backwards the characters stored in the array.

```
printf(".\n\nhave a nice day!\n\n");
```

A period is printed at the end of the current line followed by two newline characters followed by . . . .

Pointers

A pointer is just an address of something in memory. Because an array name is itself a pointer, the uses of arrays and pointers are intimately related. The following program is designed to illustrate some of these relationships.

```
main ()
{
    char    c = 'A', *p, s[100], *strcpy();

    p = &c;
    printf ("\n%c%c%c", *p, *p + 1, *p + 2);
    s[0] = 'A';    s[1] = 'B';    s[2] = 'C';    s[3] = '\0';
    p = s;
    printf ("\n%s%s%c%s", s, p, *(p + 1), p + 1);
    strcpy (s, "\nshe sells sea shells by the seashore");
    printf ("%s", s);
    p += 17;
    for ( ; *p != '\0'; ++p) {
        if (*p == 'e')
            *p = 'E';
        if (*p == ' ')
            *p = '\n';
    }
    printf ("%s\n\n", s);
}
```

The output of this program is

```
ABC
ABCABCBBC
she sells sea shells by the seashore
she sells sea shElls
by
thE
sEashorE
```

DISSECTION OF THE *ABC* PROGRAM

```
char    c = 'A', *p, s[100], *strcpy();
```

c is a variable of type char and is initialized with the value 'A'; p is a variable of type pointer to char; s is an array of 100 elements of type char; strcpy() is a function in the standard library that returns a pointer to char. If a function returns a value other than an int, the type of the value returned must be declared.

```
p = &c;
```

The symbol & is the address operator; the value of the expression &c is the address in memory of the variable c, and the address of c is assigned to p. We now think of p as "pointing to c".

```
printf("\n%c%c%c", *p, *p + 1, *p + 2);
```

The format %c is used to print the value of an expression as a character. The symbol * is the dereferencing or indirection operator. The expression *p has the value of whatever p is pointing to; since p is pointing to c and c has the value 'A', this is the value of the expression *p and an A is printed. The value of the expression *p + 1 is one more than the value of *p, causing a B to be printed. The value of the expression *p + 2 is two more than the value of *p, causing a C to be printed.

```
s[0] = 'A';   s[1] = 'B';   s[2] = 'C';   s[3] = '\0';
```

These statements cause the values 'A', 'B', and 'C' to be assigned to the first three elements of s, respectively; the fourth element is assigned the end-of-string sentinel '\0'. The array s can be thought of in memory as

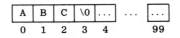

```
p = s;
```

The array name s is itself a pointer; we can think of s as pointing to s[0], or we can think of s as being the base address of the array, which is the address of s[0]. The pointer s is assigned to the pointer variable p; note carefully that even though s is a pointer, it is not a pointer variable, but rather a pointer constant; the statement

```
        s = p;
```

would result in a syntax error.

```
printf("\n%s%s%c%s", s, p, *(p + 1), p + 1);
```

s is printed in the format of a string, causing ABC to be printed; p is printed in the format of a string causing ABC to be printed. Since p points at s[0], p + 1 points at s[1], and the value of the expression *(p + 1) is the value of what p + 1 points to, which is the value of s[1]; this value is printed in the format of a character, causing a B to be printed. The expression p + 1 is printed in the format of a string; since p + 1 points at s[1], successive characters are printed until a \0 is encountered; this causes a BC to be printed.

strcpy(*ptr1*, *ptr2*)

strcpy() is a function in the standard library. It takes as arguments two pointers to char; the string pointed to by its second argument is copied in memory beginning at the position pointed to by its first argument. All characters up to and including a null character are copied. It is assumed that the first argument points to enough space to hold all the characters being copied; the effect is to copy one string into another.

```
"\nshe sells sea shells by the seashore"
```

In the program this constant string appears as the second argument to `strcpy()`. A constant string, like any other string, is a pointer to `char`; it points to its first element, in this case a newline character. A constant string ends with a null character so that even the null string `""` contains one character, namely `\0`.

```
strcpy(s, "\nshe sells sea shells by the seashore");
```

The string in the second argument is copied into the string `s`.

```
printf("%s", s);
```

The string `s` is printed in the format of a string; this causes a newline to be printed followed by

```
        she sells sea shells by the seashore
```

```
p += 17;
```

The pointer value of `p` is incremented so that `p` is now pointing at the place in memory corresponding to 17 characters further along than its starting position. Since `p` was previously pointing at `s[0]`, it is now pointing at `s[17]` (this is the e in `shells`);

```
for ( ; *p != '\0'; ++p) {
    if (*p == 'e')
        *p = 'E';
    if (*p == ' ')
        *p = '\n';
}
```

As long as the value of what `p` is pointing at is not `'\0'`, the body of the `for` loop is executed. If the value of what `p` is pointing to is `'e'`, then that value is changed to `'E'`; if the value of what `p` is pointing to is `' '`, then that value is changed to `'\n'`.

```
printf("%s\n\n", s);
```

The variable `s` is printed in the format of a string followed by two newline characters. Since the previous `for` loop changed the values of some of the elements of `s`, the following is printed:

```
        she sells sea shElls
        by
        thE
        sEashorE
```

Arrays, strings, and pointers are closely related. A declaration such as

```
char *p, s[100];
```

creates the identifier `p` as a pointer to `char` and the identifier `s` as an array of 100 elements of type `char`. Since an array name is itself a pointer, both `p` and `s` are pointers to `char`. However, `p` is a variable pointer, whereas `s` is a constant pointer that points to `s[0]`. The statement

```
p = s;
```

is syntactically correct, but the statement

```
s = p;
```

results in a syntax error. The two expressions

    `s[i]`   and   `*(s + i)`

are equivalent. The expression `s[i]` has the value of the *i*th element of the array, whereas `s + i` points `i` character positions past `s`. Then the dereferencing operator `*` is used to get the value of what is being pointed at. In a similar fashion the two expressions

    `*(p + i)`   and   `p[i]`

are equivalent. Note that the expression `++p` makes sense since `p` is being replaced by the value of `p + 1`, but because `s` is a constant pointer, the expression `++s` is wrong.

As a final example for this section we consider the following task:

1. Find successive words in a file.

2. Capitalize the lowercase letters in each word.

3. Keep track of the number of characters in each word, etc.

4. Print the words with relevant information as a list.

The following program accomplishes the task. Our definition of "word" is any string of characters separated by white space.

```
#include    <stdio.h>
#define     MAXWORD     100

main()
{
      char    *find_next(), word[MAXWORD];
      int     char_cnt = 0, word_cnt = 0, word_length = 0;

      while (find_next(word) != NULL) {
            capitalize(word);
            ++word_cnt;
            word_length = strlen(word);
            char_cnt += word_length;
            printf("\n%12d      %s", word_length, word);
      }
      printf("\n\n%12d  characters in  %d  words\n\n",
            char_cnt, word_cnt);

}
```

```
char *find_next (word)
char    word[];
{
        int    c, i;

        while ((c = getchar ()) == ' ' || c == '\n' || c == '\t')
                ;       /* skip white space */
        if (c != EOF) {
            i = 0;
            while (c != ' ' && c != '\n' && c != '\t' && c != EOF) {
                word[i++] = c;
                c = getchar ();
            }
            word[i] = '\0';
            return (word);
        }
        else
            return (NULL);
}

capitalize(p)
char    *p;
{
        for ( ; *p != '\0'; ++p)
            if ('a' <= *p && *p <= 'z')
                *p += 'A' - 'a';
}
```

Suppose that we compile this program and put the executable code into the file *list_ words*. If we create a file named *sea_shells* with the following words

```
she sells sea shells by the seashore
```

and then give the command

list_words < *sea_shells*

the following appears on the screen:

```
3       SHE
5       SELLS
3       SEA
6       SHELLS
2       BY
3       THE
8       SEASHORE

30   characters in  7  words
```

Only a few new ideas are present in this program.

DISSECTION OF THE *list_words* PROGRAM

```
char    *find_next(), word[MAXWORD];
```

> The function `find_next()` is declared to return a pointer to `char`; the identifier word is an array with MAXWORD elements.

```
word_length = strlen(word);
```

> The function `strlen()` is in the standard library; it takes as an argument a pointer to `char` (a string) and returns the number of characters in the string as an `int`.

```
char *find_next(word)
char    word[];
{
    .  .  .  .  .
}
```

> This defines the function `find_next()`. The `char *` in the header tells the compiler that the function returns a pointer to `char`; the second line in the header declares the identifier word in the argument list to be of type pointer to `char`. The code in the body of the function is straightforward; first white space is skipped; if the value of the character c is not EOF, then successive characters are collected into the elements of word until a white space character or an EOF is encountered. At that point a \0 is appended to mark the end of the string, and the pointer value word is returned; if the value of the character c is EOF, then the pointer value NULL is returned.

```
capitalize(p)
char    *p;
{
    .  .  .  .  .
}
```

> This defines the function `capitalize()`. By default it returns an `int`, but since no `return` statement is present in the body of the function, no useful value is returned. The argument p is declared to be of type pointer to `char`.

1.10 FILES

Files are easy to use in C. To open the file named *my_file*, the following code could be used:

```
#include  <stdio.h>

main()
{
    int    c;
    FILE   *fp, *fopen();

    fp = fopen("my_file", "r");
    .  .   .   .   .
```

The second line in the body of main() declares fp to be a pointer to FILE and declares the function fopen() to return a pointer to FILE. The function fopen() is in the standard library. FILE is defined symbolically as a particular structure within the standard header file *stdio.h*. To make use of the construct, a user need not know any details about it. However, the header file must be made available by means of a #include line before any reference to FILE is made. The function fopen() takes two strings as arguments, and it returns a pointer to FILE. The first argument is the name of the file, and the second argument is the mode in which the file is to be opened.

Three modes for a file

"r"	for read
"w"	for write
"a"	for append

When a file is opened for writing and it does not exist, it is created. If it already exists, its contents are destroyed and the writing starts at the beginning of the file. If for some reason a file cannot be accessed, the pointer value NULL is returned by fopen(). *After a file has been opened, all references to it are via its file pointer.* Upon completion of a program, the system automatically closes all open files. Most systems allow only a small number of files, typically 20, to be open simultaneously. When using many files, it is important to explicitly close any files not currently in use. The standard library function fclose() is used to close files.

One thing that is easy to do with text is to make a frequency analysis of the occurrence of the characters and words making up the text. This has been a useful tool in many disciplines, from the study of hieroglyphics to the study of Shakespeare. To keep things simple, we will write a program that counts the occurrences of just the uppercase letters. Among our files is one named *chapter1*, which is the current version of this chapter. We will start with the idea of doing the analysis on this file.

```
#include    <stdio.h>

main()
{
     int     c, i, letter[26];
     FILE    *fp, *fopen();

     fp = fopen("chapter1", "r");
     for (i = 0; i < 26; ++i)     /*  initialize array to zero  */
     letter[i] = 0;
     while ((c = getc(fp)) != EOF)
     if ('A' <= c && c <= 'Z')
          ++letter[c - 'A'];
     for (i = 0; i < 26; ++i) {
     if (i % 6 == 0)
          printf("\n");
     printf("%5c:%5d", 'A' + i, letter[i]);
     }
     printf("\n\n");
}
```

The output of this program is

A:	153	B:	179	C:	240	D:	47	E:	249	F:	55
G:	7	H:	17	I:	370	J:	1	K:	2	L:	140
M:	32	N:	59	O:	61	P:	366	Q:	4	R:	44
S:	98	T:	262	U:	26	V:	7	W:	44	X:	17
Y:	4	Z:	7								

Notice that the relative occurrence of many of the letters seems to be different from what might be found in ordinary text.

The C language provides a connection to the arguments on the command line that invoked the program. Typically, to make use of the connection one would code

```
main(argc, argv)
int     argc;
char    *argv[];
{
          .    .    .    .    .
```

The parameter argc stands for "argument count," and its value is the number of arguments in the command line used to execute the program. The parameter argv stands for "argument variable." It is an array of pointers to char (array of strings), and successive elements of the array point to successive words in the command line used to execute the program. Thus argv[0] is a pointer to the name of the command itself. As an example of how this facility is used, we will modify the last program, compile it, and put the executable code into the file *letters*. The intent of the command line

letters chapter1 outfile

will be to invoke the program *letters,* with the two files *chapter1* and *outfile* as parameters. The program should read the file *chapter1* and write to the file *outfile.* If we give a different command, say

> *letters chapter2 temp*

then the program should read *chapter2* and write to file *temp.* Here is the program to do this.

```
#include    <stdio.h>

main(argc, argv)
int     argc;
char    *argv[];
{
     int    c, i, letter[26];
     FILE   *ifp, *ofp, *fopen();

     if (argc != 3)
          printf("\nusage:  %s  infile  outfile\n\n", argv[0]);
     else {
          ifp = fopen(argv[1], "r");
          ofp = fopen(argv[2], "w");
          for (i = 0; i < 26; ++i)        /* initialize array to zero */
               letter[i] = 0;
          while ((c = getc(ifp)) != EOF)
               if ('A' <= c && c <= 'Z')
                    ++letter[c - 'A'];
          for (i = 0; i < 26; ++i) {
               if (i % 6 == 0)
                    fprintf(ofp, "\n");
               fprintf(ofp, "%5c:%5d", 'A' + i, letter[i]);
          }
          fprintf(ofp, "\n\n");
     }
}
```

DISSECTION OF THE *letters* PROGRAM

```
FILE   *ifp, *ofp, *fopen();
```

We often use the identifiers ifp and ofp, which stand for "infile pointer" and "outfile pointer," respectively.

```
if (argc != 3)
     printf("\nusage:  %s  infile  outfile\n\n", argv[0]);
```

If the number of words on the command line is not three, then the program is being used incorrectly. Suppose the command line

> *letters chapter1 abc abc*

is typed; since the line contains four words, `argc` will have value 4, and this will cause the message

```
usage:  letters  infile  outfile
```

to appear on the screen.

```
ifp = fopen(argv[1], "r");
ofp = fopen(argv[2], "w");
```

Assume that the command line

> *letters chapter1 outfile*

was typed to execute this program; then `argv[0]` points to the string `"letters"`, `argv[1]` points to the string `"chapter1"`, and `argv[2]` points to the string `"outfile"`; thus, the file *chapter1* is opened for reading with file pointer `ifp`, and the file *outfile* is opened for writing with file pointer `ofp`.

```
while ((c = getc(ifp)) != EOF)
```

The function `getc()` is provided by the standard library; it is similar to `get_char()` except that it takes as an argument a pointer to `FILE`. When the function is invoked, it gets the next character from that file.

```
fprintf(ofp, "%5c:%5d", 'A' + i, letter[i]);
```

The function `fprintf()` is provided by the standard library; it is similar to `printf()` except that it takes as its first argument a pointer to `FILE`. When the function is invoked, it writes to the indicated file rather than to the screen.

1.11 AN EXAMPLE: RANDOM NUMBERS AND A BEST POSSIBLE ALGORITHM

A random number generator is a function that returns a nonnegative integer each time it is invoked. Sequences of such numbers appear to be random. They have many uses in computer science, engineering, and mathematics. For some applications it is convenient to be able to create a file of random numbers. We wish to be able to create such files, which then can be used as input to the programs we write. A detailed discussion of the theory and use of random numbers is beyond the scope of this text; see *The Art of Computer Programming, Vol. 2 (Seminumerical Algorithms)* by Donald Ervin Knuth (Reading, Mass.: Addison-Wesley, 1969).

On our system, the random number generator rand() is in the standard library. Most C systems have such a function in the standard library, although some small systems may not. If your system does not provide a random number generator, you can easily write your own function. Only a few lines of code are needed; see Chapter 5, where we have written the function random(). The following program uses rand() to create a file of random numbers interactively.

```
#include    <stdio.h>

main()
{
    char    file_name[100];
    int     i, n;
    FILE    *fp;

    printf("\nthis program creates random numbers.");
    printf("\n\nhow many would you like?    ");
    scanf("%d", &n);
    printf("in what file would you like them?    ");
    scanf("%s", file_name);
    if (strcmp(file_name, "stdout") == 0)
        fp = stdout;
    else
        fp = fopen(file_name, "w");
    for (i = 1; i <= n; ++i) {
        if (i % 6 == 1)
            fprintf(fp, "\n");
        fprintf(fp, "%12d", rand());
    }
    printf("\n\n");
}
```

DISSECTION OF THE *create_rand* PROGRAM

```
scanf("%s", file_name);
```

The %s format is used to read into memory a string. When scanf() reads a string, white space, if any, is skipped and then a sequence of characters is read into memory until a white space character or EOF is encountered; at that point a \0 character is put into memory to terminate the string being read in. The string is placed at the address indicated by the argument to scanf() corresponding to the format; here the argument is file_name, which is a pointer to char (an address).

```
if (strcmp(file_name, "stdout") == 0)
    fp = stdout;
```

The function `strcmp()` is in the standard library; it compares two strings and returns a negative, zero, or positive integer, depending on whether the first string is lexicographically less than, equal to, or greater than the second string. Here, a test is being made to see if the string variable `file_name` is equal to the constant string `"stdout"`; if it is, then `fp` is assigned the value `stdout`, which is a pointer to FILE that refers to the screen. `stdout` is provided by the system and is always available for writing; the name stands for "standard output."

```
fp = fopen(file_name, "w");
```

The file whose name has been entered at the keyboard and stored in `file_name` is opened for writing.

```
if (i % 6 == 1)
    fprintf(fp, "\n");
```

Every sixth time through the `for` loop a newline character is printed in the file pointed to by `fp`.

```
fprintf(fp, "%12d", rand());
```

In the file pointed to by `fp` the random number returned by the function `rand()` is printed in the format `%12d`.

To see a few random numbers printed on the screen, we run the program and input `11` and `stdout` when prompted:

```
this program creates random numbers.

how many would you like?  11
in what file would you like them?  stdout

    1103527590    377401575    662824084   1147902781   2035015474    368800899
    1508029952    486256185   1062517886    267834847    180171308
```

To create a large file of random numbers, we run the program and respond with `10000` and `file_of_rand`. Suppose we wish to find the minimum and maximum values of all the integers in `file_of_rand`. The following function can be used to do this:

```
minmax(min_ptr, max_ptr)
int    *min_ptr, *max_ptr;
{
       int    cnt = 0, min, max, x;

       if (scanf("%d", &x) == 1) {
            ++cnt;
            min = max = x;
            while (scanf("%d", &x) == 1) {
                 ++cnt;
                 if (min > x)
                      min = x;
                 else if (max < x)
                      max = x;
            }
       }
       *min_ptr = min;
       *max_ptr = max;
       return (cnt);
}
```

This function is designed to pass three values back to the calling environment. The count of the integers processed is passed back via a return statement. Because arguments are passed "call by value," it is necessary to use pointers in the argument list to pass the min and max values back to the calling environment. The following main() function can be used to invoke minmax() and print results:

```
main()
{
       int    cnt, min, max;

       cnt = minmax(&min, &max);
       if (cnt == 0)
            printf("\n\nno data was input\n\n");
       else {
            printf("\n\nmin  =%12d\nmax  =%12d", min, max);
            printf("\n\nnumber of integers processed:%7d\n\n", cnt);
       }
}
```

In 1972 in the article "A Sorting Problem and Its Complexity" (*Communications of the ACM*, *Vol. 15, No. 6*), one of the authors, Ira Pohl, published the best possible algorithm for finding minimum and maximum values. The criterion for "best" is the least number of comparisons needed. The algorithm is somewhat longer than the one just given, but hand simulating that it correctly computes the desired values is easy. It is not at all obvious that the algorithm is "best," but this is proven to be so in the article cited. In processing a file of n integers, the algorithm given above makes approximately $2n$ comparisons, whereas the "best" algorithm makes approximately $3n/2$ comparisons.

```
/***  the best possible minmax algorithm  -  Pohl, 1972   ***/

minmax(min_ptr, max_ptr)
int   *min_ptr, *max_ptr;
{
      int   cnt = 0, min, max, x, y;

      if (scanf("%d", &x) == 1) {
            ++cnt;
            min = max = y = x;
            while (scanf("%d", &x) == 1) {
                  ++cnt;
                  if (scanf("%d", &y) == 1) {
                        ++cnt;
                        if (x < y) {
                              if (min > x)
                                    min = x;
                              if (max < y)
                                    max = y;
                        }
                        else {
                              if (min > y)
                                    min = y;
                              if (max < x)
                                    max = x;
                        }
                  }
                  else
                        break;
            }
      }
      if (cnt % 2 == 0)       /* extra element */
            if (min > x)
                  min = x;
            else if (max < x)
                  max = x;
      *min_ptr = min;
      *max_ptr = max;
      return (cnt);
}
```

The only new idea used in the algorithm is the break statement:

```
break;
```

which causes control to immediately pass out of the enclosing while loop. After
scanf() fails to find another integer, we want to avoid calling scanf() again. If the
break statement is not present, this can happen. The algorithm basically gets two
integers, puts them into x and y, and then processes them. Why not use

```
while (scanf("%d%d", &x, &y) == 2) {
```

to get both values at once? Well, eventually scanf() has to fail to get another pair of integers, and when this happens it may not be clear whether no integers were found or only one integer was found.

1.12 SUMMARY

1. Programming is the art of communicating algorithms to computers. An algorithm is a computational procedure whose steps are completely specified and elementary.

2. The functions printf() and scanf() from the standard library can be used for output and input, respectively. printf() can print out explicit text and can use conversion specifications that begin with the character % to print out values from the argument list that follows the control string. scanf() is analogous to printf(), but it needs addresses in its argument list, and it returns as an int the number of successful conversions made.

3. Every program contains a main() function. The body of a function is contained within the braces { and }. The first part of a function contains declarations. All variables must be declared. The second part of a function consists of executable statements such as assignment statements or calls to functions such as printf().

4. The cc compiler has built into it a preprocessor. A #define line beginning in column 1 can be used to define symbolic constants, and a #include line beginning in column 1 can be used to copy the contents of a file into the code.

5. Statements are ordinarily executed sequentially. Special statements such as if, if-else, for, and while statements can alter the sequential flow of control during execution of a program.

6. The function getchar() reads a character from the keyboard, and the function putchar() writes a character to the screen. These functions are used typically to manipulate character data.

7. A program consists of one or more functions in one or more files. Execution begins with the function main(). The cc command followed by a list of files that constitutes a program creates an executable file.

8. All arguments to functions are passed "call by value." Thus, there is no direct way for variables to have their values altered in the calling environment by passing arguments to a function. When a return statement is encountered in a function, control is passed back to the calling environment. If an expression is present, then its value is passed back as well.

9. The use of many small functions as a programming style aids modularity and documentation of programs. Moreover, programs composed of many small functions are easier to debug.

10. Arrays, strings, and pointers are intimately related. A string is an array of type char, and an array name is itself a pointer that points to its first element. By convention the character \0 is used as an end-of-string sentinel. A constant string such as "ABC" can be considered a pointer to type char. The string has four characters in it, the last one being \0.

1.13 EXERCISES

1. Write on the screen the words

        she sells sea shells by the seashore

   (a) all on one line, (b) on three lines, (c) inside a box.

2. Use a hand calculator to verify that the output of the marathon program is correct. Create another version of the program by changing the floating constant 1760.0 to an integer constant 1760. Compile and execute the program and notice that the output is not the same as before. This is because integer division discards any fractional part.

3. Write a version of the marathon program in which all constants and variables are of type double. Is the output of the program exactly the same as that of the original program?

4. The following program has a run-time error in it.

```
main()
{
    int   x, y = 0;

    x = 1 / y;
}
```

   Check to see that it compiles without any error messages. Run the program to see what the effect of the error is. Try to rewrite the program without the variable y, but keeping the error in the program. What happens when you try to compile it?

5. Write a version of the *pacific_sea* program that makes use of the #include facility. If you configure your program so that it starts as follows, will it work?

```
main(
#include   "pacific.h"
) {
       .   .   .   .   .   .
```

6. Create the file *pacific_sea.c* with source code in it. Make sure that the code compiles with no errors. Now rename the file *pacific_sea.c* as *pacific_sea* and try the command

    cc pacific_sea

    The compiler will complain about the file not ending in *.c*. On some systems the complaint is quite cryptic.

7. The following program writes a large letter *I* on the screen.

```
#define  HEIGHT  17

main()
{
    int   i;

    printf("\nIIIIIIII");
    for (i = 0; i < HEIGHT; ++i)
        printf ("\n  III");
    printf("\nIIIIIIII\n\n");
}
```

    Compile and run this program so that you understand its effect. Write a similar program that prints a large letter *C* on the screen.

8. Take a working program and omit each line in turn and run it through the compiler. Record the error messages each such deletion causes. As an example, consider the following code in the file *nonsense.c*.

```
/* forgot main */
{
    printf("nonsense\n");
}
```

    When this code(?) is run through the compiler, the following messages are generated:

```
"nonsense.c", line 2: syntax error
"nonsense.c", line 3: illegal character: 134 (octal)
"nonsense.c", line 3: cannot recover from earlier errors: goodbye!
```

9. The text editor *vi* provides several facilities to aid in writing code. For example, when the cursor is sitting on a { character, typing the % key causes the cursor to go to the matching brace symbol, if there is one. This allows you to conveniently check if your left and right braces are properly matched. This facility works in a similar fashion for brackets and parentheses. If *vi* is available to you, check this feature. Also, find out how to set and make use of "autoindent" and "showmatch" in *vi*. If you are using some other text editor, find out what special features, if any, the editor provides to help you write code.

10. Write a program that asks interactively for your *name* and *age* and responds with

    ```
    Hello name, next year you will be next_age.
    ```

    where *next_age* is *age* + 1.

11. Write a program that neatly prints a table of powers. The first few lines of the table might look like this.

    ```
    ::::: a table of powers :::::

    integer      square       cube     quartic     quintic
    -----------------------------------------------------------
        0            0            0          0           0
        1            1            1          1           1
        2            4            8         16          32
        3            9           27         81         243
    ```

12. Write a `prn_string()` function which uses `putchar()` to print a string passed as an argument. Remember that strings are terminated by the null character `\0`.

13. Suppose the source code for the program that capitalizes lowercase letters is in a file named *capital.c*. Compile the program and put the executable code into the file named *capital*. What will happen when the UNIX command

    capital < capital.c

    is given? Use the UNIX command

    capital < capital.c > try.c

    to redirect the output of the command to the file *try.c*. Can you compile the file *try.c*?

14. Rewrite the following code as a single `for` loop with a body that consists of a simple statement (not a compound statement):

    ```
    i = 0;
    while (c != ' ' && c != '\n' && c != '\t' && c != EOF) {
        word[i++] = c;
        c = getchar();
    }
    ```

15. Create a file of 10000 random numbers. Check to see that the two `minmax()` functions given at the end of this chapter both find the same minimum and maximum values in the file. Modify each function so that a count of the number of comparisons made is printed out. Are the two counts consistent with the theory stated in the text?

2
Syntax and the
Lexical Level

A C program is a sequence of characters that will be converted by a C compiler to a target language on a particular machine. On most systems the target language will be a form of machine language that can be run or interpreted. For this to happen the program must be a syntactically legal string of the language. The compiler first collects the characters into *tokens*, which comprise the basic vocabulary of the language.

The compiler checks that the tokens can be formed into legal strings according to the syntax of the language. Most compilers are very precise in their requirements. Unlike human readers of English, who are able to understand the meaning of a sentence with an extra punctuation mark or a misspelled word, a C compiler will fail to provide a translation of a syntactically incorrect program, no matter how trivial the error. This, of course, is generally true of all computer languages. Hence, the programmer must learn to be precise in writing code.

The compilation process

C program	→	group characters into tokens
	→	translate to target code

2.1 CHARACTERS AND TOKENS

A C program is constructed out of a sequence of characters that include

lowercase letters	a b c . . . z
uppercase letters	A B C . . . Z
digits	0 1 2 3 4 5 6 7 8 9
special characters	+ = _ − ( ) * & % $ # ! | < > . , ; : " ' / ? { } ˜ \ [ ] ˆ
nonprinting characters (white space),	

which include *blank, newline,* and *tab*

These characters are collected by the compiler into syntactic units called tokens, which include identifiers, keywords, constants, strings, operators, and other separators. Let us look at a simple program and informally pick out some of its tokens before we go on to a strict definition of C syntax.

```
/***    read in two integers and print their sum    ***/

main()
{
      int    a, b, sum;

      printf("\ninput  a  and  b :   ");
      scanf("%d%d", &a, &b);
      printf("\na  is  %d  and  b  is  %d", a, b);
      sum = a + b;
      printf("\n\nthe sum of  a  and  b  is   %d\n\n", sum);
}
```

DISSECTION AT THE LEXICAL LEVEL OF THE *sum* PROGRAM

```
/***    read in two integers and print their sum    ***/
```

Comments are delimited by /* and */ and are treated as white space by the compiler.

```
main()
{
      int    a, b, sum;
```

The function name main is an identifier; " (", ") ", and "{" are separators; int is a keyword; a, b, and sum are identifiers; " , " and " ; " are separators.

```
printf("\ninput  a  and  b :   ");
scanf("%d%d", &a, &b);
```

printf and scanf are identifiers, and the parentheses following them tell the compiler that they are functions. If, in the link phase of *cc*, the linker cannot find these functions elsewhere, it will take them from the standard library; a programmer would not normally redefine these identifiers.

```
"\ninput  a  and  b :   "
```

Constant strings are tokens.

```
&a,  &b
```

& is an operator.

```
sum = a + b;
```

The symbols = and + are operators. White space here will be ignored, so we could have written

```
      sum=a+b;
```

or

```
      sum    =    a    +    b  ;
```

but not

s u m = a + b;

In this example, `main`, `sum`, `a`, `b`, `scanf`, and `printf` are all tokens. The token `int` is a keyword. The characters such as `=` `+` `{` and `}` are also tokens. They are interpreted as operators or have other special meaning. Blanks or comments may be inserted anywhere except in tokens. White space is used by the compiler in many instances to determine how to separate tokens. Another use of white space is to provide a more legible program for the reader. Program text is implicitly a single stream of characters, but to a human reader it is a two-dimensional tableau.

One must be especially careful with C programs because there are several ways to group symbols, and different groupings may have different interpretations. An example would be

a+++b

Since `+` and `++` are operators, the meaning could be either

a++ +   b   or   a +   ++ b

depending on how the tokens were grouped. Normally at the lexical level the two pluses would be grouped and passed to the compiler to see if this was syntactically correct.

2.2 SYNTAX RULES

The syntax of C will be described using a rule system derived from Backus-Naur Form (BNF). These schemes were first used in 1960 to describe ALGOL 60. While they will not be adequate by themselves to describe the legal strings of C, when used in conjunction with some explanatory remarks they are a standard form of describing modern high-level languages.

A syntactic category will be written as *category* and defined by productions, also called rewriting rules, such as

digit ::= 0 | 1 | 2 | 3 | 4 | 5 | 6 | 7 | 8 | 9

This should be read as

The syntactic category *digit* is rewritten as either
the symbol 0, the symbol 1, . . . , or the symbol 9.

The vertical bar separates alternate choices. Symbols not in italics are taken to be terminal symbols of the language to which no further productions are applied.

Symbols to be used in productions

italics	indicate syntactic categories
:: =	"to be rewritten as" symbol
|	vertical bar to separate choices
{ }$_1$	choose 1 of the enclosed items
{ }$_{0+}$	repeat the enclosed items 0 or more times
{ }$_{1+}$	repeat the enclosed items 1 or more times
{ }$_{opt}$	optional items

Other items are terminal symbols of the language.

Let us define a category *letter_or_digit* to mean any lowercase or uppercase letter of the alphabet or any decimal digit. Here is one way that this can be accomplished.

lowercase_letter :: = a | b | c | . . . | z
uppercase_letter :: = A | B | C | . . . | Z
letter :: = *lowercase_letter* | *uppercase_letter*
digit :: = 0 | 1 | 2 | 3 | 4 | 5 | 6 | 7 | 8 | 9
letter_or_digit :: = *letter* | *digit*

Now let us create a category *alphanumeric_string* to be an arbitrary sequence of letters or digits.

alphanumeric_string :: = {*letter_or_digit*}$_{0+}$

Using these productions, we see that strings of one character such as "5" or "x" and strings of many characters such as

"THISisONEsuchSTRINGgo000123999"

as well as the null string "", are all alphanumeric strings.

If we wish to guarantee that a string has at least one character, we must define a new syntactic category, such as

alpha_string_1 :: = {*letter_or_digit*}$_{1+}$

and if we want strings that start with an uppercase letter, we could define

u_alpha_string :: = *uppercase_letter* {*letter_or_digit*}$_{0+}$

or equivalently,

u_alpha_string :: = *uppercase_letter* *alphanumeric_string*

To illustrate the { }$_{opt}$ notation, let us define the if-else conditional statement.

conditional_statement :: = if (*expression*) *statement*
{else *statement*}$_{opt}$

Because *expression* and *statement* have not yet been supplied with rewriting rules, this category is not defined completely. These rewriting rules are complicated, and we are not ready to present them here. In any case, some examples are

```
if (big_big_big > 999)
    huge = giant + a_lot;        /*  no else part immediately follows  */

if (normalized_score >= 65)
    pass = 1;
else            /*  this else part is associated with the preceding if  */
    pass = 0;
```

2.3 IDENTIFIERS

An identifier is a sequence of letters, digits, and the special character _, which is called an "underscore". A letter or underscore must be the first character of an identifier. In most implementations of C the upper- and lowercase letters are treated as distinct. It is good programming practice to choose identifiers that have mnemonic significance so that they contribute to the readability and documentation of the program.

$$identifier ::= \{letter \mid \_\}_1 \{letter \mid \_ \mid digit\}_{0+}$$

Some examples are

```
n
x
_id
iamanidentifier
so_am_i
me222
```

but not

```
not#me      /*  special character  #  not allowed  */
101south    /*  must not start with a digit  */
-plus       /*  do not mistake  -  for  _  */
```

Identifiers are created to give unique names to various objects in a program. Some identifiers are reserved as special to the C language; they are called *keywords*. Although not technically part of the C language, the identifiers scanf and printf are already known to the C system as input/output functions in a standard library. The identifier main is also special in that C programs always begin execution at the function called main.

Good programming style requires the programmer to choose names that are meaningful. If you were to write a program to figure out various taxes, you might have identifiers such as tax_rate, price, and tax, so that the statement

```
tax = price * tax_rate;
```

would have an obvious meaning. The underscore _ is used to create a single identifier from what would normally be a string of words separated by spaces. If a group of identifiers has a related use, the identifiers are frequently distinguished by ending in consecutive digits. For example, the identifiers tax1, tax2, tax3, and tax4 might be used to represent taxes computed on four separate items. Meaningfulness and avoiding confusion go hand in hand with readability to constitute the main guidelines for a good programming style.

2.4 KEYWORDS

Keywords are explicitly reserved words that have a strict meaning as individual tokens in C. They cannot be redefined or used in other contexts.

Keywords

auto	break	case	char	continue	default
do	double	else	enum	extern	float
for	goto	if	int	long	register
return	short	sizeof	static	struct	switch
typedef	union	unsigned	void	while	

Some implementations may have additional keywords such as

```
ada    asm    fortran    pascal
```

In comparison to other major languages, C has only a small number of keywords. Ada, for example, has 62 keywords. It is a characteristic of C that it does a lot with relatively few special symbols and keywords.

2.5 OPERATORS AND SEPARATORS

There are many special characters that have particular meaning. Examples include the arithmetic operators

```
+        -        *        /
```

which stand for the usual arithmetic operations of addition, subtraction, multiplication, and division, respectively. In a C program these often separate tokens.

```
a+b        /*  this means identifier  a  plus identifier  b  */
a_b        /*  whereas this is a three-character identifier  */
```

Some symbols have several meanings depending on context.

```
printf("%d", a)
a % 5
        /***
        %  is a format control character in printf() that tells
        the system to print the value of the identifier  a   as a
        decimal digit string;
        %  is also the modulus operator
        ***/
```

Special characters along with white space serve to separate tokens, and some special characters are used in many different contexts. The context itself can determine which token is being used. For example, the expressions

```
a + b          ++a          a += b
```

all use + as a character, but ++ is a single token, as is +=. Having the meaning of a symbol depend on context makes for a small symbol set and a terse language.

2.6 STRINGS

A sequence of characters enclosed in a pair of double quote marks " is a string. Note that " is just one character, not two. If the character " itself is to occur in a string, it must be preceded by the character \. The following are examples of strings.

```
"a string of text"
"              "                 /*  a string of blank characters  */
"z"
",.1kM87Ytt  -  gibberish"
"a string with  \"  double quotes within"
" a = b + c;    x = sin(y);  "        /*  nothing is executed  */
" "                                   /*  the null  string  */
```

Strings are tokens. Character sequences that would have meaning if outside a string are just a sequence of characters when surrounded by double quotes. In the previous example, a string contained what appears to be the statement a = b + c;, but since it occurs surrounded by double quotes, it is explicitly this sequence of characters. A string is a particular type of constant within a C program, technically an array of characters, and this will be discussed in detail in Chapter 7.

2.7 COMMENTS

Comments are arbitrary strings of symbols placed between the delimiters /* and */. We have already seen examples such as

```
/*  a comment  */       /***  another comment  ***/      /*****/
```

Another example is

```
/***
 ***   a very long comment
 ***   can be written in this fashion
 ***   to set it off from the surrounding
 ***   code
 ***/
```

The following style can be used to give prominence to comments.

```
/***************************
*    if you wish, you can    *
*    put comments in a box.  *
***************************/
```

Comments are treated as white space by the compiler. They are not part of the executable program, but are used by the programmer as a documentation aid. In a production environment, the ideal aim of documentation is to explain clearly to oneself, to users, and to program maintenance people how the program works, its intended use, and its limitations. Comments frequently contain an informal argument demonstrating the correctness of the program. Comments will be used throughout this text wherever examples of code occur.

Comments should be written simultaneously with program text. Frequently beginners leave the inserting of comments as a last step. There are two problems with this. The first is that once the program is running, the tendency is either to omit or abbreviate the comments. The second is that ideally the comments should serve as an ongoing dialogue with the programmer, indicating program structure and contributing to program clarity and correctness. They cannot serve this purpose if they are inserted after the coding is finished.

2.8 CONSTANTS

As we have seen in some simple introductory programs, C manipulates various kinds of values. Integers such as 29 and floating numbers such as 3.14159 are examples of constants. In Chapter 3 we will go into detail on how C understands numbers. Strings such as "i am a . . . " are constants of a particular kind (see Chapter 7). Also, there are character constants such as 'a', 'b', . . . , and they are distinctly different from strings. For example, 'a' and "a" are not the same. Some character constants are of a special kind, such as the newline character, written '\n'. The backslash has a special meaning in this context and '\n' is a single-character constant even though the characters \ and n are being used to describe it. These constants are all collected by the compiler as tokens.

We leave the detailed discussion of the various types of constants to later sections that discuss the corresponding data types. Constants that are syntactically expressible may not be available on a particular machine because of implementation limits. For example, an integer may be too large to be expressible in a machine word.

Integers are finite strings of decimal digits. Because there are octal and hexadecimal integers, as well as decimal integers, we have to be careful to distinguish between the different kinds. For example, 17 is a decimal integer constant, 017 is an octal integer constant, and 0x17 is a hexadecimal integer constant. Details about octal and hexadecimal integers are given in Chapter 3. Also, negative constant integers such as -33 are considered constant expressions.

positive_digit ::= 1 | 2 | 3 | 4 | 5 | 6 | 7 | 8 | 9
decimal_integer ::= 0 | *positive_digit* {*digit*}$_{0+}$
integer ::= *decimal_integer*

Some examples of constant integers are

```
0
123
49
```

but not

```
0123        /*  an octal integer       */
-49         /*  a constant expression  */
123.0       /*  a floating constant    */
```

While we have already used floating constants such as 39.7, their meaning in terms of machine accuracy and use in expressions is complicated enough to require a thorough discussion, which is provided in the next chapter.

2.9 SUMMARY

1. Tokens are the basic syntactic units of C. They include identifiers, keywords, strings, constants, operators, and other separators. Comments and blanks (or other white space such as tabs) are separators that are otherwise ignored.

2. Syntax is precisely specified by BNF productions, also called rewriting rules.

3. Identifiers are tokens that the programmer uses chiefly to name variables and functions. They begin with a letter or _ and are chosen to be meaningful to the human reader.

4. Some identifiers are already known to the system because they are predefined system functions. These include the input/output functions `printf()` and `scanf()`, and such mathematical functions as `sqrt()`, `sin()`, `cos()`, `tan()`, etc.

5. A keyword, also called a reserved word, has a strict meaning. There are 29 keywords in C. They cannot be redefined.

6. Operators and separators are numerous in C and can mean different things in different contexts.

7. Strings are arbitrary sequences of characters, including white space, that are placed inside double quotes, such as `"she sells sea shells . . . "`. They occur as the first argument in the input/output functions `printf()` and `scanf()`. They are also considered character array constants.

8. Comments are critical for good program documentation. They are enclosed by the bracket pair `/*` and `*/`. Comments should assist the reader to both use and understand the program.

9. Constants include characters, strings, and various kinds of number constants.

2.10 EXERCISES

1. Give an example of three types of tokens.

2. Use BNF productions to define the integers 0, 1, 2, . . . , 99999.

3. Use BNF productions to define a class of identifiers that has only letters at the beginning and may have digits at the end. Thus `abc`, `a678`, `a5`, `intf`, and `res43` are allowed, but `aa2d` and `5id` are not.

4. Which of the following are not identifiers and why?

`3id`	`__yes`	`o_no_o_no`	`00_go`	`star*it`
`1_i_am`	`one_i_aren't`	`me_to-2`	`xYshouldI`	`int`

5. List five keywords and explain their use.

6. Take a symbol such as + and illustrate the different ways it can be used in a program.

7. Design a standard form of introductory comment that will give a reader information about who wrote the program and why.

8. Can you have the following as a comment?

   ```
   /*  This is an attempt /* to nest */  a comment */
   ```

9. The following code, although not very readable, should compile and execute. Test it to see if that is true.

   ```
   main(
   ){float qx,
   zz,
   tt;printf("gimme 3"
   );scanf
   (    "%f%f        %f",&qx,&zz

   ,&tt);printf("averageis=%f",(qx+tt+zz)/3.0);}
   ```

10. Rewrite the above program with white space and comments to make it more readable and well documented.

3

Declarations, Expressions, Assignment, Data Types

We begin this chapter with a discussion of declarations and the fundamental data types. After a brief look at expressions, statements, and assignment, a detailed explanation concerning each of the fundamental data types is given. In addition, the use of the arithmetic operators is explained, with particular attention being paid to the concepts of precedence and associativity of operators. In expressions with operands of different types, certain implicit conversions occur. The rules for conversion are explained, including the cast operator, which forces explicit conversion.

3.1 DECLARATIONS

Variables and constants are the objects that a program manipulates. In general, all variables must be declared before they can be used. For example,

```
int     i, j, k;
float   length, height;
char    c;
```

are declarations that specify that i, j, and k are variables of type int, that length and height are variables of type float, and that c is a variable of type char. A variable name is an identifier, and a declaration is a type followed by a list of variable names terminated with a semicolon.

$int\_declaration ::=$ int $identifier$ {, $identifier$}$_{0+}$;

In the next section a more general syntax is given.

The beginning of a program might look like

```
main()
{
    int     a, b;              /*  declaration  */
    char    cc1, cc2, cc3;     /*  declaration  */
    float   bignum;            /*  declaration  */

    a = 0;                     /*  assignment statement  */
    .   .    .    .   .        /*  etc  */
}
```

The braces { and } surround a block. They are used to enclose declarations and statements. The declarations, if any, must occur before the statements. Declarations serve two purposes. First, they tell the compiler to set aside an appropriate amount of space in memory to hold values associated with variables; and second, because they specify the data types associated with variables, they enable the compiler to instruct the machine to perform specified operations correctly. Consider the code

```
int      a, b, c;
float    x, y, z;       /*  floating types represent real values  */

a = 3;
b = -7;
c = a + b;              /*  addition of two variables of type int  */
x = 3.3;
y = -7.7;
z = x + y;              /*  addition of two variables of type float  */
```

In the statement c = a + b; the operation + is being applied to two variables of type int, which at the machine level is a different operation than + applied to variables of type float, as occurs in the statement z = x + y;. Of course, the programmer need not be concerned that the two + operations are mechanically different, but the C compiler has to recognize the difference and give the appropriate machine instructions.

3.2 FUNDAMENTAL DATA TYPES

C provides several fundamental types.

Fundamental data types

char	short int	int	long int
unsigned char	unsigned short int	unsigned int	unsigned long int
float	long float		

These are all keywords, and therefore their use is reserved. They may not be used as names of variables. Of course, char stands for "character" and int stands for "integer," but only char and int can be used as keywords. Other data types such as arrays, pointers, and structures are derived from the fundamental types. They are presented in later chapters.

The keywords short int, long int, and unsigned int may be, and usually are, shortened to just short, long, and unsigned, respectively. Also, double and long float are equivalent, but double is the keyword usually used. (Shorter names are easier to type.) With these conventions we obtain a new list:

Fundamental data types

char	short	int	long
unsigned char	unsigned short	unsigned	unsigned long
float	double		

Now we can give the syntax for a fundamental type, and use that information to give a more general syntax for a declaration.

type ::= char | short | int | long
| unsigned char | unsigned short | unsigned
| unsigned long | float | double

declaration ::= *type* *identifier* {, *identifier*}$_{0+}$;

Various subsets of the fundamental types are given collective names.

integral types: char, short, int, long, unsigned char, unsigned short, unsigned, unsigned long
floating types: float, double
arithmetic types: *integral types* + *floating types*

These collective names are a convenience. In Chapter 7, for example, when we discuss arrays, we will explain that only integral expressions are allowed as subscripts, meaning that only expressions involving integral types are allowed. Later in this chapter when we discuss the arithmetic operators, we will explain that they are used with the arithmetic types, meaning any of the integral or floating types.

We want to describe in detail how the fundamental data types are used, and the simplest place to begin is to introduce integer and floating arithmetic. But to understand in detail even simple examples of code, we need to have a sense of what an expression is, to know that expressions have value, and to understand how the assignment operator = is used to assign values to variables. The following section covers the topics expressions, statements, and assignment so that the simple code given in the succeeding sections is understandable.

3.3 EXPRESSIONS, STATEMENTS, AND ASSIGNMENT

Expressions are combinations of constants, variables, operators, and function calls. Some examples of expressions are

```
a + b
3.0 * x - 9.66553
3.77 + sin(3.11 * x - 7.33001)
tan(17.777)
```

Most expressions have a value. For example, the expression a + b has an obvious value, depending on the values of the variables a and b. If a has value 1 and b has value 2, then a + b has value 3.

The equal sign, =, is the basic assignment operator in C. An example of an assignment *expression* is

```
i = 7
```

The variable i is assigned the value 7, and the expression as a whole takes that value as well. When followed by a semicolon, an expression becomes a statement. Some examples of statements are

```
i = 7;
x = 3.1 + sin(22.2);
printf("the sun shines at high noon");
```

The following two statements are perfectly legal, but they do no useful work.

```
3.777;
a + b;
```

Simple assignment statements are of the form

> *variable = expression*;

The value of the expression on the right side of the equal sign is computed and then assigned to the variable on the left side of the equal sign. For example, the code

```
int   a, b, c;

a = 7;
b = 2;
c = a + b;
```

declares a, b, and c to be variables of type int, then assigns the value 7 to a, the value 2 to b, and the value of the expression a + b to c. Since the value of a + b is 9, that is the value that is assigned to c.

Even though assignment statements sometimes resemble mathematical equations, the two notions are distinct and should not be confused. The mathematical equation

> $x + 2 = 0$

does not become an assignment statement by typing

```
x + 2 = 0;      /* wrong */
```

The left side of the equal sign is an expression, not a variable, and this expression may not be assigned a value. Now consider the assignment statement

```
x = x + 1;
```

The interpretation is that the current value of x is assigned the old value of x plus 1. If the old value of x is 2, then the value of x after execution of the statement will be 3. Observe that as a mathematical equation

> $x = x + 1$

is meaningless; after subtracting x from both sides of the equation, we obtain

> $0 = 1$

In C the assignment operation is the principal way to change the value of a variable.

We must specifically think of = as an operator. To put the situation into perspective, consider + for comparison. The binary operator + takes two operands as in the expression a + b. The value of the expression a + b is just the sum of the values of a and b. A simple assignment expression is of the form

> *variable = right_side*   /* no ; here */

where *right_side* is itself an expression. The assignment operator = has the two operands *variable* and *right_side*. The value of *right_side* is assigned to *variable*, and that value becomes the value of the assignment expression as a whole. To illustrate this, consider

```
int   x, y, z;

x = (y = 5) + (z = 7);
```

The two assignment expressions y = 5 and z = 7 have value 5 and 7, respectively, and these values are added to obtain the value 12, which is then assigned to x. This example would usually be written instead as

```
int   x, y, z;

y = 5;
z = 7;
x = y + z;
```

However, there are many situations where assignment occurs naturally as part of an expression. One typical example is

```
int   x, y, z;

x = y = z = 0;
```

The operator = associates "right to left" so that

```
x = y = z = 0;
```

is equivalent to

```
x = (y = (z = 0));
```

First, z is assigned the value 0 and the expression (z = 0) has value 0. Then y is assigned the value 0 and the expression (y = (z = 0)) has value 0. Finally, x is assigned the value 0 and the expression x = (y = (z = 0)) has value 0. Many languages do not use assignment in such an elaborate way. In this respect C is different. In section 3.5 the concepts of precedence and associativity of operators are explained, and the assignment operator along with the arithmetic operators is seen in a more complete context.

3.4 THE DATA TYPE int

In C the data type int is the principal working type of the language. This type, along with the types short, long, and unsigned, is designed for working with the integer values that are representable on a machine.

In mathematics the natural numbers are 0, 1, 2, 3, . . . , and these numbers, along with their negatives, comprise the integers. On a machine only a finite portion of these integers is representable for a given integral type.

The syntax for integer constants representable in decimal notation is the following. (For hexadecimal and octal notation see section 3.14.)

$$digit ::= 0 \mid 1 \mid 2 \mid 3 \mid 4 \mid 5 \mid 6 \mid 7 \mid 8 \mid 9$$
$$positive\_digit ::= 1 \mid 2 \mid 3 \mid 4 \mid 5 \mid 6 \mid 7 \mid 8 \mid 9$$
$$decimal\_integer\_constant ::= 0 \mid positive\_digit \ \{digit\}_{0+}$$

The negative integers are considered expressions, with the unary minus operator being applied to integer constants. Some examples of decimal integer constants are

```
0
7
123
123456789123456789        /*  too big for the machine?  */
```

but not

```
1.777   /*  a floating constant  */
4.0     /*  a floating constant  */
0x66    /*  a hexadecimal integer, not decimal  */
066     /*  an octal integer, not decimal  */
1,209   /*  comma not allowed  */
-33     /*  this is a constant expression  */
```

In any machine it is impossible to represent all the integers; there are too many of them. A variable i of type int can take on integer values in the range

$$N_{min\_int} \leq i \leq N_{max\_int}$$

where the integers N_{min_int} and N_{max_int} are machine dependent. On a VAX

1 byte = 8 bits   1 word = 4 bytes = 32 bits

and a variable of type int is stored in one word. A word having 32 bits can take on 2^{32} different states. Half of these states, 2^{31} in number, are used to represent the nonnegative integers

$$0,1,2, \ldots , 2^{31} - 1$$

while the remaining states are used to represent the negative integers

$$-2^{31}, \ -2^{31} + 1, \ldots , \ -3, -2, -1$$

Hence, on a VAX

$$N_{min\_int} = -2^{31} = -2147483648 \approx -2 \ billion$$
$$N_{max\_int} = 2^{31} - 1 = +2147483647 \approx +2 \ billion$$

The following code

```
int  a, b, c;

a = 2000000000;
b = 2000000000;
c = a + b;                  /*  out of range  */
```

is syntactically correct, but at run-time the variable c may be assigned an incorrect value. The logical value of a + b is 4 billion, and that is greater than N_{max_int}. This condition is called *integer overflow*, and what actually happens is machine dependent.

A not uncommon occurrence is for nothing to happen except that the program gives logically incorrect results.

3.5 ARITHMETIC OPERATORS WITH int DATA

The binary arithmetic operators

$$+ \qquad - \qquad * \qquad / \qquad \%$$

correspond to the usual mathematical operations of addition, subtraction, multiplication, division, and modulus, respectively. They are called binary operators because they each take two operands, as in the expression a + b. There is also a unary minus operator, as in the expression − a. There is no unary plus operator. Integer division returns the integer value obtained by discarding any fractional part. For example, 1/2 has value 0, 3/2 has value 1, and − 7/3 has value − 2. The expression a % b is read "a modulo b." If a and b are positive integers, then a % b yields the remainder after dividing a by b. For example, 7 % 2 has value 1, and 12 % 3 has value 0. If a and/or b are negative, then a % b is defined, but the result is machine dependent. The value of b should not be zero, for that would lead to division by zero. The operator % is used mostly with positive operands. If a and b are positive integers, then the expression

```
((a / b) * b) + (a % b)
```

has value a. You should hand simulate the expression with some simple values for a and b so that you understand why this is so. The following simple program is designed to help you test, on your own machine, the arithmetic operators as applied to integer data.

```
/*** integer arithmetic ***/

main()
{
    int   x, y;

    printf("\n\ninteger arithmetic:  experiment with your machine");

    while (1) {
        printf("\n\ninput two integers:   ");
        scanf("%d %d", &x, &y);
        printf("\nx = %d\ny = %d\n\n", x, y);
        printf("x + y = %d\nx - y = %d\n", x + y, x - y);
        printf("x * y = %d\nx / y = %d\n", x * y, x / y);
        printf("(x / y) * y = %d\n", (x / y) * y);
        printf("x (mod y) = %d\n", x % y);
        printf("(x / y) * y  +  x (mod y) = %d", x / y * y + x % y);
        /** precedence and associativity of operators must be known
            to correctly interpret the last expression **/
    }
```

Operators have rules of *precedence* and *associativity,* which determine precisely how expressions are evaluated. Since expressions inside parentheses are evaluated first, parentheses can be used to clarify or change the order in which operations are performed. Consider the expression 1 + 2 * 3. In C the operator * has higher precedence than +, so multiplication is performed first, and then addition. Hence the expression has the value 7. An equivalent expression is 1 + (2 * 3). On the other hand, since expressions inside parentheses are evaluated first, the expression (1 + 2) * 3 has value 9. The operators + and - have the same precedence. Therefore, the associativity rule "left to right" is used to determine how an expression such as

        1 - 2 + 3 - 4 - 77

is evaluated. The "left to right" rule means that the operations are performed from left to right. Parentheses can be used to give the equivalent expression

        (((1 - 2) + 3) - 4) - 77

The following table gives the rules of precedence and associativity for the arithmetic operators, the assignment operator =, and the operators ++ and --, which are discussed in section 3.6.

Operators	*Associativity*
- (unary) ++ --	right to left
* / %	left to right
+ -	left to right
=	right to left

All operators on the same line, such as *, /, and %, have equal precedence, and all operators on a given line have higher precedence than those on the lines below them. The associativity rule for all the operators on a given line appears on the right side of the table. We are now in a position to illustrate how the rules are used by writing down some expressions, then the corresponding expressions with parentheses, and finally the value of the expressions.

Declarations and assignments

```
int   a, b, c, d;
a = 2; b = -3; c = 7; d = -19;
```

Expression	Equivalent expression	Value
a / b	a / b	0
c / b / a	(c / b) / a	-1
c % a	c % a	1
a % b	a % b	/* machine dependent */
d / b % a	(d / b) % a	0
- a * d	(- a) * d	38
a % - b * c	(a % (- b)) * c	14
9 / c + - 20 / d	(9 / c) + ((- 20) / d)	2
- d % c - b / a * 5 + 5	(((- d) % c) - ((b / a) * 5)) + 5	15
7 - a % (3 + b)	7 - (a % (3 + b))	/* error */
- - - a	- (- (- a))	-2
a = b = c = -33	a = (b = (c = (-33)))	-33

3.6 INCREMENT AND DECREMENT OPERATORS
WITH int DATA

The increment operator ++ and decrement operator -- are unary operators with the
same precedence as the unary -, and they all associate from right to left. Both ++
and -- can be applied to variables, but not to constants or expressions. Moreover, they
can occur in either prefix or postfix position, with possibly different effects occurring.

> *increment_or_decrement_expression* ::=
> ++ *variable* | -- *variable* | *variable* ++ | *variable* --

Some examples are

```
++ count
-- kk
index ++
going_down --
```

but not

```
777 ++                      /*  constants cannot be incremented  */
++ (black / knight)         /*  expressions cannot be incremented  */
```

The statement

```
++ i;    is equivalent to   i = i + 1;
```

Also, the statement

```
i ++;    is equivalent to   i = i + 1;
```

and in a similar fashion

```
-- i;    is equivalent to   i = i - 1;
i --;    is equivalent to   i = i - 1;
```

In simple situations one can consider ++ and -- operations as just a concise notation
for incrementing and decrementing a variable. However, in some expressions the
situation is more complicated. Both ++ and -- can be used as either prefix or postfix
operators, and the effect can be different. The expressions ++a and a++ both increment
a by 1. Similarly, --a and a-- both decrement a by 1. However, when ++a is used in
an expression, the value of a is incremented *before* the expression is evaluated, whereas
when a++ is used, the expression is evaluated with the current value of a and *then* a
is incremented. Similarly with --a and a--. The following code illustrates the situation.

```
/***    increment and decrement expressions    ***/

main()
{
    int    a, b, c;

    a = b = c = 0;
    a = ++b + ++c;
    printf("\n %d %d %d", a, b, c);     /*  2 1 1  is printed  */
    a = b++ + c++;
    printf("\n %d %d %d", a, b, c);     /*  2 2 2  is printed  */
    a = ++b + c++;
    printf("\n %d %d %d", a, b, c);     /*  5 3 3  is printed  */
    a = b-- + --c;
    printf("\n %d %d %d", a, b, c);     /*  5 2 2  is printed  */
    a = ++c + c;
    printf("\n %d %d %d", a, b, c);     /*  machine dependent  */
    printf("\n\n");
}
```

An expression such as a + b has a value that depends on the values of a and b, but the values of a and b in memory are in no way affected by the expression. However, the expression ++a is different. It has a value that depends on the value of a, and moreover, the expression changes the value of a in memory. This phenomenon is called a *side effect*. In certain constructions a side effect can produce unintended results. Consider the statement

```
a = ++c + c;          /*  machine dependent code  */
```

Here ++ is prefixed to c, meaning that c is supposed to be incremented before it is used. But c occurs twice in the statement, and when c is incremented it changes the value of c in both places in the statement. The computation of the value of the expression ++c + c is machine dependent, and such expressions are considered bad programming practice. It is considered better to write code that isolates the effect of the ++ operator, such as

```
++c;
a = c + c;
```

or

```
a = 2 * (++c);
```

These latter pieces of code strictly determine the sequence of evaluation and assignment.

Declarations and assignments		
int a, b, c, d, e, f, g, h, i, j, k, m, n; a = b = c = d = e = f = g = h = i = j = k = m = n = 3;		
Expression	*Equivalent expression*	*Value*
--- a	- (- (- a))	-3
- -- a	- (-- a)	-2
-- - a	-- (- a)	/* illegal */
b - -- c	b - (-- c)	1
d -- - e	(d --) - e	0
d --- e	?	/* illegal */
- f -- - g	(- (f --)) - g	-6
f ++ = g	(f ++) = g	/* illegal */
h ++ / ++ i * -- j	(((h ++) / (++ i)) * (-- j)	0
++ k / m ++ * -- n	((((++ k) / (m ++)) * (-- n)	2

3.7 THE INTEGRAL TYPES short, long, AND unsigned

In C the data type int is considered the "natural" or "usual" type for working with integers. The other integral types: char, short, long, and the unsigned types, are intended for more specialized use. For example, the data type short might be used in situations where storage is of concern. The compiler may provide less storage for a short than for an int, although it is not required to do so. The situation varies from machine to machine. On a VAX a short is stored in 2 bytes (= 16 bits). Thus, a short variable s can take on integer values in the range

$$N_{min\_short} \leq s \leq N_{max\_short}$$

where

$$N_{min\_short} = -2^{15} = -32768 \approx -32 \; thousand$$
$$N_{max\_short} = 2^{15} - 1 = +32767 \approx +32 \; thousand$$

The data type long is provided for situations where a larger range of integer values is desired. The compiler may provide more storage for a long than for an int, although it is not required to do so. On a VAX a long is stored in 4 bytes, the same as for an int. On microcomputers with 16-bit architectures, such as machines based on an Intel 8086 or 8088 microprocessor, short's and int's usually are stored in 2 bytes and long's in 4 bytes.

Variables of type unsigned are stored in the same number of bytes as an int. However, as the name implies, the integer values stored have no sign. If, on a particular machine, an int is stored in a word, then a variable u of type unsigned takes values in the range

$$0 \leq u \leq 2^{wordsize} - 1$$

On a VAX we have

$$N_{min\_unsigned} = 0$$
$$N_{max\_unsigned} = 2^{32} - 1 = 4294967295 \approx 4 \text{ billion}$$

Arithmetic on unsigned variables is performed modulo $2^{wordsize}$.

The operator sizeof is built in as part of the C language, and it will be described in more detail later. The operator returns an integer that represents the number of bytes used to store an object. The following program uses this operator, and it will tell you how many bytes are used on your own machine to store variables of a given type.

```
/***   compute the size of the fundamental types   ***/

main()
{
      printf("\n      char:  %d  byte ",  sizeof(    char));
      printf("\n     short:  %d  bytes",  sizeof(   short));
      printf("\n       int:  %d  bytes",  sizeof(     int));
      printf("\n      long:  %d  bytes",  sizeof(    long));
      printf("\nunsigned:  %d  bytes",  sizeof(unsigned));
      printf("\n     float:  %d  bytes",  sizeof(   float));
      printf("\n    double:  %d  bytes",  sizeof(  double));
      printf("\n\n");
}
```

All that is guaranteed by the C language is that

```
sizeof(char)  = 1
sizeof(short) ≤ sizeof(int) ≤ sizeof(long)
sizeof(unsigned)  = sizeof(int)
sizeof(float) ≤ sizeof(double)
```

3.8 THE FLOATING TYPES

Two floating types, float and double, are provided in C to deal with numbers such as

```
1.7      0.001      3.14159
```

Some of the integers are representable as floating constants, but they must be written with a decimal point as in

```
0.0,   1.0,   2.0,   .  .   .
```

as opposed to

```
0,   1,   2,   3,   .  .   .
```

Also, there is an exponential notation, as in the example 1.092332e5. This corresponds to the scientific notation 1.092332×10^5. Recall that

$$1.092332 \times 10^5 = 1.092332 \times 10 \times 10 \times 10 \times 10 \times 10$$
$$= 1.092332 \times 100000$$
$$= 109233.2 \qquad (\textit{decimal place shifted five places})$$

In a similar fashion, the number

```
1.092332e-3
```

calls for shifting the decimal point three places to the left to obtain the equivalent constant

```
0.001092332
```

Now we want to describe the exponential notation very precisely. A floating constant such as

```
333.77777e-22
```

may not contain any embedded blanks or special characters. Each part of the constant is given a name:

```
333    ≡ integer part
77777  ≡ fractional part
e-22   ≡ exponential part
```

A floating constant may contain an integer part, a decimal point, a fractional part, and an exponential part. A floating constant *must* contain either a decimal point or an exponential part or both. If a decimal point is present, either an integer part or fractional part or both *must* be present. If no decimal point is present, then there must be an integer part along with an exponential part.

$$integer\_part ::= \{digit\}_{1+}$$
$$fractional\_part ::= \{digit\}_{1+}$$
$$exponential\_part ::= \{e \mid E\}_1 \{+ \mid -\}_{opt} \{digit\}_{1+}$$
$$floating\_constant ::=$$

        integer_part . fractional_part exponential_part
    | *integer_part . fractional_part*
    | *integer_part .*
    | *. fractional_part*
    | *integer_part exponential_part*
    | *. fractional_part exponential_part*

Some examples of floating constants are

```
3.14159
314.159e-2
314159e-5
0.00314159e+3
0.00314159e3
.00314159e003      /*  first six floating constants are equal  */
0.0
0e0                /*  equivalent to 0.0  */
.0e0               /*  equivalent to 0.0  */
```

```
1.0
1e0                     /*  equivalent to 1.0  */
1.                      /*  equivalent to 1.0, but harder to read  */
```

but not

```
3.14,159                /*  comma not allowed  */
3.1415 9                /*  embedded space not allowed  */
314159                  /*  decimal point or exponential part needed  */
.e0                     /*  integer part or fractional part needed  */
-3.14159                /*  this is a floating constant expression  */
```

Typically, a C compiler will provide more storage for a variable of type `double` than for one of type `float`, although it is not required to do so. All floating constants are of type `double`.

The possible values that a floating type can be assigned are described in terms of attributes called *range* and *precision*. The range describes the limits of the largest and smallest *positive* floating values that can be represented in the machine. The precision describes the number of significant decimal places that a floating value carries.

On a VAX a variable of type `float` has an approximate precision of six significant figures, and an approximate range of 10^{-38} to 10^{+38}. This means that for convenience we may think of a `float` as represented in the machine in the form

$$\pm\ .d_1\, d_2\, d_3\, d_4\, d_5\, d_6\ \times\ 10^n$$

where

each d_i is a decimal digit,
the first digit d_1 is positive,
and $-38 \leqslant n \leqslant +38$.

A variable of type `double` has an approximate precision of 16, and a range identical to that of a `float`. Thus we may think of a `double` as represented in the machine in the form

$$\pm\ .d_1\, d_2 \cdots d_{16}\ \times\ 10^n$$

where

each d_i is a decimal digit,
the first digit d_1 is positive,
and $-38 \leqslant n \leqslant +38$.

For example, if x is a variable of type `double`, then the statement

```
x = 123.45123451234512345;          /*  20  significant digits  */
```

will result in x being assigned a value that is stored in the form (only approximately true)

$$0.1234512345123451 \times 10^{+3} \quad \textit{(16 significant digits)}$$

The main points that one must be aware of are (1) that not all real numbers are representable, and (2) that floating arithmetic operations, unlike the integer arithmetic operations, need not be exact. For small computations this is usually of no concern. For very large computations, such as numerically solving a large system of ordinary differential equations, a good understanding of rounding effects, scaling, etc., may be necessary. This is the domain of numerical analysis.

The arithmetic types are composed of the integral types and the floating types; the arithmetic operators

$$+ \qquad - \qquad * \qquad / \qquad \%$$

are used with the arithmetic types, although the modulus operator is restricted to just the integral types. The following program illustrates the use of the arithmetic operators with floating variables.

```
/***  compute areas of triangles, squares, and circles  ***/

#define   PI        3.1415926535897932384
#define   SQRT_3    1.7320508075688772935

main()
{
      double   x;

      printf("\nthis program asks for a length,");
      printf("\nstores the value in the variable  x ,");
      printf("\nand then computes the areas of the following figures");
      printf("\n    (1)   an equilateral triangle of side  x ,");
      printf("\n    (2)   a square of side  x ,");
      printf("\n    (3)   a circle of radius  x .");

      while (1) {
            printf("\n\ninput a length:   ");
            scanf("%lf", &x);
            printf("\nx = %.16f\n", x);
            printf("\n triangle:   %.16f", 0.5 * x * SQRT_3 / 2.0 * x);
            printf("\n   square:   %.16f", x * x);
            printf("\n   circle:   %.16f", PI * x * x);
      }
}
```

The statement

```
scanf("%lf", &x);
```

is telling the system to read in a long float (a double) for x. The formula for the area of a triangle is given by

$$\frac{1}{2} \times base \times height$$

Therefore, since an equilateral triangle of side 1 has height $\sqrt{3}/2$, the formula for the area of an equilateral triangle of side x is given by

$$\frac{1}{2} \times x \times \frac{\sqrt{3}}{2} \times x$$

This formula was used in the above program. Note that we looked up the square root of 3 in a table and included it as a constant in the program. The next section describes how one can make use of mathematical functions such as sqrt() in a library.

3.9 MATHEMATICAL FUNCTIONS

In C there are no built-in mathematical functions. Functions such as

    sqrt()   exp()   log()   sin()   cos()   tan()

usually occur in a special library. If a programmer wishes to use these functions, the library must be made available to the compiler. For example, on our system the command

    cc program.c −lm

uses the flag −*lm* to make a mathematical library accessible. The system will load those mathematical functions that are called for in *program.c*. We will assume that the mathematical functions just given are available. They all take an argument of type double and return a value of type double. The following program prints out short trigonometric tables.

```
/***  trigonometric tables  ***/

main()
{
    int     i;
    double  x, h, sin(), cos(), tan();

    printf("\n:::::  trigonometric tables  :::::\n");
    printf("\neach time through the loop you must input ");
    printf("a starting value and a step.");
    while (1) {
        printf("\n\ninput a starting value and a step:   ");
        scanf("%lf%lf", &x, &h);
        printf("\n\n x \t sin(x) \t cos(x) \t tan(x)");
        printf(" \t pythagorean discrepancy");
        for (i = 0; i < 10; ++i) {
            printf("\n%g \t %g \t %g \t %g \t %g",
                x, sin(x), cos(x), tan(x),
                sin(x)*sin(x) + cos(x)*cos(x) - 1.0);
            x += h;
        }
    }
}
```

Some new formatting commands have been used. In `printf()` the tab character `\t` has been used in an attempt (not entirely successful) to make the output of the program line up properly. See the exercises for further formatting ideas. The statement

```
printf("\n %g \t %g \t  .  .  . ", x, sin(x),  .  .  .);
```

is telling the system to print out the values for `x`, `sin(x)`, . . . in the format `%g`, which means to use an e-format or f-format, whichever is shorter. Formatting is explained in detail in Chapter 11.

3.10 THE DATA TYPE char

Constants and variables of type `char` are used to represent characters, and each character is stored in 1 byte. A byte composed of 8 bits is capable of storing 2^8 or 256 distinct values, but only a small subset of these values represents actual printing characters. These include the lowercase letters, uppercase letters, digits, punctuation, and special characters such as +, *, and %. The character set also includes the white space characters blank, tab, and newline.

Most machines use either ASCII or EBCDIC character codes. A table for ASCII code is in an appendix. In the discussion that follows we will be using the ASCII code. For any other code the numbers will be different, but the ideas are completely analogous.

A `char` is stored in 1 byte according to its ASCII code, and it is considered to have the corresponding integer value. A constant of type `char` is written between single quotes as in `'a'`. Some examples are given in the following table.

Some constants of type **char** *and their corresponding integer values*

Constants of type char	:	'a'	'b'	'c'	. . .	'z'
Corresponding integer values:		97	98	99	. . .	112
	:	'A'	'B'	'C'	. . .	'Z'
	:	65	66	67	. . .	90
	:	'0'	'1'	'2'	. . .	'9'
	:	48	49	50	. . .	57
	:	'&'	'*'	'+'		
	:	38	42	43		

Observe that there is no particular relationship between the value of the character constant representing a digit and the digit's intrinsic integer value. That is, the value of `'3'` is *not* 3. The fact that the values of `'a'`, `'b'`, `'c'`, and so on, occur in order is an important property. It makes convenient the sorting of characters, words, and lines into lexicographical order. Character arrays (Chapter 7) are needed for this kind of work. Character constants and variables can be treated as "small integers."

```
printf("%d", 'a' + 'b' + 'c');      /*  294  is printed  */
```

Note carefully that a character constant and a string constant such as

    'a'   and   "a"

are *not* the same. The string constant `"a"` is an array of type `char`.

In the functions `printf()` and `scanf()` a %c is used to designate the character format. The following program illustrates input and output of characters and their corresponding integer values.

```
/***  char and int input-output on ascii machines  ***/

main()
{
     int     i;
     char    a_single_char = 'A';
     char    bell = '\007';              /*  ascii code for the bell  */

     printf("\n%c", a_single_char);            /*  A   is printed  */
     printf("\n%c", a_single_char + 1);        /*  B   is printed  */
     printf("\n%c", a_single_char + 2);        /*  C   is printed  */
     printf("\n%d", a_single_char);            /*  65  is printed  */
     i = 65;
     printf("\n%c\n\n", i);                    /*  A   is printed  */
     a_single_char = 'a';
     for (i = 0; i < 26; ++i)
          printf("%c", a_single_char++);       /*  abc ...  printed  */
     printf("\n\n  %d  %d  %d  %d", 'a', ' ', '\t','\n');
          /*  97  32  9  10  is printed  */
     printf("\n\n ring the bell%c\n\n", bell);
}
```

Some nonprinting and hard-to-print characters require an escape sequence. For example, the newline character is written as `'\n'` in a program, and even though it is being described by the two characters \ and n, it represents a single ASCII character. The backslash character \ is also called the *escape character* and is used to escape the usual meaning of the character that follows it. The following table contains some nonprinting and hard-to-print characters.

Name of character	Written in C	Integer value
null	'\0'	0
backspace	'\b'	8
tab	'\t'	9
newline	'\n'	10
formfeed	'\f'	12
carriage return	'\r'	13
double quote	'\"'	34
single quote	'\''	39
backslash	'\\'	92

Another way to write a constant of type char is by means of a one-, two-, or three-octal-digit escape sequence, as in ' \007 '. This character is the *bell* (used in the previous program), and it can also be written as '\07' or '\7'. The null character, written '\0', has value 0 and is used to signal the end of strings. The type char is used mostly for treating text. String handling functions are described in Chapter 7 after arrays and pointers have been introduced.

3.11 ASSIGNMENT OPERATORS

An expression such as

```
k = k + 2
```

will add 2 to the old value of k and assign the result to k, and the expression as a whole will have that value. The expression

```
k += 2
```

makes use of the assignment operator += to accomplish the same task. The following list contains all the assignment operators:

Assignment operators

| = | += | −= | *= | /= | %= | >>= | <<= | &= | ^= | \|= |

All these operators have the same precedence and "right to left" associativity. The semantics is specified by

variable op= expression

being equivalent to

variable = variable op (expression)

with the exception that if *variable* is itself an expression, it is evaluated only once. Thus, an assignment expression such as

```
k *= 3 + x
```

is equivalent to

```
k = k * (3 + x)
```

rather than

```
k = k * 3 + x          /*  wrong  */
```

Similarly, if a is an array of integers, then

```
a[i] /= 5 + 7          and          a[i] = a[i] / (5 + 7)
```

are equivalent statements. However,

```
a[++i] += 3;          and          a[++i] = a[++i] + 3;
```

are not equivalent. The reason for this is that an expression on the left side of an assignment operator is only evaluated once. (Moreover, because its effects are compiler dependent, the last statement on the right is considered undesirable code.)

Declarations and assignments		
int i, j, k, m, n; i = j = k = m = n = 3;		
Expression	*Equivalent expression*	*Value*
i += ++ j + 3	i = (i + ((++ j) + 3))	10
k %= m = 1 + n / 2	k = (k % (m = (1 + (n / 2))))	1
1 + 3 * n += 7 / 5	(1 + (3 * n)) += (7 / 5)	/* illegal */
1 + 3 * (n += 7) / 5	1 + (3 * (n = (n + 7)) / 5)	7

3.12 CONVERSIONS AND CASTS

An arithmetic expression such as x + y computes a value of a certain type. For example, if x and y are both variables of type int, then the value of x + y is also of type int. However, if x and y are different types, then x + y is a *mixed expression*. Suppose x is a short and y is an int. Then the value of x is converted to an int and the value of x + y is of type int. Note carefully that the value of x as stored in memory is unchanged. It is only a temporary copy of x that is converted during the computation of the value of the expression. Now suppose that both x and y are of type short. Even though x + y is not a mixed expression, automatic conversions again take place; both x and y are promoted to int and the expression is of type int. The general rules are straightforward.

Automatic conversion in an arithmetic expression   x op y

First: Any char or short is promoted to int.
        Any unsigned char or unsigned short is promoted to unsigned.

Second: If after the first step the expression is of mixed type,
        then according to the hierarchy of types

           int < unsigned < long < unsigned long < float < double

        the operand of lower type is promoted to that of the higher type and the value
        of the expression has that type.

This process goes under various names:

      implicit conversion   coercion   promotion   widening

With the following declarations

```
char c;        double d;      float f;        int i;
long l;        short s;       unsigned u;
```

we can list some expressions and their corresponding types.

Expression	Type
c - s / i	int
u * 3 - i	unsigned
u * 3.0 - i	double
f * 3 - i	float
c + 1	int
c + 1.0	double
3 * s * l	long

An implicit conversion also can occur across an equal sign. For example,

```
d = i
```

will convert the value of the int i to a double and assign it to d, and this will be the value and type of the assignment expression as a whole. A promotion or widening such as d = i will usually be well behaved, but a narrowing or demotion such as i = d can lose information. Here, the fractional part of d will be discarded. Precisely what happens in each case is machine dependent. As a general rule, conversions among all the integral types work in an expected way. In

```
c = i
```

the high-order bytes in i are discarded. In

```
i = c
```

one of two cases will occur. If the ASCII value of c is greater than or equal to zero, then the bits in the high-order bytes in i are padded with zeros. If the ASCII value of c is negative, then either the bits in the high-order bytes of i are padded with zeros or they are padded with ones. The case where they are padded with ones is called *sign extension*. Some machines sign extend, others do not. In any case the C language guarantees that the usual characters, in whatever character set is provided, will have nonnegative values. The effect of this is that if c has a value such as 'x' or ';' or '+', then the two statements

```
i = c;
c = i;
```

will leave c unchanged.

In addition to implicit conversions, which can occur across an equal sign and which occur automatically in mixed expressions, there are explicit conversions called *casts*. If i is an int, then

```
(double) i
```

will cast the value of i so that the expression has type `double`. The value of i in memory remains unchanged. Casts can be applied to any expression. The syntax is given by

> *cast_expression* ::= *(type) expression*

Some examples are

```
(char)  (3 - 3.14 * x)
k = (int)  ((int)  x + (double)  i + j)
(float)  (x = 77)
```

but not

```
(float)  x = 77      /*  equivalent to  ((float)  x) = 77  */
```

The cast operator *(type)* is a unary operator having the same precedence as other unary operators, and the same associativity, namely, "right to left." Thus the expression

```
(float)  i + 3
```

is equivalent to

```
((float)  i) + 3
```

because the cast operator *(type)* has higher precedence than +.

3.13 CONSTANTS

Constants occur in such expressions as

```
c = 'Y'
2 * (x + 7) - 33
kilometers = 1.609344 * miles
```

In addition to having value, a constant also has an associated data type. Which data types can occur for constants is system dependent. The usual situation is that constants of type `short`, `unsigned`, and `float` do not exist. Although the situation may be different on small machines, we will assume that the usual situation pertains.

The data type associated with a constant depends on how the constant is written. The following list contains all the data types that admit constants, along with some examples:

Examples of constants of various types

int:	0	77	5013
long:	0L	77L	5013L
double:	0.003	1.0	0.5013e-2
char:	'a'	'b'	'c'
string:	"this is a string constant"		

Note that constants of type short, unsigned, and float are not in this list. A constant of type long is obtained by appending the letter L or l to the number. Since the number 1 and the letter l look very much alike, it is advisable to use only L to designate a long constant. Also, a constant integer that is too big for an int will automatically be considered a constant of type long. For example, on a machine where an int is stored in 2 bytes and a long in 4 bytes, the number 44000 will be a long.

A constant expression is an expression containing only constants, and the C compiler will evaluate such expressions at compile time, rather than during execution. For example, in the statement

```
seconds = 60 * 60 * 24 * days;
```

the constant expression 60 * 60 * 24 will be evaluated as 86400 by the compiler. Therefore, even if the statement gets repeatedly evaluated during execution of the program, the constant expression is computed only once. For anyone who reads the program, including the programmer, this statement is much clearer than the equivalent statement

```
seconds = 86400 * days;
```

3.14 HEXADECIMAL AND OCTAL CONSTANTS

A positive integer written in decimal notation is a string of digits of the form

$$d_n \, d_{n-1} \cdots d_2 \, d_1 \, d_0$$

where each d_i is a decimal digit. The value of such an integer is

$$d_n \times 10^n + d_{n-1} \times 10^{n-1} + \cdots + d_2 \times 10^2 + d_1 \times 10^1 + d_0 \times 10^0$$

For example,

$$75301 \equiv 7 \times 10^4 + 5 \times 10^3 + 3 \times 10^2 + 0 \times 10^1 + 1 \times 10^0$$

Such a system is a positional notation in base 10.

Machine words can be considered as strings of binary digits that are grouped into bytes. A binary, or base 2, positional number is written in the form

$$b_n \, b_{n-1} \cdots b_2 \, b_1 \, b_0$$

where each b_i is a binary digit, either 0 or 1. It has the value

$$b_n \times 2^n + b_{n-1} \times 2^{n-1} + \cdots + b_2 \times 2^2 + b_1 \times 2^1 + b_0 \times 2^0$$

For example,

$$10101 \equiv 1 \times 2^4 + 0 \times 2^3 + 1 \times 2^2 + 0 \times 2^1 + 1 \times 2^0$$

which is $16 + 4 + 1$ or 21 in decimal notation.

A number represented by a positional notation in base 16 is called a hexadecimal number. There are 16 hexadecimal digits.

Hexadecimal digits and their corresponding decimal values

Hexadecimal digit:	0	1	. . .	9	A	B	C	D	E	F
Decimal value :	0	1	. . .	9	10	11	12	13	14	15

A positive integer written in hexadecimal notation is a string of hexadecimal digits of the form

$$h_n \; h_{n-1} \cdots h_2 \; h_1 \; h_0$$

where each h_i is a hexadecimal digit. The value of such an integer is

$$h_n \times 16^n + h_{n-1} \times 16^{n-1} + \cdots + h_2 \times 16^2 + h_1 \times 16^1 + h_0 \times 16^0$$

For example,

$$
\begin{aligned}
\text{A0F3C} &\equiv \text{A} \times 16^4 + 0 \times 16^3 + \text{F} \times 16^2 + 3 \times 16^1 + \text{C} \times 16^0 \\
&\equiv 10 \times 16^4 + 0 \times 16^3 + 15 \times 16^2 + 3 \times 16^1 + 12 \times 16^0 \\
&\equiv 659260
\end{aligned}
$$

Some hexadecimal numbers and their decimal equivalents are given in the following table:

Some hexadecimal numbers and their conversion to decimal

2A	$2 \times 16 + \text{A} = 2 \times 16 + 10 = 42$
B3	$\text{B} \times 16 + 3 = 11 \times 16 + 3 = 179$
113	$1 \times 16^2 + 1 \times 16 + 3 = 275$
ABC	$\text{A} \times 16^2 + \text{B} \times 16 + \text{C}$
	$= 10 \times 16^2 + 11 \times 16 + 12 = 2748$

On machines that have 8-bit bytes, a byte is conveniently represented as two hexadecimal digits. Moreover, the representation has two simultaneously valid interpretations. First, one may consider the 8 bits in a byte as representing a number in base 2 notation. That number can be expressed uniquely as a hexadecimal number with two hexadecimal digits. The following table lists 8-bit bytes and corresponding two-digit hexadecimal numbers. For convenience, decimal numbers are listed, and for later reference, octal numbers are also listed.

Decimal	Binary	Hexadecimal	Octal
0	00000000	00	000
1	00000001	01	001
2	00000010	02	002
3	00000011	03	003
4	00000100	04	004
. . . .			
7	00000111	07	007
8	00001000	08	010
9	00001001	09	011
10	00001010	0A	012
11	00001011	0B	013
. . . .			
15	00001111	0F	017
16	00010000	10	020
17	00010001	11	021
. . . .			
31	00011111	1F	037
32	00100000	20	040
. . . .			
188	10111100	BC	274
. . . .			
254	11111110	FE	376
255	11111111	FF	377

Another interpretation of this correspondence is also useful. By definition a *nibble* consists of 4 bits, so that a byte is made up of two nibbles. Each nibble has a unique representation as a single hexadecimal digit, and 2 nibbles, making up a byte, are representable as 2 hexadecimal digits. For example,

    1011 1100   corresponds to   BC

Note that this same correspondence occurs in the above table. All of this is useful when manipulating the values of variables in bit form.

The octal digits are 0 , 1 , . . . , 7. A positive integer written in octal notation is a string of digits of the form

$$o_n \, o_{n-1} \cdots o_2 o_1 o_0$$

where each o_i is an octal digit. The value of such an integer is

$$o_n \times 8^n + o_{n-1} \times 8^{n-1} + \cdots + o_2 \times 8^2 + o_1 \times 8^1 + o_0 \times 8^0$$

For example,

$$75301 \equiv 7 \times 8^4 + 5 \times 8^3 + 3 \times 8^2 + 0 \times 8^1 + 1 \times 8^0$$

On machines that have words consisting of 24 or 48 bits, it is natural to have words consisting of "bytes" with 6 bits, each "byte" made up of two "nibbles" of 3 bits each. In this case, a "nibble" has a unique representation as a single octal digit, and a "byte" has a unique representation as two octal digits.

In C code positive integer constants prefaced with 0 represent integers in octal notation, and positive integer constants prefaced with 0x or 0X represent integers in hexadecimal notation. Just like decimal integer constants, octal and hexadecimal constants may have l or L appended to them to designate a constant of type long. The letters A through F and a through f are used to code hexadecimal digits.

octal_digit ::= 0 | 1 | . . . | 7
octal_integer_constant ::= 0 {*octal_digit*}$_{1+}$
hexadecimal_digit ::= 0 | 1 | . . . | 9 | a | A | . . . | f | F
hexadecimal_integer_constant ::= { 0x | 0X }$_1$ {*hexadecimal_digit*}$_{1+}$

The following program illustrates these ideas:

```
/***  decimal, hexadecimal, octal conversions  ***/

main()
{
    /*  the output of each statement is appended as a comment  */
    printf("\n%d  %x  %o", 19, 19, 19);          /*  19   13   23  */
    printf("\n%d  %x  %o", 0x1c, 0x1c, 0x1c);    /*  28   1c   34  */
    printf("\n%d  %x  %o", 017, 017, 017);       /*  15    f   17  */
    printf("\n%d", 11 + 0x11 + 011);             /*  37           */
    printf("\n%x", 2097151);                     /*  1fffff       */
    printf("\n%d", 0x1FfFFf);                     /*  2097151      */
    printf("\n\n");
}
```

In printf() the format %o is for octal output and %x is for hexadecimal output. Details are given in Chapter 11. Note that integers printed out in octal and hexadecimal notation are *not* prefaced with 0 or 0x. The 0 and 0x preface convention applies to C code only. Neither the output for printf() nor the input for scanf() is written with this convention.

3.15 ORDER OF EVALUATION

C has fully defined rules for forming expressions that include precedence and associativity. For example, we have seen that * is of higher precedence than + and both associate left to right. But beware! These rules do not dictate the order in which parts of expressions are evaluated. Expressions involving one of the commutative operators such as + or * can be reordered at the convenience of the compiler *even though they have been parenthesized in the program*. For example, in the statement

```
x = (a + b) + c;
```

the variables can be summed by the compiler in some unspecified order. If for some reason the order of evaluation is important, then the programmer can assign intermediate values to temporary variables. Thus

```
temp = a + b;
x = temp + c;
```

would force the compiler to do the operations in a specific order. Expressions subject to reordering by the compiler are those involving just one of the following commutative operators:

*	+	&	∧	|

3.16 SUMMARY

1. The fundamental data types are char, short, int, long, unsigned versions of these, and two floating types. The type char is a 1-byte integral type mostly used for representing characters.

2. The type int is designed to be the "natural" or "working" integral type. The types short, long, and unsigned are provided for more specialized situations.

3. Two floating types, float and double, are provided to represent real numbers. Typically, a float will be stored in one word and a double in two words. Unlike integer arithmetic, floating arithmetic is not always exact.

4. Precedence and associativity of operators determine precisely how expressions are evaluated.

5. Assignment is an operator and can occur as part of an expression. This is one of many distinctive features of the C language.

6. The operator ++ increments a variable, and the operator -- decrements it. Each can be either a prefix operator or a postfix operator. As a prefix operator it acts *before* the expression is evaluated, and as a postfix operator it acts *after* the expression is evaluated. The side effects of these operators can cause unexpected results.

7. Mathematical functions are not part of the C language, but they are usually available in a library.

8. A variety of assignment operators such as += and *= are available. They allow the compiler to provide somewhat better machine code. The expression

    i += 3   as opposed to   i = i + 3

    is more concise.

9. Automatic conversions occur in mixed expressions and across an equal sign. Casts can be used to force explicit conversions.

10. Integer constants beginning with 0x and 0 designate hexadecimal and octal integers, respectively. Integer constants of type long are specified by appending an L.

3.17 EXERCISES

1. Not all real numbers are machine representable. Because of this, the numbers that are available on a machine have a "graininess" to them. For example, the two numbers

```
123.45123451234512345
123.45123451234512300    /*  last two digits are different  */
```

are mathematically different, but their representation in a VAX is the same. What can you say about the two numbers

```
123.45123451234512345
123.45123451234510000    /*  last four digits are different  */
```

or

```
123.45123451234512345
123.45123451234000000    /*  last six digits are different  */
```

Explain your answer.

2. If a function in a library is not declared, the compiler assumes that it returns an `int` value. The following program (when correctly written) illustrates the mathematical fact that

$$\cos^2(x) + \sin^2(x) = 1 \quad \text{for all } x \text{ real}$$

The correct declaration in the program is

```
double  sin(), cos(), x;
```

Code and run the program correctly first so that you understand its proper effects. Then experiment to see what the effect is when the `sin()` function is not declared. Finally, change the program so that the values of `sin(x)` and `cos(x)` are printed out, but `sin()` is left undeclared. If a new phenomenon occurs, explain why.

```
/***  what is the effect when sin() is not declared?  ***/

main()
{
    double   cos(), x;      /*  sin() is missing  */

    while(1) {
        printf("\n\ninput a number:   ");
        scanf("%lf", &x);
        printf("\n%s%.16f\n%s%.16e\n%s%.16e",
            "x  =  ", x, "x  =  ", x,
            "sin(x) * sin(x)  +  cos(x) * cos(x)  =   ",
            sin(x) * sin(x)  +  cos(x) * cos(x));
    }
}
```

3. On some systems the following program prints a double set of characters. On other systems it will wreck havoc with the terminal (locking keyboards, sending screen dumps, etc.). If you are brave, see what happens on your system and try to explain the effects of the program.

```
/*** print everything possible ***/

main()
{
        char    c = '\0';
        int     i;

        for (i = 0; i < 256; ++i)
                printf("%c", c++);
        printf("\n\n");
}
```

4. Create a test program with this line in it.

```
a = a++;    /* what is supposed to happen? */
```

Since the effect of this statement is compiler dependent, *lint* should give you a warning. On the other hand, since the statement is syntactically correct, your C compiler should not complain. Run your test program through both *lint* and your compiler to see what warnings, if any, you get. Of course, any code that produces effects that are compiler dependent is considered undesirable.

5. As you experiment with the program that prints trigonometric tables, you will find that the tabs in the printf() statements do not always format the table in a desirable fashion. One way to achieve more robust formatting is to replace the statement

```
printf("\n %g\t %g\t %g\t %g\t %g",
       x, sin(x), cos(x), tan(x),
       sin(x)*sin(x) + cos(x)*cos(x) - 1.0);
```

in the program by

```
printf("\n%15.9f%15.9f%15.9f%15.9f%15.9f",
       x, sin(x), cos(x), tan(x),
       sin(x)*sin(x) + cos(x)*cos(x) - 1.0);
```

Try this, and then line up the headings appropriately. Note that even though all the arithmetic in the program is being done in double precision, only six significant digits are printed in the original program, and nine significant digits in the above modification. The default precision with %f and %g is 6. If the %g's are all changed to %.16g or %.16f, then 16 decimal places will be printed, but the table becomes unwieldy to print on a typical CRT. Try it.

6. Write a test program to find out whether the printf() function truncates or rounds when writing a float or double with fractional part.

7. The line of code

```
printf ("%c", '\007');
```

will ring the bell. What happens with the line

```
printf ("%c", 0x7);
```

Explain your answer.

8. Write a test program to find out the effect of the following statement:

```
printf ("\n%d%u\n\n", 2000000000 + 2000000000, 2000000000 + 2000000000);
```

9. Write a test program to find out the effect of the following code:

```
int     big_big;

big_big = 2000000000 + 2000000000;
printf ("\n%d\n%u\n\n", big_big, big_big);
```

Compare the output with that of the previous problem. Explain what is happening. Does the output change if big_big is declared to be unsigned instead of int?

10. Explain the output of the following program. What is the effect of changing the declaration of x from unsigned to int? What is the effect of changing the format from %u to %d?

```
/***   compute powers of 2   ***/

main()
{
        int        i = 0;
        unsigned   x = 1;

        while (i < 35) {
            printf ("\n%5d: %12u", i, x);
            /*  %u  is unsigned decimal format  */
            ++i;
            x *= 2;
        }
        x = -1;
        printf ("\n\nminus one = %u\n\n", x);
}
```

11. Reformat the output of the program in exercise 10 so that the powers of 2 are all lined up on the units digit.

12. Print out a list of powers of 2 in decimal, hexadecimal, and octal numbers. The function printf() uses %d, %x, and %o, for decimal, hexadecimal, and octal output, respectively.

13. Experiment to see if your compiler admits the types unsigned char, unsigned short, and unsigned long.

14. Consider the following program.

```
main()      /* mystery? */
{
      printf("\nwhy is   21 + 31   equal to   %d ?\n\n", 21 + 31);
}
```

Here is its output.

```
why is 21 + 31 equal to 5?
```

Can you deduce the moral?

15. In the program that computes areas, experiment to see the effect of replacing the line

```
printf("\ntriangle: %.16f", 0.5 * x * SQRT_3 / 2.0 * x);
```

with each of the following:

```
printf("\ntriangle: %.16f", 1 / 2 * x * SQRT_3 / 2 * x);
printf("\ntriangle: %.16f", x / 2 * SQRT_3 / 2 * x);
```

Give an explanation for what happens.

16. In the program that does integer arithmetic, change the declaration

```
int  x, y;
```

to

```
short  x, y;
```

What happens when 32000 is added to 32000? Now change the declaration to

```
char  x, y;
```

What happens when 127 is added to 127? Your machine may be doing modulo arithmetic in the range -128 to 127. Experiment to see if this is the case. Is modulo arithmetic being performed in all cases? If so, over what ranges?

17. In mathematics the Greek letter ϵ, called "epsilon," is often used to represent a small positive number. It can be arbitrarily small in mathematics, but on a machine there is no concept of "arbitrarily small." In numerical analysis the convention is to declare eps (for "epsilon") as a variable of type double, and to assign to eps the smallest positive number with the property that

```
1.0 < 1.0 + eps
```

is *true*. This number is machine dependent, but one can expect, for example, that if eps is assigned the value 1e-33, then the above relational expression is *false*. See if you can find eps on your machine.

18. Explain the output of the following program:

```
main()
{
    char    a = 127, b = 128;

    printf("\n%d  %d  %d\n\n", a, a + 1, b);
    printf("\n%d  %d  %d\n\n", a, a += 1, b);
}
```

Does interchanging the arguments in the last `printf()` statement make any difference?

19. What gets printed?

```
int   k = -7;
printf("\n%d\n\n", 0 < !k);
```

4

Flow of
Control

In this chapter we will discuss the relational, equality, and logical operators, and then show how they are used to affect flow of control. In the execution of a program, control will flow sequentially from one statement to the next unless explicit change of control is effected. For example, an if statement can rely on relational or equality or logical expressions to decide the order of execution of program statements. Flow of control is also controlled by grouping statements together into a compound statement.

Interesting computations require programs that take different courses of action, depending on data and calculations. This chapter will develop in detail the meaning and use of the if statement and the if-else statement, which select from different next statements. Finally, the various iterative statements, namely the while statement, the do-while statement, and the for statement will be explained and their use illustrated by examples.

4.1 RELATIONAL, EQUALITY, AND LOGICAL OPERATORS

The following table contains the operators that are most often used to affect flow of control:

Relational, equality, and logical operators

relational operators:	less than:	<
	greater than:	>
	less than or equal:	<=
	greater than or equal:	>=
equality operators:	equal:	==
	not equal:	! =
logical operators:	(unary) negation:	!
	logical and:	&&
	logical or:	| |

Just as with other operators, the relational, equality, and logical operators have rules of precedence and associativity that determine precisely how expressions involving these operators are evaluated.

99

Operators	Associativity
! - (unary) ++ -- sizeof (*type*)	right to left
* / %	left to right
+ -	left to right
< <= > >=	left to right
== !=	left to right
&&	left to right
||	left to right
= += -= *= *etc*	right to left
, (comma operator)	left to right

The ! operator is unary. All the other relational, equality, and logical operators are binary. They operate on expressions and yield either the int value 0 or the int value 1. The reason for this is that in the C language *false* is represented by the value zero and *true* is represented by any nonzero value. The value for *false* can be either 0 or 0.0, and the value for *true* can be any value other than 0 or 0.0. Intuitively, an expression such as a < b is either *true* or *false*. In C this expression will yield the int value 1 if it is *true* and the int value 0 if it is *false*.

4.2 RELATIONAL OPERATORS AND EXPRESSIONS

The relational operators

    <   >   <=   >=

are all binary. They each take two expressions as operands and yield either the int value 0 or the int value 1.

> *relational_expression*   ::=   *expression < expression*
> | *expression > expression*
> | *expression <= expression*
> | *expression >= expression*

Some examples are

```
a < 3
a > b
-7.7 <= -99.335
-1.3 >= (2.0 * x + 3.3)
a < b < c                /* syntactically correct, but confusing;
                           this is explained in detail below */
```

but not

```
a =< b          /*  out of order  */
a < = b         /*  space not allowed  */
a >> b          /*  this is a shift operation  */
```

Consider a relational expression such as a < b. Intuitively, if the value of a is less than the value of b, then the expression is *true*. Since *true* is represented in C by any nonzero value, it is natural that a < b has the int value 1. If the value of a is not less than the value of b, then the expression is *false* and a < b has the int value 0. The relational operators follow the standard arithmetic conversion rules. Observe that the value of a < b is the same as the value of a - b < 0. Because the precedence of the relational operators is less than that of the arithmetic operators, the expression

a - b < 0   is equivalent to   (a - b) < 0

On most machines, an expression such as a < b is implemented as the equivalent expression a - b < 0. The semantics of all the relational operators is given in the following table:

values of: *e1 - e2*	*e1 < e2*	*e1 > e2*	*e1 <= e2*	*e1 >= e2*
positive	0	1	0	1
zero	0	0	1	1
negative	1	0	1	0

The following table illustrates the use of the rules of precedence and associativity to evaluate relational expressions:

Declarations and assignments		

`char    c;`
`int     i, j, k;`
`double  x, y;`
 	
`c = 'w'; i = 1; j = 2; k = -7; x = 7e+33; y = 0.001;`		

Expression	**Equivalent expression**	**Value**
`'a' + 1 < c`	`('a' + 1) < c`	1
`- i - 5 * j >= k + 1`	`((- i) - (5 * j)) >= (k + 1)`	0
`3 < j < 5`	`(3 < j) < 5`	1
`/* an expression such as a < b < c should not be used in code */`		
`x - 3.333 <= x + y`	`(x - 3.333) <= (x + y)`	1
`x < x + y`	`x < (x + y)`	0
`/* see the explanation given below */`		

Two expressions in this table give surprising results in that they do not conform to rules as written mathematically. In mathematics one writes

$$3 < j < 5$$

to indicate that the variable j has the property of being greater than 3 and less than 5. It can also be considered as a mathematical statement which, depending on the value of j, may or may not be true. For example, if $j = 4$, then the mathematical statement

$$3 < j < 5$$

is true, but if $j = 7$, then the mathematical statement is false. Now consider the C code

```
j = 7;
printf ("\n%d", 3 < j < 5);
```

By analogy with mathematics one might expect that the expression is *false* and that 0 is printed. However, that is not the case. Since relational operators have "left to right" associativity,

$3 < j < 5$	is equivalent to	$(3 < j) < 5$

Since the expression $3 < j$ is *true*, it has value 1. Thus

$(3 < j) < 5$	is equivalent to	$1 < 5$

which has value 1, and 1 is the integer that gets printed. The correct way in C to write a test for both $3 < j$ and $j < 5$ is

$$3 < j \ \&\& \ j < 5$$

Because the relational operators have higher precedence than the binary logical operators, this is equivalent to

$$(3 < j) \ \&\& \ (j < 5)$$

and as we will see below, this expression is *true* if and only if both operands of the && expression are *true*.

In mathematics the relation

$x < x + y$	is equivalent to	$0 < y$

Mathematically, if y is positive this relation is logically true. Computationally, if x is a floating variable with a large value such as 7e+33 and y is a floating variable with a small value such as 0.001, then it can happen that the relational expression

$$x < x + y$$

is *false*, even though mathematically it is true. An equivalent expression is

$$(x - (x + y)) < 0.0$$

and it is this expression that the machine implements. However, to machine accuracy the values of x and x + y are equal. Therefore, the expression will yield the int value 0.

4.3 EQUALITY OPERATORS AND EXPRESSIONS

The equality operators == and ! = are binary operators acting on expressions, and they yield either the int value 0 or the int value 1. The usual arithmetic conversions are applied to expressions that are the operands of the equality operators.

   equality_expression ::= *expression* == *expression* | *expression* != *expression*

Some examples are

```
c == 'w'
x != -2.77
22 == 33
x + 2.0 * y != 3.3 / z
```

but not

```
a = b            /*  an assignment statement  */
x = = y - 1      /*  space not allowed  */
x =! 44          /*  equivalent to x = (!44)  */
x + y =! 44      /*  equivalent to  (x + y) = (!44)—syntax error  */
```

The operator semantics is given by the following table:

values of: *exp1* - *exp2*	*exp1* == *exp2*	*exp1* != *exp2*
zero	1	0
nonzero	0	1

Intuitively, an equality expression such as a == b is either *true* or *false*. An equivalent expression is a - b == 0, and this is what is actually implemented at the machine level. If the value of a equals the value of b, then a - b has value 0 and 0 == 0 is *true*. In this case, the expression a == b will yield the int value 1. If the value of a is not equal to the value of b, then a == b will yield the int value 0. In a similar fashion the expression a != b is evaluated, except that the test here is for inequality rather than for equality. Observe that the expression

   a != b   is equivalent to   ! (a == b)

Note carefully that the two expressions

   a == b   and   a = b

are *visually* similar. They are close in form, but radically different in function. The expression a == b is a test for equality, whereas a = b is an assignment expression. One of the more common programming mistakes is to code something like

```
if  (i = 1)
        .    .    .    .         /*  do something  */
```

instead of

```
if  (i == 1)
        .    .    .    .         /*  do something  */
```

The expression in the first if statement is always *true*, and an error such as this can be very difficult to find.

The following table shows how the rules of precedence and associativity are used to evaluate some expressions with equality operators:

Declarations and assignments		
char c; int i, j, k; double x, y; c = 'w'; i = 1; j = 2; k = -7; x = 7e+33; y = 0.001;		
Expression	*Equivalent expression*	*Value*
'v' == c - 1	'v' == (c - 1)	1
i + j + k == - 2 * j	((i + j) + k) == ((- 2) * j)	1
k == j - 9 == i	(k == (j - 9)) == i	1
/* such an expression should not be used */		
x + x != x * y	(x + x) != (x * x)	1
x != x + y	x != (x + y)	0
/* machine accuracy is limited */		

4.4 LOGICAL OPERATORS AND EXPRESSIONS

The logical operators !, &&, and || when applied to expressions yield either the int value 0 or the int value 1. In this section we will give syntax, examples, and explanations for each of the logical operators.

Logical negation can be applied to an arbitrary expression. If an expression has value 0 or 0.0, then its negation will yield the int value 1. If the expression has a nonzero value, then its negation will yield the int value 0.

logical_negation_expression ::= ! *expression*

Some examples are

```
! 5
! a
! 'z'
! (x + 7. 7)
! (2 * (x + a) - 3 - 'z')
```

but not

```
a ! = b    /* ! = is the token for the equality operator "not equal"  */
```

The usual arithmetic conversion rules are applied to expressions that are the operands of ! . In the example

```
! (2 * (x + a) - 3 - 'z')
```

the expression

```
(2 * (x + a) - 3 - 'z')
```

will be of type int if both x and a are of type int, and this will require the conversion of the character 'z' to its int value. If either x or a is of type double, then all the variables and constants in the expression will be converted to type double, and that will be the type of the expression. In either case, if the expression has zero value, then the logical expression

```
! (2 * (x + a) - 3 - 'z')
```

will have the int value 1; otherwise it will have the int value 0 . The semantics for the operator ! is given by the following table:

values of: expression	! *expression*
zero	1
nonzero	0

While logical negation is a very simple operator, there is one subtlety. The operator ! in C is unlike the *not* operator in mathematics. If *s* is a mathematical statement, then

not (not s) = s

whereas in C the value of ! ! 5, for example, is 1. The operator ! is unary, and it has the same precedence and "right to left" associativity as the other unary operators. Thus

```
! ! 5              is equivalent to              ! (! 5)
```

and ! (! 5) is equivalent to ! (0) , which has value 1. In a similar fashion an expression such as

```
! -! -3            is equivalent to              ! (- (! (-3)))
```

The following table shows how some expressions with logical negation are evaluated:

Declarations and assignments		
char c; int i, j; double x, y; c = 'w'; i = j = 7; x = 0.0; y = 2.3;		
Expression	*Equivalent expression*	*Value*
! c	! c	0
! (i - j)	! (i - j)	1
! i - j	(! i) - j	-7
! - i - j	(! (- i)) - j	-7
x * ! y	x * (! y)	0.0
! x * ! y	(! x) * (! y)	0
x / ! y	x / (! y)	/* error */
x / ! ! y	x / (! (! y))	0.0
! ! x	! (! x)	0
! ! ! x	! (! (! x))	1

The binary logical operators && and || also act on expressions and yield either the int value 0 or the int value 1. The syntax for a logical expression is given by

```
logical_expression    ::=      logical_negation_expression
                        |     logical_or_expression
                        |     logical_and_expression
logical_or_expression ::= expression || expression
logical_and_expression ::= expression && expression
```

Some examples are

```
2 || 3
a && b
a || b
a && 1
x || !3.77
3 && (-2 * a + 7)
```

but not,

```
a &&          /*  one operand missing */
a | b         /*  this is a bitwise operation  */
a | | b       /*  extra space not allowed  */
&a            /*  address of  a  */
```

```
a & b          /*  this is a bitwise operation  */
a & & b        /*  equivalent to  a & (& b)-syntax error  */
```

The operator semantics is given by the following table:

values of: *exp1*	*exp2*	*exp1* && *exp2*	*exp1* || *exp2*
zero	*zero*	0	0
zero	*nonzero*	0	1
nonzero	*zero*	0	1
nonzero	*nonzero*	1	1

The precedence of && is higher than ||, but both operators are of lower precedence than all unary, arithmetic, and relational operators. Their associativity is "left to right." The following table shows how the rules of precedence and associativity are used to compute the value of some logical expressions:

Declarations and assignments		

`char     c;`
`int      i, j, k;`
`double   x, y;`
`c = 'w';    i = j = k = 3;    x = 0.0;    y = 2.3;`		

Expression	**Equivalent expression**	**Value**
i && j && k	(i && j) && k	1
x && i || j - 3	(x && i) || (j - 3)	1
x || i && j - 3	x || (i && (j - 3))	0
i < j && x < y	(i < j) && (x < y)	0
i < j || x < y	(i < j) || (x < y)	1
i == j && x <= y	(i == j) && (x <= y)	1
x != y && j + 1 == ! k + 4	(x != y) && ((j + 1) == ((! k) + 4))	1
'A' <= c && c <= 'Z'	('A' <= c) && (c <= 'Z')	0
c - 1 == 'v' || c + 1 == 'v'	((c - 1) == 'v') || ((c + 1) == 'v')	1
i == 2 || j == 4 || k == 6	((i == 2) || (j == 4)) || (k == 6)	0
i == 2 || j == 4 || k = 6	((i == 2) || (j == 4)) || (k = 6)	1

The usual arithmetic conversion rules are applied to expressions that are the operands of logical operators. Note that many of the above expressions are of mixed type. Whenever this occurs, certain values are promoted to match the highest type present in the expression.

In the evaluation of expressions that are the operands of && and ||, the evaluation process stops as soon as the outcome *true* or *false* is known. Suppose that *exp1* and *exp2* are expressions. If *exp1* has zero value, then in

> *exp1* && *exp2*

exp2 will not be evaluated because the value of the logical expression is already determined to be 0. Similarly, if *exp1* has nonzero value, then in

> *exp1* || *exp2*

exp2 will not be evaluated because the value of the logical expression is already determined to be 1. The following program illustrates this.

```
/*** evaluation stops as soon as true/false is determined ***/

main()
{
    int    i = 0, j = 0, x, y;

    x = 0 && (i = j = 999);
    printf("%d  %d  %d\n", i, j, x);      /* 0 0 0 is printed */
    y = 1 || (i = ++j);
    printf("%d  %d  %d\n", i, j, y);      /* 0 0 1 is printed */
}
```

The property that the processing of operands within a logical expression stops as soon as *true* or *false* is known is important. Consider the code

```
/* process just the first 3  characters of the file */
i = 0;
while (i++ < 3  && (c = getchar()) != EOF)
       .    .    .    .    .             /*  do something  */
```

When i has value 3, the next call to getchar() will not be made. When program control passes out of the while loop, the next character available in the file is the fourth one (unless EOF is encountered). If the operator && always evaluated both of its operands, the fifth character would be next.

4.5 THE COMPOUND STATEMENT

A compound statement is a series of statements surrounded by the braces { and }.

> *compound_statement* ::= { {*declaration*}$_{0+}$ {*statement*}$_{0+}$ }

The chief use of the compound statement is to group statements into an executable unit. When declarations come at the beginning of a compound statement, the statement is called a block. Blocks will be explained in Chapter 5. In C, wherever it is syntactically correct to place a statement, it is also syntactically correct to place a compound statement. *A compound statement is itself a statement.* An example of a compound statement is

```
{
    a = 7;
    b = a + 3;
    printf("\na + b = %d   and   a - b = %d", a + b, a - b);
}
```

and another example is

```
{
    a = 1;
    b = 2;
    {
        c = 3;
        d = 4;
    }
}
```

but not

```
{
    x = 3.11;
    {
        y = -7.7;
        c = 'a';
}                                    /*  a brace is missing  */
```

Grouping of statements is used to achieve the desired flow of control in such constructs as the if statement and the while statement.

4.6 THE EMPTY STATEMENT

The empty statement is written as a single "; ". It is useful where a statement is needed syntactically, but no action is required semantically. As we shall see, this is sometimes useful in statements that affect flow of control, such as an if statement or a for statement.

4.7 THE if AND THE if-else STATEMENTS

In a construction of the form

> if (*expression*)
> >   *statement1*
> *next statement*

If *expression* is nonzero (*true*), then *statement1* is executed; otherwise *statement1* is skipped and control passes to *next statement*. In the example

```
if (grade >= 90)
    printf("\ncongratulations!");
printf("\nyour grade is %d", grade);
```

a congratulatory message is printed only when a grade is greater than or equal to 90. The second `printf()` is always executed. The syntax is given by

if_statement ::= if *(expression) statement*

Commonly, the expression in an `if` statement is a relational or equality or logical expression, but as the syntax shows, an expression from any domain is permissible. Some other examples of `if` statements are

```
if (x != 0.0)
    y /= x;

if (c == ' ') {
    ++blank_cnt;
    printf("\nanother blank");
}
```

but not

```
if b == a                /* parentheses missing */
    area = a * a;

if (c != EOF && 'a' <= c && c <= 'z')
    c += 'A' - 'a'   /* semicolon missing  -  not a statement */
```

Where appropriate, compound statements should be used to group a series of statements under the control of a single `if` expression. The following code

```
test = (j < k);
if (test)
    min = j;
if (test)
    printf("\nj  is smaller than  k");
if (test)
    if (j < 0)
        printf("\nj  is negative");
```

can be written more efficiently and more understandably by making use of a compound statement.

```
if (j < k) {
    min = j;
    printf("\nj  is smaller than  k");
    if (j < 0)
        printf("\nj  is negative");
}
```

The if-else statement is closely related to the if statement. It has the form

```
if (expression)
      statement1
else
      statement2
next statement
```

If *expression* is nonzero, then *statement1* is executed and *statement2* is skipped; if *expression* is zero, then *statement1* is skipped and *statement2* is executed. In both cases control then passes to *next statement*. Consider the code

```
if (x < y)
      min = x;
else
      min = y;
```

If x < y is *true*, then min will be assigned the value of x, and if it is *false*, then min will be assigned the value of y. The syntax is given by

if_else_statement   ::=   if (*expression*) *statement*
                            else *statement*

Some examples are

```
if (c == 'e')
      ++e_cnt;
else
      ++other_cnt;

if ('a' <= c && c <= 'z') {
      ++lc_cnt;
      printf("\nanother lower case letter");
}
else {
      ++other_cnt;
      printf("\nc  is not a lower case letter");
}

if ((c = getchar()) != EOF)
      putchar(c);
else if (c > 'z')
      ;                       /* use of empty statement */
else if (c >= 'a')
      ++lower_case;
else
      ++other;
```

but not

```
if (i != j) {
     i = 1;
     j = 2;
} ;
else i += j;        /*  syntax error  */
```

The syntax error in this example occurs because the semicolon following the right brace creates an empty statement and consequently the `else` has nowhere to attach.

Since an `if` statement is itself a statement, it can be used as the statement part of another `if` statement. Consider the code

```
if (a == 1)
     if (b == 2)
          printf ("\n***");
```

This is of the form

```
if (a == 1)
     statement
```

where *statement* is the following `if` statement

```
if (b == 2)
     printf ("\n***");
```

In a similar fashion an `if-else` statement can be used as the statement part of another `if` statement. Consider, for example,

```
if (a == 1)
     if (b == 2)
          printf ("\n***");
     else
          printf ("\n###");
```

Now we are faced with a semantic difficulty. This code illustrates the *dangling else problem*. It is not clear from the syntax what the `else` part is associated with. Do not be fooled by the format of the code. As far as the machine is concerned, the following code is equivalent:

```
if (a == 1)
     if (b == 2)
          printf ("\n***");
else
     printf ("\n###");
```

The rule is:

an `else` *attaches to the nearest* `if`

Thus the code is correctly formatted as

```
if (a == 1)
    if (b == 2)
        printf ("\n***");
    else
        printf ("\n###");
```

which is of the form

```
if (a == 1)
    statement
```

where *statement* is the if-else statement

```
if (b == 2)
    printf ("\n***");
else
    printf ("\n###");
```

Various combinations of if and if-else statements can occur, and if the situation is complicated, the logic can be difficult to understand. One common construction is the following:

```
if (expression1)
    statement1
else if (expression2)
    statement2
else if (expression3)
    statement3

    .   .   .   .   .

else if (expressionN)
    statementN
else
    default statement
next statement
```

This whole giant construction, except for *next statement*, is a single if statement. Suppose, for example, that *expression1* and *expression2* are both zero (*false*) and that *expression3* is nonzero (*true*). Then *statement1* and *statement2* will be skipped and *statement3* will be executed; then control will pass to *next statement*. No other intervening statement will be executed. If we suppose that all of the expressions are zero, then only *default statement* will be executed. In some circumstances, the execution of a default statement is not wanted. In this case a construction such as the above would be used without the two lines

```
else
    default statement
```

These ideas are illustrated in the following program:

```
/*** count blanks, digits, letters, newlines, and others ***/

#include <stdio.h>

main()
{
    int    c, blank_cnt, digit_cnt, letter_cnt, nl_cnt, other_cnt;

    blank_cnt = digit_cnt = letter_cnt = nl_cnt = other_cnt = 0;

    while ((c = getchar()) != EOF)      /* braces not necessary */
        if (c == ' ')
                ++blank_cnt;
        else if ('0' <= c && c <= '9')
                ++digit_cnt;
        else if ('a' <= c && c <= 'z' || 'A' <= c && c <= 'Z')
                ++letter_cnt;
        else if (c == '\n')
                ++nl_cnt;
        else
                ++other_cnt;

    printf("\n%12s%12s%12s%12s%12s%12s",
            "blanks", "digits", "letters", "lines", "others", "total");
    printf("\n\n%12d%12d%12d%12d%12d%12d\n\n",
            blank_cnt, digit_cnt, letter_cnt, nl_cnt, other_cnt,
            blank_cnt + digit_cnt + letter_cnt + nl_cnt + other_cnt);
}
```

4.8 THE while STATEMENT

Repetition of action is one reason we rely on computers. When there are large amounts of data, it is very convenient to have control mechanisms that repeatedly execute specific statements.

Although we have used the while statement in many examples, we now want to explain precisely how this looping mechanism works. Its syntax is given by

> *while_statement* ::= while (*expression*) *statement*

Some examples are

```
while (i++ < n)
        factorial *= i;

while ((c = getchar() != EOF) {
    if ('a' <= c && c <= 'z')
            ++lower_case_letter_cnt;
    ++total_cnt;
}
```

but not

```
while (++i < LIMIT) do {       /* syntax error */
    j = 2 * i + 3;
    printf("\n%d", j);
}
    /* many other languages require "do", but not  C  */
```

In a construction of the form

```
while (expression)
    statement
next statement
```

expression is first evaluated. If it is zero (*false*), then control is passed directly to *next statement*. If it is nonzero (*true*), then *statement* is executed and control is passed back to the beginning of the while loop. Thus *statement* is repeatedly executed until *expression* is zero, at which point control is passed to *next statement*. The effect of this is that *statement* can be executed zero or more times. It is possible to inadvertently specify an expression that never becomes zero, and unless other means of escaping the while loop are introduced, the program is stuck in an infinite loop. Care should be taken to avoid this difficulty. As an example, consider the code

```
int   n;

printf("\ninput an integer:   ");
scanf("%d", &n);
while (--n) {
    .   .   .   .   .           /* do something */
}
```

The intent is for a positive integer to be entered and assigned to the variable n. Then the statements in the while loop are to be executed repeatedly until the expression --n is eventually zero. However, if a negative integer is inadvertently assigned to n, then the loop will be infinite. To guard against this possibility, it would be better to code instead

```
while (--n > 0) {
    .   .   .   .   .           /* do something */
}
```

It is sometimes appropriate for a while loop to contain only an empty statement. A typical example would be

```
while ((c = getchar()) == ' ')
    ;                 /* null statement */
```

This code will cause blank characters in the input stream to be skipped. We could have written this as

```
while ((c = getchar()) == ' ');
```

However, it is considered good programming style to place the semicolon on the next line by itself so that it is clearly visible as a null statement.

4.9 THE for STATEMENT

The for statement is closely related to the while statement, and is used just about as much. The following code, for example, will sum the integers from 1 to 10.

```
int    i, sum;

sum = 0;
for (i = 1; i <= 10; ++i)
      sum += i;
```

The construction

```
for  (expression1;  expression2;  expression3)
      statement
next statement
```

is semantically equivalent to

```
expression1;
while (expression2) {
      statement
      expression3;
}
next statement
```

provided that *expression2* is nonempty, and provided that a continue statement is not in the body of the for loop. This last special case is treated in Chapter 6. The above construction shows that the semantics of the for statement is the following. First *expression1* is evaluated. Typically, *expression1* is used to initialize the loop. Then *expression2* is evaluated. If it is nonzero (*true*), then *statement* is executed, *expression3* is evaluated, and control passes back to the beginning of the for loop again, except that evaluation of *expression1* is skipped. Typically, *expression2* is a logical expression controlling the iteration. This process continues until *expression2* is zero (*false*), at which point control passes to *next statement*.

The syntax of a for statement is given by

for_statement ::= for (*expression*; *expression*; *expression*)
      statement

Some examples are

```
for (i = 1; i <= n; ++i)
      factorial *= i;

for (j = 2; k % j == 0; ++j) {
      printf("\n%d  is a divisor of  %d", j, k);
      sum += j;
}
```

but not

```
for (i = 0, i < n, i += 3)       /*   semicolons  needed   */
     sum += i;
```

Any or all of the expressions in a for statement can be missing, but the two semicolons must remain. If *expression1* is missing, then no initialization step is performed as part of the for loop. The code

```
i = 1;
sum = 0;
for ( ; i <= 10; ++i)
     sum += i;
```

will compute the sum of the integers from 1 to 10, and so will the code

```
i = 1;
sum = 0;
for ( ; i <= 10 ; )
     sum += i++;
```

When *expression2* is missing, the special rule is that the test is always *true*. Thus, the for loop in the code

```
i = 1;
sum = 0;
for ( ; ; ) {
     sum += i++;
     printf ("\n%d", sum);
}
```

is an infinite loop.

A for statement can be used as the statement part of an if, if-else, while, or another for statement. For example, the construction

```
for ( .   . . )
     for ( .   . . )
          for ( .   . . )
               statement
```

is a single for statement.

Since program control can be accomplished by use of either while or for statements, which gets used is often a matter of taste. One major advantage of a for loop is that control and indexing can both be kept right at the top. When loops are deeply nested, this can facilitate the reading of the code. The program in the next section illustrates this.

4.10 AN EXAMPLE: BOOLEAN VARIABLES

Boolean algebra plays a big role in the design of computer circuits. In this algebra all variables have only the values one or zero. Transistors and memory technologies implement zero-one value schemes with currents, voltages, and magnetic orientations. Frequently the circuit designer has a function in mind and needs to check whether, for all possible zero-one inputs, the output has the desired behavior.

Suppose for five boolean variables, say

        b1,   b2,   b3,   b4,   b5,

we want to create a table of values for the functions

        b1 || b3 || b5   and   b1 && b2 || b4 && b5

and the majority function. The majority function is 1 if more than half of all the variables have the value 1.

```
/***   a table of values for some boolean functions   ***/

main()
{
    int    b1, b2, b3, b4, b5;      /*  boolean variables  */
    int    cnt = 0;

    printf("\n%5s%5s%5s%5s%5s%5s%13s%13s%12s\n",
           "cnt", "b1", "b2", "b3", "b4", "b5",
           "function1", "function2", "majority");

    for (b1 = 0; b1 <= 1; ++b1)
        for (b2 = 0; b2 <= 1; ++b2)
            for (b3 = 0; b3 <= 1; ++b3)
                for (b4 = 0; b4 <= 1; ++b4)
                    for (b5 = 0; b5 <= 1; ++b5)
                        printf("\n%5d%5d%5d%5d%5d%5d%9d%13d%12d",
                               ++cnt, b1, b2, b3, b4, b5,
                               b1 || b3 || b5,
                               b1 && b2 || b4 && b5,
                               b1 + b2 + b3 + b4 + b5 >= 3);
    printf("\n\n");
}
```

This program prints a table of values for all possible inputs and corresponding outputs. It illustrates a typical use of nested `for` loops. Here is some of the output from the program.

cnt	b1	b2	b3	b4	b5	function1	function2	majority
1	0	0	0	0	0	0	0	0
2	0	0	0	0	1	1	0	0
3	0	0	0	1	0	0	0	0
.	.	.	.	.	.			
23	1	0	1	1	0	1	0	1
24	1	0	1	1	1	1	1	1
.	.	.	.	.	.			
30	1	1	1	0	1	1	1	1
31	1	1	1	1	0	1	1	1
32	1	1	1	1	1	1	1	1

4.11 THE COMMA OPERATOR

Of all the operators in C the comma operator has the lowest precedence. It is a binary operator with expressions as operands.

comma_expression ::= *expression , expression*

In a comma expression of the form

expression1 , expression2

expression1 is evaluated first, then *expression2*; the comma expression as a whole has the value and type of its right operand. An example would be

```
sum = 0, i = 1
```

If i has been declared an int, then this comma expression has value 1 and type int.

The comma operator is sometimes used in for statements. It allows multiple initializations and multiple processing of indices. For example, the code

```
for (sum = 0, i = 1; i <= n; ++i)
    sum += i;
printf("\n%d", sum);
```

will print the sum of the integers from 1 to n. Carrying this idea further, we can stuff the entire for loop inside the for parentheses. The previous code could be written as

```
for (sum = 0, i = 1; i <= n; sum += i, ++i)
    ;              /* empty statement */
printf("\n%d", sum);
```

but not as

```
for (sum = 0, i = 1; i <= n; ++i, sum += i)
    ;              /* empty statement */
printf("\n%d", sum);
```

In the comma expression

```
++i, sum += i
```

the expression ++i is evaluated first, and this will cause a different value to be printed.

To find the sum of the first n even integers and the sum of the first n odd integers, we could write

```
even_sum = odd_sum = 0;
for (cnt = 0, j = 2, k = 1; cnt < n; ++cnt, j += 2, k += 2) {
    even_sum += j;
    odd_sum += k;
}
printf("%7d%7d", even_sum, odd_sum);
```

The comma operator associates from left to right.

Declarations and initializations		
`int        i, j, k = 3;` `double     x = 3.3;`		
Expression	*Equivalent expression*	*Value*
`i = 1, j = 2, ++ k + 1`	`((i = 1), (j = 2)), ((++ k) + 1)`	5
`k != 1, ++ x * 2.0 + 1`	`(k != 1), (((++ x) * 2.0) + 1)`	9.6

Most commas in programs do not represent comma operators. Commas used to separate expressions in argument lists of functions or used within initializer lists are not comma operators. If a comma operator is to be used in these places, the comma expression in which it occurs must be enclosed in parentheses.

4.12 THE do STATEMENT

The do statement can be considered a variant of the while statement. Instead of making its test at the top of the loop, it makes it at the bottom. Its syntax is given by

> *do_statement* ::= do   *statement*   while (*expression*) ;

An example is

```
do {
    sum += i;
    scanf("%d", &i);
} while (i > 0);
```

In a construction of the form

> do
> > *statement*
>
> while (*expression*);
> *next statement*

statement is executed, then *expression* is evaluated, and if it is nonzero (*true*), then control passes back to the beginning of the do statement and the process repeats itself. When *expression* is zero (*false*), then control passes to *next statement*. As an example, suppose you want to read in a positive integer, and you want to insist that the integer is positive. Then the following code will do the job:

```
do {
      printf("\n\ninput a positive integer:    ");
      scanf("%d", &n);
} while (n <= 0);
```

As long as a nonpositive integer is entered, the user will be notified with a request for a positive integer. Control will exit the loop when a positive integer has been entered.

Only a small percentage of the loops in C code tend to be do loops. Because of this, it is considered good programming style to use braces even when they are not needed. The braces in the construct

```
do {
      a single statement
} while ( .    .    . );
```

make it easier for the reader to realize that you have written a do statement rather than a while statement followed by an empty statement.

Now that we have discussed in detail the if statement, the if-else statement, and the various looping statements, we want to pass along the following tip, which applies to all of their control expressions. It is considered a good programming style to use a relational expression, when appropriate, rather than an equality expression. In many cases the code will be more robust if you do so. For expressions of type float or double, an equality test can be beyond the accuracy of the machine. Here is an example of this.

```
/*** a test that fails ***/

main()
{
      int        cnt = 0;
      double     sum = 0.0, x;

      for (x = 0.0; x != 9.9; x += 0.1) {      /* test not robust */
            sum += x;
            printf("\ncnt   =%5d", ++cnt);
      }
      printf("\nsum   =   %f", sum);
}
```

On most machines this program results in an infinite loop.

4.13 AN EXAMPLE: FIBONACCI NUMBERS

The sequence of Fibonacci numbers is defined recursively as

$$x_0 = 0,$$
$$x_1 = 1,$$
$$x_{j+1} = x_j + x_{j-1} \quad \text{for} \quad j = 1, 2, \ldots$$

Except for x_0 and x_1, every element in the sequence is the sum of the previous two elements. It is easy to write down the first few elements of the sequence.

0, 1, 1, 2, 3, 5, 8, 13, 21, 34, 55, 89, 144, 233, . . .

Fibonacci numbers have lots of uses and many interesting properties. One of the properties has to do with the Fibonacci quotients defined by

$$q_j = \frac{x_j}{x_{j-1}} \quad \text{for} \quad j = 2, 3, \ldots$$

It can be shown that the sequence of quotients converges to the golden mean, which is the real number

$$\frac{1}{2} (1 + \sqrt{5})$$

We want to write a program that prints Fibonacci numbers and quotients. If `f1` contains the value of the current Fibonacci number and `f0` contains the value of the previous Fibonacci number, then we can

Save the value of `f1` (the current Fibonacci number) in a temporary.

Add `f0` and `f1` and store the value in `f1`, the new Fibonacci number.

Store the value of the temporary in `f0` so that `f0` will contain the previous Fibonacci number.

Print, and then repeat this process.

The following construct will do this.

```
for ( .   .   . ) {
        temp = f1;
        f1 += f0;
        f0 = temp;
        print the new Fibonacci number and quotient
}
```

The use of the variable `temp` is essential. The following construct is wrong.

```
for ( .   .  . ) {       /*  wrong code  */
     f1 += f0;
     f0 = f1;            /*  f0  does not contain the
                             previous Fibonacci number  */
```
print the new Fibonacci number and quotient
```
}
```

Here is the complete program. The Fibonacci numbers grow very large very fast, so not too many of them are computed.

```
/***  print fibonacci numbers and quotients  ***/

#define   LIMIT   46

main()
{
     int    f0 = 0, f1 = 1, n, temp;

     /*  print headings and the first two cases  */
     printf("\n%7s%19s%29s", "", "fibonacci", "fibonacci");
     printf("\n%7s%19s%29s\n", "n", "number", "quotient");
     printf("\n%7d%19d", 0, 0);
     printf("\n%7d%19d", 1, 1);

     for (n = 2; n <= LIMIT; ++n) {
          temp = f1;
          f1 += f0;
          f0 = temp;
          printf("\n%7d%19d%29.16f",
               n, f1, (double) f1 / (double) f0);
     }
     printf("\n\n");
}
```

Here is the partial output of the program.

n	fibonacci number	fibonacci quotient
0	0	
1	1	
2	1	1.0000000000000000
3	2	2.0000000000000000
.	.	.
7	13	1.6250000000000000
8	21	1.6153846153846154
9	34	1.6190476190476190
10	55	1.6176470588235294
.	.	.
44	701408733	1.6180339887498948
45	1134903170	1.6180339887498948
46	1836311903	1.6180339887498948

4.14 AN EXAMPLE: PRIME NUMBERS

Let *d* and *k* be nonzero integers. We say that *d* is a divisor of *k* if

$$k = d \times j \quad \text{for some integer } j$$

For example,

$$
\begin{array}{rll}
2 & \text{is a divisor of} & 4 \\
-3 & \text{is a divisor of} & -21
\end{array}
$$

but

$$
\begin{array}{rll}
5 & \text{is not a divisor of} & 17 \\
88 & \text{is not a divisor of} & -89
\end{array}
$$

A prime number *p* is an integer greater than or equal to 2 with the property that its only positive divisors are 1 and *p* itself. It was known even to the ancient Greeks that there are an infinite number of primes. The first few are

$$2, 3, 5, 7, 11, 13, 17, 19, 23, 29, \ldots$$

We want to write a program that will count all the primes less than some large number, call it LIMIT, and print them out. We begin by doing this in the simplest way possible. For each integer k between 2 and LIMIT we want to see if k has any positive divisors other than 1 and k itself. This will determine whether or not k is a prime. Since a divisor of k cannot be bigger than k, we need test only whether the integers j between 2 and k are divisors of k. These ideas are embodied in the following construct:

```
j = 2;
while (k % j != 0)
    ++j;
if (j == k)
    the integer k is a prime, print it
```

An alternative construct would be

```
for (j = 2; k % j != 0; ++j)
    ;
if (j == k)
    the integer k is a prime, print it
```

Here is the complete program:

```
/***   print all primes less than LIMIT   ***/

#define   LIMIT   1000

main()
{
    int    cnt = 0, j, k;

    for (k = 2; k < LIMIT; ++k) {
        j = 2;
        while (k % j != 0)
            ++j;
        if (j == k) {
            ++cnt;                       /*  a prime has been found  */
            if (cnt % 6 == 1)
                printf("\n");
            printf("%12d", k);
        }
    }
    printf("\n\nthere are   %d  prime numbers less than   %d\n\n",
        cnt, LIMIT);
}
```

In this program, the while loop is contained within the for statement. For each increment to k in the for statement the entire while statement is executed. The while statement is called the inner loop and the for statement is called the outer loop. Nesting of loops is a common construction in programming, but care should be taken to make the inner loops efficient.

4.15 SUMMARY

1. Relational, equality, and logical operators have an int value of 0 or 1.

2. Negation is a unary operator, and all unary operators are of higher precedence than all binary operators.

3. Relational, equality, and logical operators make a comparison of two expressions. Automatic type conversions may occur when the expressions are compared.

4. A chief use of relational, equality, and logical expressions is to test data to affect flow of control.

5. The grouping construct { . . . } is a compound statement. It allows enclosed statements to be treated as a single unit.

6. An if statement gives a means of choosing whether or not to execute a statement.

7. The else part of an if-else statement associates with the nearest available if. This resolves the *dangling else* problem.

8. The while, for, and do statements provide looping mechanisms. The body of a do statement executes at least once.

9. To prevent an unwanted infinite loop, the programmer must make sure that the expression controlling the loop eventually becomes zero. The miscoding of controlling expressions is a common error.

10. In many situations the code can be naturally written using either a while statement or a for statement. In situations where clarity dictates that indexing control be kept visible at the top of the loop, the for statement is the natural choice.

11. The comma operator is occasionally useful in for statements. Of all the operators in C it has the lowest priority.

4.16 EXERCISES

1. Give equivalent logical expressions without negation.

```
! (a > b)            ! (a <= b + 3)       ! (a < b && c < d)
! (a + 1 == b + 1)  ! (a > 2 || a < 5)  ! (a < 1 || b < 2 && c < 3)
```

2. What are the values of the expressions in the following table?

Declarations and assignments	

int   a, b, c, d, e;
double   x, y;
 	
a = 0; b = 1; c = 2; d = 3; e = -1;
x = 1.65; y = 0.0;	

Expression	**Value**
a > b	
a <= y	
(c < d) || a	
c < (d || a)	
2 < !d + d	
2 < ! (d + d)	
! (! (!e))	
! (! (!y))	
a + c <= !d + b	
x <= 1 + 2/3	

3. Write a program that reads characters from a file until EOF is encountered. Use the variables `digit_cnt` and `other_cnt` to count the number of digits and the number of other characters.

4. Write a program that counts the number of times the first three letters of the alphabet (a, A, b, B, c, C) occur in a file. Do not distinguish between lower- and uppercase.

5. Write a program that contains the loop

```
while (scanf ("%lf", &salary) == 1) {
    .  .  .  .  .
}
```

Within the loop compute a 15% withholding tax, print each `salary` and its corresponding tax, and accumulate the sums of all salaries and taxes printed. Print these sums after the program exits the `while` loop. Run the program on your system.

6. What does the following program print?

```
main ()
{
    char    c = 'w';
    int     i = 5, j = 0, k = -7;
    double  x = 2.3, y = 0.0;

    printf ("\n%c   %d", c, !c);
    printf ("\n%d   %d", i, !i);
    printf ("\n%d   %d", - ! j, ! - j);
    printf ("\n%d   %d", !i, !!i);
    printf ("\n%d   %d", !!x, !!!x);
    printf ("\n%d   %d", !!y, !!!y);
    printf ("\n%d   %d", (k - k), ! (k - k));
    printf ("\n%d   %d", (k - k, !k - k);
    printf ("\n\n");
}
```

7. Complete the following table:

Declarations and assignments
| ```
char    X;
int     a, b, c, d;
double  x, y;
X = 'X';   a = 2;   b = -3;   c = 7;   d = -19;   x = 5.77;   y = -7.33;
``` |

Expression	Equivalent expression	Value
a && b && c	(a && b) && c	
a && b || c		
a || b && c		
a || b && c || d + 19		
a && b || c && d + 19		
a && b && c && d + 19		
! a + ! b && x + y		
! a + ! b || x + y		
X && b + c - 4 || 0.0 * x		
X || b + c - 4 && 0.0 * x		
x = a && b || c		
x = ! a && b || ! c	x = (((! a) && b) || (! c)))	

8. Explain the effect of the following code.

```
{
      int   i;

      .  .   .   .   .
      while (i = 2) {
            printf("\nsome even numbers are:   %d   %d   %d",
                  i, i + 2, i + 4);
            i = 0;

      }
      .   .    .    .    .
```

Contrast this code with the following:

```
{
      int   i;

      .   .    .    .    .
      if (i = 2) {
            printf("\nsome even numbers are:   %d   %d   %d",
                  i, i + 2, i + 4);
      }

      .   .    .    .    .
```
```

Both pieces of code are logically wrong. The run-time effect of one of them is so striking that the error is easy to spot; the other piece of wrong code has a subtle effect that is much harder to spot. Explain.

9. What does the following program print?

```
main()
{
        char      c;
        int       i, j, k;
        double    x, y;

        c = 'w';      i = 1;       j = 2;        k = -7;
        x = 7e+33;    y = 0.001;

        printf("\n%d   %d", c == 'a', c != 'b');
        printf("\n%d   %d", i == j, j != k);
        printf("\n%d   %d", 2*i - j == k + 7, 0 != !k);
        printf("\n%d      ", c == 'a' && c > 'j');
        printf("\n%d      ", c != 'a' && c > 'j');
        printf("\n%d      ", x != y || x <= 0.0);
        printf("\n%d      ", 1 == i == j - 1);
        printf("\n\n");

}
```

10. What gets printed?

```
int    i, j;

i = j = 2;
if (i == 1)
        if (j == 2)
               printf("\n%d", i = i + j);
else
        printf("\n%d", i = i - j);
printf("\n%d", i);
```

11. The syntax error in the following piece of code does not really show up on the line listed. Run a test program with this piece of code in it, find out which line is flagged with a syntax error, and explain why.

```
while (++i < LIMIT) do {     /* syntax error */
        j = 2 * i + 3;
        printf("\n%d", j);

}
        /* many other languages require "do", but not  C  */
```

12. Can the following code ever lead to an infinite loop?

```
printf("\ninput two integers:  ");
scanf("%d%d", &i, &j);
while (i * j < 0 && ++i != 7 && j++ != 9) {
    .  .  .  .  .        /* do something */
}
```

13. Write a program that reads in an integer n and then sums the integers from n to 2 * n if n is nonnegative, or from 2 * n to n if n is negative. Write the code in two versions, one using only for loops and the other using only while loops.

14. The system function putchar() returns the int value of the character that it writes. What does the following code print?

```
for (putchar('1'); putchar('2'); putchar('3'))
    putchar('4');
```

15. Answer the following true-false questions.

In the C language:
Every statement ends in a semicolon.
Every statement contains at least one semicolon.
Every statement contains at most one semicolon.
There exists a statement with precisely 33 semicolons.
There exists a statement made up of 35 characters
 which contains 33 semicolons.

16. Examine the output of the program that prints a table of values for some boolean functions. For the 32 different inputs, exactly half of them (16 in number) have majority value 1. Write a program that prints a table of values for the majority function for, say, 7 boolean variables. Of the 128 different inputs, how many have majority value 1? State the general case as a theorem and try to give a proof. (Your machine can help you find theorems by checking special cases, but in general it cannot give a "proof.")

17. Write a program that reads in a positive integer n and prints the sum of the first n even integers and the sum of the first n odd integers. Write the code in three versions, one using a single for statement with comma operators, the second using two for statements with no comma operators, and the third using only while statements.

18. Of the three programs written in the preceding exercise, choose one of them and incorporate into it the following piece of code:

```
do {
        printf("\n\ninput a positive integer:    ");
        scanf("%d", &n);
        if (n <= 0) {
            printf("\n\n%d  is nonpositive", n);
            printf("\na positive integer is required");
        }
} while (n <= 0);
```

Then write another version of the program that uses a while statement instead of a do statement to accomplish the same effect.

19. The following loop prints TRUE across the screen until interrupted by a control-c.

```
main()
{
    while (1)
        printf("TRUE    ");
}
```

Write an equivalent program using the for statement, where the statement controlled by the for is the empty statement "; ".

20. The semantics of logical expressions imply that order of evaluation is critical in some computations. The fact that certain subexpressions may not be evaluated inside a logical "and" expression or a logical "or" expression has a bearing on efficiency. Why? Explain which of the following two alternate expressions is most likely the correct one:

(a)

```
if ((x != 0.0) && ((z - x) / x * x < 2.0))
        .    .    .    .    .
```

(b)

```
if (((z - x) / x * x < 2.0) && (x != 0.0))
        .    .    .    .    .
```

21. Suppose that we have three statements called *st1*, *st2*, *st3*. We wish to write an if-else statement that will test the value of an int variable i and execute different combinations of the statements accordingly. The combinations are given in the following tables.

(a)	i	execute	(b)	i	execute	(c)	i	execute
	1	*st1*		1	*st2*		1	*st1, st2*
	2	*st2*		2	*st1, st3*		2	*st1, st2*
	3	*st3*		3	*st1*		3	*st2, st3*

Write programs that read in the values of i interactively and use appropriate printf() statements to check that the flow of control mimics the action described in the tables. For example, statements of the following kind

```
if (i == 1)
    printf("\nstatement_1 executed");
```

will provide the feedback so that you can see if your program runs correctly.

22. A polynomial in x of at most degree 2 is given by

$$a x^2 + b x + c$$

Its *discriminant* is defined to be

$$b^2 - 4 a c$$

We are interested in the square root of the discriminant; see exercise 23. If the discriminant is nonnegative, then

$$\sqrt{b^2 - 4 a c}$$

has its usual interpretation, but if the discriminant is negative, then

$$\sqrt{b^2 - 4 a c} \quad \text{means} \quad i\sqrt{-(b^2 - 4 a c)}$$

where i is the imaginary number satisfying

$$i^2 = -1 \quad \text{or equivalently} \quad i = \sqrt{-1}$$

Write a program that reads in the values of a, b, c and then prints the value of the square root of the discriminant. For example, if `1.0`, `2.0`, and `3.0` are read in, then

```
i 2.828427
```

should be printed.

23. Write a program that repeatedly reads in the values for a, b, c and then finds the roots of the polynomial

$$a x^2 + b x + c$$

Recall that the roots are numbers, real or complex, that solve the equation

$$a x^2 + b x + c = 0$$

When both $a = 0$ and $b = 0$ we will consider the case "extremely degenerate" and leave it at that. When $a = 0$ and $b \neq 0$, we will consider the case "degenerate." In this case the equation reduces to

$$b x + c = 0$$

and it has one root given by

$$x = -\frac{c}{b}$$

When $a \neq 0$ (the general case), the roots are given by

$$root_1 = \frac{1}{2a}(-b + \sqrt{b^2 - 4 a c})$$

$$root_2 = \frac{1}{2a}(-b - \sqrt{b^2 - 4ac})$$

The expression under the square root sign is the *discriminant*; see exercise 22. If the discriminant is positive, then two real roots exist. If the discriminant is zero, then the two roots are real and equal. In this case we say that the polynomial (or the equation) has *multiple real roots*. If the discriminant is negative, then the roots are complex. Your program should print, as appropriate, the following messages:

```
extremely degenerate
degenerate
two real roots
multiple real roots
two complex roots
```

along with the computed root(s). For example, if 1.0, 2.0, and 3.0 are read in for the values of a, b, c, respectively, then

```
two complex roots:   root1  =  -1.000000  +  i 1.414214
                     root2  =  -1.000000  -  i 1.414214
```

should be printed.

24. A *truth table* for a boolean function is a table consisting of all possible values for its variables and the corresponding values of the boolean function itself. In this chapter we created a truth table for the majority function, along with two other functions. In that table we used 0 and 1 to represent *false* and *true*, respectively. Create separate truth tables for the following boolean functions:

    (a) b1 || b2 || b3 || b4
    (b) b1 && b2 && b3 && b4
    (c) ! (!b1 || b2) || (!b3 || b4)

    Instead of using 0 and 1, use false and true (print out the words) in the tables. *Hint:* Use the #define mechanism to define a BOOLEX, and write your program to operate on an arbitrary BOOLEX.

25. Write a program that prints out those Fibonacci numbers that are prime.

26. Write a program to check proper pairing of braces. The program will have two variables, one to keep track of left braces and the other to keep track of right braces. They both start at value 0 and the appropriate one is incremented each time a brace is encountered. If the right brace variable ever exceeds the value of the left brace variable, the program inserts the character pair ?? at that point in the output. If, at the end of the input file, the left brace variable is greater than the right brace variable, the output should print a message that includes the number of right braces missing as a series of that many }'s. Use the library functions getchar() and putchar() to do your input/output. Try it on some of your own C programs.

27. Extend your program in the previous problem so that it deals with both braces and parentheses simultaneously.

28. (Advanced) Let a be a positive real number. Define the sequence x_j of positive numbers recursively as follows.

$$x_0 = 1,$$

$$x_{j+1} = \frac{1}{2}(x_j + \frac{a}{x_j}) \qquad \text{for} \qquad j = 0, 1, 2, \dots$$

It can be shown mathematically that

$$x_j \rightarrow \sqrt{a} \qquad \text{as} \qquad j \rightarrow \infty$$

This algorithm is derived from the Newton-Raphson method in numerical analysis. Write a program that reads in the value of a interactively and uses this algorithm to compute the square root of a. As you will see, the algorithm is very efficient. (Nonetheless, it is not the algorithm used in the system function `sqrt()`.) Your program should have two variables of type `double`, say, `x0` and `x1`. Start with `x0` having value 0.0 and `x1` having value 1.0. Inside a loop do the following:

```
x0 = x1;              /* save the current value of x1 */
x1 = 0.5 * (x1 + a / x1);  /* compute a new value of x1 */
```

The loop should continue as long as `x0` is not equal to `x1`. Print out the values of a, `x1` (the square root of a), a - `x1` * `x1` (this computation is a check on accuracy), and the number of iterations required to compute the square root.

29. (Advanced) Modify the program you wrote for exercise 28 so that the square roots of

```
1.0,   2.0,   3.0,   .   .   .   ,   LIMIT
```

are all computed. Print the number, the square root of the number, and the number of iterations needed to compute it. (You can look in a numerical analysis text to discover why the technique is so efficient. It is characterized as *quadratically convergent*.)

30. (Advanced) The constant e, which is the base of the natural logarithms, is given to 41 significant figures by

$$e = 2.71828\ 18284\ 59045\ 23536\ 02874\ 71352\ 66249\ 77572$$

Define

$$x_n = (1 + \frac{1}{n})^n \qquad \text{for} \qquad n = 1, 2, \dots$$

It can be shown mathematically that

$$x_n \rightarrow e \qquad \text{as} \qquad n \rightarrow \infty$$

Investigate how to calculate *e* to arbitrary precision using this algorithm. You may use other algorithms, if you so desire.

31. The following program is machine dependent. If it does the unexpected on your machine, see if you can explain what is happening.

```
main()
{
    char    c;

    c = 0xff;
    if (c == 0xff)
        printf("\ntruth!\n\n");
    else
        printf("\nthis needs to be explained!\n\n");
}
```

32. Modify the program in this chapter that counts blanks, digits, and letters to count lowercase and uppercase letters separately.

33. Is the number of primes less than 10000 itself a prime?

34. If *p* and *q* are both primes and *q* = *p* + 2, then the pair *p,q* are called *twin primes*. For example 3,5 are twin primes. Write a program which lists all the twin primes less than LIMIT. (It is not known whether the number of twin primes is finite or infinite.)

5

Functions

The heart of effective problem solving is problem decomposition. Taking a problem and breaking it up into small, manageable pieces is critical to writing large programs. The function facility provides a construction to implement this "top down" method of programming. Each program consists of one or more files of functions, one of them being a main() function. A program begins execution with main() and can include the use of library functions such as printf() and sqrt(). Functions operate with program variables, and those variables available for use in a function are determined by scope rules. This chapter will discuss function definition, function invocation, scope rules, and storage classes.

5.1 FUNCTION DEFINITION

A function definition consists of a header and a body. The body is explicitly a block or compound statement. Declarations, if any, must appear before any executable statements at the beginning of the block. The header can simply be an identifier and a parenthesis pair. A simple example is

```
/***   a function with a simple header and body   ***/

wrt_address()       /*   header   */
                    /*   the body is everything between the braces   */
{
    printf("\n\n%s\n%s\n%s\n%s\n%s\n\n",
        "      *******************",
        "      **   SANTA  CLAUS   *",
        "      **   NORTH  POLE    *",
        "      **   EARTH          *",
        "      *******************");
}
```

Wherever a program knows this function, the expression

```
wrt_address()
```

causes the function to be invoked. For example, if the code

```
for (i = 0; i < 3; ++i)
    wrt_address();
```

occurs in a main() function written in the same file as wrt_address(), then it will be invoked, or called, three times. Thus, functions act as useful abbreviating schemes.

A function definition has a name and a parenthesis pair containing zero or more parameters and a body. For each parameter there should be a corresponding declaration that occurs before the body. Any parameter not declared is taken to be an int by default. It is good programming practice to declare all parameters. They act as place holders for values that are passed when the function is invoked. To emphasize their role as place holders, these parameters are called the *formal parameters* of the function. The function body is a block, or compound statement, and it too may contain declarations. Some examples are

```
nothing() { }      /* this function does nothing */

static double twice(x)
double    x;
{
    return (2.0 * x);
}

all_add(a, b, c, x, y, z)
int       a, b, c;
double    x, y, z;
{
    int    i, j, k;
    .   .    .    .
    return (a + b + c + i + j + k + x + y + z);
}
```

Any variables declared in the body of a function are said to be "local" to that function. Other variables not declared either as arguments or in the function body are considered "global" to the function and must be defined externally. An example would be

```
int   i = 33;      /* i is external and initialized to 33 */

main() {
    printf("\ni = %d\n\n", i);      /* i is global to main() */
}
```

There are several important reasons for writing programs as collections of many small functions. It is simpler to correctly write a small function that does one job. Both writing and debugging are made easier. It is also easier to maintain or modify such a program. One can readily change just the set of functions that need to be rewritten expecting the rest of the code to work correctly. Also, small functions tend to be self-documenting and highly readable. A useful heuristic for writing good programs is to write each function so that its code fits on a single page.

We have already used predefined mathematical functions such as `sqrt()`, which take as an argument an expression of type `double` and return a value of type `double`. Here are some examples of how the argument to `sqrt()` might appear:

```
y = sqrt(4.0)    /* the argument is a constant of type double */
y = sqrt(4)      /* error  -  the argument is of type int      */
y = sqrt(x)      /* the argument is a variable of type double */
y = sqrt(b*b - 4.0*a*c)      /* an expression of type double */
```

The system does *not* check to ensure that parameters to functions have the right type. It is the responsibility of the programmer to supply the right number of arguments of the right type. The function call `sqrt(4)` will return nonsense. Similarly, if i is a variable of type `int`, then `sqrt(i)` will return nonsense.

A function such as `sqrt()` is written as follows.

```
double sqrt(x)
double    x;
{              /* the body is everything between the braces */
    .  .  .  .
    return ( .   . . );          /* a value is returned */
}
```

The first `double` is the *type specifier* of the function. It specifies the type of the value returned by the function. If the type specifier is absent, then, by default, it is `int`. Thus, for example, the function definition

```
f() { .   .  . }
```

is equivalent to

```
int f() { .   .  . }
```

In the function definition of `sqrt()`, the identifier x is placed in the parameter list between parentheses, and its declaration is given after the right parenthesis and before the left brace. The header consists of everything before the left brace, the block comprises the body, and the header and body together make up the function definition for `sqrt()`. A value is passed back to the external calling environment by a `return` statement.

5.2 THE `return` STATEMENT

The `return` statement may or may not include an expression.

return_statement ::= return; | return *expression*;

Some examples are

```
return;
return (377);
return (a * b);
return (++x);
return ++x;              /*  correct, but bad style  */
```

It is considered good programming practice to always enclose the expression in a return statement in parentheses so as to clearly indicate what value is being computed.

The return statement terminates the execution of the function and passes control back to the calling environment. If the return statement contains an expression, then the value of the expression is passed back to the calling environment as well. Moreover, this value will be converted to the type given by the type specifier of the function.

```
double g(a, b, c)
char    a, b, c;
{
      int i;
      .  .  .  .  .
      return (i);      /* value will be converted to a double */
}
```

There can be zero or more return statements in a function. If there is no return statement, then control passes back to the calling environment when the closing brace of the body of the function is encountered. This is called "falling off the end." The following is an illustration of how two return statements might be used.

```
double absolute_value(x)
double    x;
{
      if (x >= 0.0)
            return (x);
      else
            return (-x);
}
```

Even though a function returns a value, a program need not make use of it.

```
while ( . . . ) {
      getchar();        /*  get a char - do nothing with it  */
      c = getchar();    /*  c  will be processed  */
      .  .  .  .  .
}
```

Suppose that we want a function that will return the square of an integer n, where n is a parameter. The function, let us call it square(), will have a parameter list consisting of a single variable of type int.

```
square(n)
int    n;
{
      return (n * n);
}
```

Now suppose that in a different function a variable i of type int has the value 3, and the statement

```
x = square(i);
```

is executed. The value of i is passed to the corresponding parameter, namely n, in the function definition for square(). The only executable statement in the function is

```
return (n * n);
```

so that with n having value 3, the value 9 is returned, which is the value that is assigned to x.

Suppose that we want a function that will return the sum of the squares of the integers from 1 to *n*, that is,

$$1^2 + 2^2 + \cdots + n^2$$

where *n* is a parameter. The function will have a parameter list consisting of a single variable of type int.

```
/***   the sum of squares of integers from  1  to  n  ***/

sum_of_squares (n)
int    n;
{
     int    i, sum = 0;

     for (i = 1; i <= n; ++i)
          sum += i * i;
     return (sum);
}
```

To test this function, we write the following:

```
/***   test sum of squares   ***/

#define   N    5

main ()
{
     int    n;

     for (n = 1; n <= N; ++n)
          printf ("\n%12d", sum_of_squares (n));
     printf ("\n\n");
}
```

After we compile these functions and create an executable program, we find that the output from the program is the following:

```
          1
          5
         14
         30
         55
```

If we want a function that will compute the sum of *k*th powers,

$$1^k + 2^k + \cdots + n^k$$

where both *k* and *n* are parameters, then the parameter list must contain two variables of type int.

```
/***   the sum of kth powers of integers from  1  to  n  ***/

sum_of_powers (k, n)
int    k, n;
{
      int    i, sum = 0;

      for (i = 1; i <= n; ++i)
            sum += power (i, k);
      return (sum);
}
```

Since this function calls power (), we must write it, too.

```
/***   m  raised to the nth power  ***/

power (m, n)
int    m, n;
{
      int    i, product = 1;

      for (i = 1; i <= n; ++i)
            product *= m;
      return (product);
}
```

Now we write a test function that creates a table of sums of *k*th powers.

```
/***   print a table of sums of kth powers  ***/

#define    K    5
#define    N    9

main()
{
      int    k, n;
      printf ("\n%12s%s\n",
            " ", ":::::  a table of sums of kth powers  :::::");
      for (n = 1; n <= N; ++n) {
            printf ("\n");
            for (k = 1; k <= K; ++k)
                  printf ("%12d", sum_of_powers (k, n));
      }
      printf ("\n\n");
}
```

After compiling these functions and creating an executable program, we find that the output from its execution is the following:

::::: a table of sums of kth powers :::::

1	1	1	1	1
3	5	9	17	33
6	14	36	98	276
10	30	100	354	1300
15	55	225	979	4425
21	91	441	2275	12201
28	140	784	4676	29008
36	204	1296	8772	61776
45	285	2025	15333	120825

Observe that it is not immediately obvious that the program does what we want. Some hand simulation is necessary to check that the output is logically correct. Note that the second column in the table corresponds to the output of the program that tested the function sum_of_squares() above.

The writing of small functions such as power() and sum_of_powers() makes it easy to correctly build up more complicated programs. This is one of the essentials of "structured programming."

5.3 INVOCATION AND CALL BY VALUE

A function is executed by invoking it. This is done by writing its name and a parenthesized argument list. The semantics of invocation use several concepts. We must know about scope. We must understand how formal parameters work. And we must understand how the return statement works.

Functions are declared as individual objects that cannot be nested. Therefore, a program consists of a series of one or more function definitions. These functions are available for use in each other's body. They can be used wherever an expression of the type given by the type specifier of the function is appropriate. (Recall that if a type specifier for a function is absent, then it is int by default.)

Functions are invoked by writing their name and an appropriate list of arguments within parentheses. Typically, these arguments will match in number and type the parameters in the parameter list in the function definition. All arguments are passed "call by value." This means that each argument is evaluated and its value is used locally in place of the formal parameter. Thus, if a variable is passed to a function, the stored value of that variable will not be changed in the calling environment.

```
main()
{
    int    i = 4, j;

    j = try_to_change_it(i);      /*  try to change  i  */
    printf("%d  %d\n", i, j);     /*  4  37  is printed  */
}

try_to_change_it(k)
int    k;
{
    printf("%d\n", k);     /*  4  is printed  */
    k += 33;               /*  the stored value of  k  is changed  */
    printf("%d\n", k);     /*  37  is printed  */
    return (k);
}
```

Function invocation means:

1. Each expression in the argument list is evaluated.

2. The value of the expression is assigned to its corresponding formal parameter at the beginning of the body of the function.

3. The body of the function is executed.

4. If a return statement is executed, then control passes back to the calling environment.

5. If the return statement includes an expression, then the value of the expression is converted (if necessary) to the type given by the type specifier of the function, and that value is passed back to the calling environment too.

6. If no return statement is present, then control is passed back to the calling environment when the end of the body of the function is reached.

7. If a return statement without an expression is executed or no return statement is present, then no useful value is returned to the calling environment.

8. All arguments are passed "call by value."

The "call by value" mechanism is in contrast to "call by reference." In Chapter 7 we will explain how to accomplish the effect of "call by reference." It is a way to pass addresses (references) of variables to a function that then allows the body of the function to make changes to the values of variables in the calling environment.

5.4 THE TYPE SPECIFIER void

A function f() is called by writing

   f (*argument list*)

and this may occur wherever it is appropriate to have an expression. If the function is not meant to return a value through the use of an expression in a return statement in its body, then it may be invoked as a statement

   f (. . .) ;

We have seen this in our use of printf(). The type specifier void is used to declare functions that are not intended to return values. Using a void function in an expression that requires a value will cause the compiler to complain.

```
main()
{
      int    k;
      void   prn_char();

      k = prn_char('w');      /*  syntax error  */
}

void   prn_char(c)
char   c;
{
      printf("%c  has value  %d\n", c, c);
}
```

Let us contrast this code with the following:

```
main()
{
      int    k;

      k = prn_char('w');    /* k  is assigned a "garbage" value */
}

prn_char(c)
char   c;
{
      printf("%c  has value  %d\n", c, c);
}
```

On our system *lint* gives a warning, but *cc* compiles the program without complaint and when it runs, it prints the line

   w has value 119

If the type specifier for a function is not explicitly given as void, most C systems will return a value when control is passed back from a function call, whether or not a return statement is present. If control is passed back by executing a return statement without an expression or by reaching the end of the function body, the value passed back will be undefined ("garbage"). If that value is used inadvertently in the calling environment, the programmer will *not* be warned. Nonetheless, it is conventional that most of the time programmers omit the type specifier void. We will follow this convention.

5.5 ELEMENTARY STATISTICS: AN EXAMPLE

We will write a program that will do some simple statistics on a series of numbers to be entered interactively. The problem will be to input data, compute the minimum, maximum, sum, and average value of the data, and to output this information accumulatively. By writing each function separately we can see how easy it would be to extend the program to include other calculations, such as standard deviation, and so on.

The code to compute the minimum and maximum of two floating numbers is straightforward:

```
double minimum(x, y)
double    x, y;
{
     if (x <= y)
          return (x);
     else
          return (y);
}

double maximum(x, y)
double    x, y;
{
     if (x >= y)
          return (x);
     else
          return (y);
}
```

The next pieces of code are designed to take care of some housekeeping chores:

```
prn_info()
{
     printf("\n%s\n%s%s",
          "this program computes and prints accumulative statistics",
          "on  n  floating numbers, where  n  is the number ",
          "of data items entered.");
}
```

```
get_n()
{
    int    n;
    printf("\n\nhow many data items are to be entered?   ");
    scanf("%d", &n);
    while (n <= 0) {
        printf("\n\nyou must input a positive integer.");
        printf("\nhow many data items are to be entered?   ");
        scanf("%d", &n);
    }
    return (n);
}

prn_heading()
{
    printf("\n\n%5s%12s%12s%12s%12s%12s\n",
        "count", "item", "minimum", "maximum", "sum", "average");
}
```

Finally, to put everything together we write a main() function:

```
/***   simple interactive statistics   ***/

main()
{
    int     i, n;
    double  x, min, max, sum, minimum(), maximum();

    prn_info();
    while (1) {
        n = get_n();
        printf("\ninput %d  data items:   ", n);
        scanf("%lf", &x);
        min = max = sum = x;
        prn_heading();
        prn_data(1, x, min, max, sum, sum);
        for (i = 2; i <= n; ++i) {
            scanf("%lf", &x);
            min = minimum(x, min);
            max = maximum(x, max);
            sum += x;
            prn_data(i, x, min, max, sum, sum / i);
        }
        prn_heading();
    }
}
```

Suppose that we run the program and type in 3 followed by 2.44, -8.44, and 5 when prompted. The following is what appears on the screen:

```
this program computes and prints accumulative statistics
on  n  floating numbers, where  n  is the number of data items entered.

how many data items are to be entered?  3

input  3  data items:  2.44   -8.44   5
```

count	item	minimum	maximum	sum	average
1	2.44000	2.44000	2.44000	2.44000	2.44000
2	-8.44000	-8.44000	2.44000	-6.00000	-3.00000
3	5.00000	-8.44000	5.00000	-1.00000	-0.33333
count	item	minimum	maximum	sum	average

```
how many data items are to be entered?
```

The collection of functions constitutes a program. Notice how other functions could be readily added. In a real sense, we are creating a new set of operations for our particular problem specification. This set, the functions defined for the problem, are now a special higher level language more convenient to the problem domain.

5.6 SCOPE RULES

The basic rule of scoping is that identifiers are accessible only within the block in which they are declared. They are unknown outside the boundaries of that block. This would be an easy rule to follow, except that programmers, for a variety of reasons, choose to use the same identifier in different declarations. We then have the question of which object the identifier refers to. Let us give a simple example of this state of affairs.

```
.    .    .    .    .
{
    int   a = 5;            /* outer block  a */
    printf ("\n%d", a);     /* 5  is printed */
    {
        int   a = 2;        /* inner block  a */
        printf ("\n%d", a); /* 2  is printed */
    }                       /* back to outer block */
    printf ("\n%d", ++a);   /* 6  is printed */
}
    .    .    .    .    .
```

An equivalent piece of code would be

```
      .    .    .    .    .
      {
              int    a_out = 5;
              printf ("\n%d", a_out);
              {
                      int    a_in = 2;
                      printf ("\n%d", a_in);
              }
              printf ("\n%d", ++a_out);
      }
      .    .    .    .    .
```

Each block introduces its own nomenclature. An outer block name is valid unless an inner block redefines it. If redefined, the outer block name is hidden, or masked, from the inner block. Inner blocks may be nested to arbitrary depths that are determined by system limitations. The following piece of code illustrates hidden variables in three nested blocks:

```
      .    .    .    .    .
      {
              int    a = 5, b = -3, c = -7;

              printf ("\n%d  %d  %d", a, b, c);              /* 5   -3   -7 */
              {
                      int      b = 8;
                      float    c = 9.9;

                      printf ("\n%d  %d  %.1f", a, b, c);    /* 5   8   9.9 */
                      a = b;
                      {
                              int    c;

                              c = b;
                              printf ("\n%d  %d  %d", a, b, c);  /* 8   8   8 */
                      }
                      printf ("\n%d  %d  %.1f", a, b, c);   /* 8   8   9.9 */
              }
              printf ("\n%d  %d  %d", a, b, c);              /* 8   -3   -7 */
      }
      .    .    .    .    .
```

The int variable a is declared in the outer block and is never redeclared. Therefore, it is available in both nested inner blocks. The variables b and c are redeclared in the first inner block, thus hiding the outer block variables of the same name. Upon exiting this block, both b and c will resume being available as the outer block variables, with their values intact from the outer block initialization. The innermost block again redeclares c, so that both c (inner) and c (outer) are hidden by c (innermost).

5.7 PARALLEL AND NESTED BLOCKS

Two blocks can come one after another, in which case the second block has no knowledge of the variables declared in the first block. Such blocks, residing at the same level, are called parallel blocks. Functions are declared in parallel at the outermost level. The following code illustrates two parallel blocks nested in an outer block.

```
      .   .    .   .    .
  {
      int    a, b;
      .   .    .   .    .
      {                         /* inner block 1 */
          float    b, x, y;
              .    .    .    .     /* int a known, but not int b */
      }
          .    .    .    .
      {                         /* inner block 2 */
          int    a;
          char    c, d;
              .    .    .    .     /* int b known, but not int a */
                      /* nothing in inner block 1 is known */
      }
          .   .    .   .    .
  }
```

Parallel and nested blocks can be combined in arbitrarily complicated schemes. The chief reason for blocks is to allow memory for variables to be created where needed. If memory is a scarce resource, then block exit will release the storage allocated locally to the block, allowing the memory to be used for some other purpose. Also, blocks associate names in their neighborhood of use, making the code more readable. Functions can be viewed as named blocks, with parameters and return statements allowed.

5.8 THE STORAGE CLASS auto

Every variable and function in C has two attributes: *type* and *storage class*. The four storage classes in C are automatic, external, register, and static, with corresponding keywords

> auto   extern   register   static

Variables declared within function bodies are by default automatic. Thus, automatic is the most common of the four storage classes. If a compound statement starts with variable declarations, then these variables can be acted on within the scope of the enclosing compound statement. A compound statement with declarations will be called a block to distinguish it from one that does not begin with declarations.

Declarations of variables within blocks are implicitly of storage class automatic. This can be explicitly specified by using the keyword `auto`, but usually it is not done. Thus the code

```
{
    char    c;
    int     i, j, k;
    .  .   .  .   .
}
```

is equivalent to

```
{
    auto char    c;
    auto int     i, j, k;
    .  .   .  .
}
```

When a block is entered, the system sets aside adequate memory for the automatically declared variables. Within that block those variables are defined, and they are considered "local" to the block. When the block is exited, the system no longer reserves the memory set aside for the automatic variables. Thus, the values of these variables are lost. If the block is reentered, the storage once again is appropriately allocated, but previous values are unknown. If a function definition contains a block, then each invocation of that function sets up a new environment.

5.9 THE STORAGE CLASS `extern`

One method of transmitting information across blocks and functions is to use external variables. When a variable is declared outside a function, storage is permanently assigned to it, and its storage class is `extern`. A declaration for an external variable looks just the same as a variable declaration occurring inside a function or block. Such a variable is considered to be global to all functions declared after it; upon block or function exit, the external variable remains in existence. The following program illustrates these ideas:

```
double    x = 1.0, y = 2.0, z;      /*  global variables  */

main()
{
    double    f();

    z = f();
    printf("%.1f   %.1f   %.1f\n", x, y, z);   /*  3.0   2.0   9.0  */
}
```

```
double    f ()
{
     double    y, z;        /*  y  and  z  are local  */
                            /*  global  y  and  z  are masked  */
     x = y = z = 3.0;
     return (x + y + z);
}
```

External variables never disappear. Since they exist throughout the execution life of the program, they can be used to transmit values across functions. They may be hidden if the identifier is redefined, as is the case for the variables y and z in the function f () above. Another way of conceiving of external variables is to think of a block that encloses all other program functions, with the external variables being declared at the head of this outermost block.

One can also use the storage class specifier extern to tell the function body or the block or the file, as the case may be, that the variable is to be expected from another place, even if the declaration is not visible within this file. By avoiding undefined variable names, this facility allows separate compilation of programs across files. The following simple program is written in two files:

In file1.c:

```
int    v;      /*  a global variable, storage is allocated  */

main()
{
     int    i;

     .   .   .   .   .

     printf("%d  %d  %d\n", i, v, f (v));
}
```

In file2.c:

```
double f (x)        /*  all functions have storage class extern  */
double    x;
{
     extern int    v;

     /*****
        the system will look for  v  externally,
        either in this file or in another file
        that will be combined into the final program
     *****/
     .   .   .   .   .

     return (3.0 * x * v);
}
```

The functions main () and f () written in *file1.c* and *file2.c*, respectively, can be compiled separately. The extern declaration of the variable v in *file2.c* tells the system that it will be declared externally, either in this file or in some other. The executable program obtained by compiling these two functions separately will act no differently than a program obtained by compiling a single file containing both functions with the external variable defined at the beginning of the file.

Information can be passed into a function in two ways: by use of external variables and by use of the parameter mechanism. Although there are exceptions, the use of the parameter mechanism is the preferred method to pass information into a function. This tends to improve the modularity of the code, and the possibility of undesirable side effects is reduced.

One form of "side effect" occurs when a function changes a global variable within its body rather than through its parameter list. Such a construction is error-prone. Correct practice is to effect changes to global variables through the parameter and return mechanisms. However, to do this we need to know how to use pointers and the address operator, material which will be covered in Chapter 7. Adhering to this practice improves modularity and readability, and since changes are localized, programs are typically easier to write and maintain.

5.10 THE STORAGE CLASS register

The storage class register, used in a declaration, indicates that if it is physically and semantically possible, the associated variables will be stored in high-speed memory registers. Since resource limitations and semantic constraints sometimes make this impossible, this class defaults to automatic whenever the compiler cannot allocate an appropriate physical register. Typically, the compiler has only a few such registers available. The VAX has 16 general-purpose storage registers. Many of these are required for system use and cannot otherwise be allocated.

Basically, the use of storage class register is an attempt to improve execution speed. When speed is of concern, the programmer may choose a few variables that are most frequently accessed and declare them to be of storage class register. Common candidates for such treatment include loop variables and function variables. An example might be

```
        .   .    .    .    .
    {
            register int    i;

            for (i = 0;  i < LIMIT;  ++i) {
                .    .    .    .    .
            }
    }           /*  block exit will free the register  */
        .    .    .    .    .
```

Note that the register variable i was declared as close to its place of use as possible. This is to allow maximum availability of the physical registers, using them only when needed. Always remember that a register declaration is taken only as *advice* to a compiler.

5.11 THE STORAGE CLASS static

Static declarations have two important and distinct uses. The more elementary use is to allow a local variable to retain its previous value when the block in which it resides is reentered. This is in contrast to ordinary automatic variables, which lose their value upon block exit and must be reinitialized. The second and more subtle use is in connection with external declarations. Along with external constructs, it provides a "privacy" mechanism very important for program modularity. By privacy, we mean visibility or scope restrictions on otherwise accessible variables or functions.

As an example of the value-retention use of static, we will write a pseudo random number generator. This function produces an apparently random sequence of integer values. (It is based on linear congruential methods that will not be explained here.) The sequence will begin with an initial value given as the constant INITIAL_ SEED. Each call to random() will produce a next value of the variable seed. Since seed has the storage class static, it will retain its value upon function exit.

```
/*** a pseudo random number generator ***/

#define    MULTIPLIER      25173
#define    MODULUS         65536
#define    INCREMENT       13849
#define    INITIAL_SEED       17

random()
{
      static int   seed = INITIAL_SEED;

      seed = (MULTIPLIER * seed + INCREMENT) % MODULUS;
      return (seed);
}
```

Now let us write a function to output numbers generated by our pseudo random number generator.

```
/*** create an array of pseudo random numbers ***/

#define    LIMIT    333

main()
{
      register int   i;

      for (i = 0; i < LIMIT; ++i)
           if (i % 6 == 0)
                printf("\n%12d", random());
           else
                printf("%12d", random());
      printf("\n\n");
}
```

This example could have been written using the extern storage class for seed. However, other references to seed in main() would then possibly alter its value. The declaration of seed as a static int inside of random() keeps it private to random(). The programmer cannot now inadvertently misuse seed, and is indeed at liberty to reuse the name "seed" as an identifier in a different context.

5.12 STATIC EXTERNAL VARIABLES

At first glance, static external variables seem unnecessary. External variables already retain their values across block and function exit. The difference is that static external variables are scope-restricted external variables. The scope is the remainder of the source file in which they are declared. Thus, they are unavailable to functions defined earlier in the file or to functions defined in other files, even if these functions attempt to use the extern storage class keyword.

```
f1()
{
        .   .   .   .   .      /*  p  is not available here  */
}

static int    p;             /*  static external variable  */

f2()
{
        .   .   .   .   .      /*  p  can be used here  */
}

f3()
{
        .   .   .   .   .      /*  p  can be used here  */
}
```

We can use this facility to provide a variable that is private to a particular family of functions. For example, let us extend our random number generator into a family of two such functions, both using the same seed.

```
/*** a family of pseudo random number generators ***/

#define    MULTIPLIER         25173
#define    MODULUS            65536
#define    INCREMENT          13849
#define    FLOATING_MODULUS   65536.0

static int   seed;        /*  external, but private to this file  */

initialize_seed(s)
int    s;
{
     seed = s;
}

random()
{
     return (seed = (MULTIPLIER * seed + INCREMENT) % MODULUS);
          /*  a value between  0  and  MODULUS  is returned  */
}

double probability()
{
     seed = (MULTIPLIER * seed + INCREMENT) % MODULUS;
     return (seed / FLOATING_MODULUS);
          /*  a value between  0.0  and  1.0  is returned  */
}
```

The `static` external variable seed is private to this file. We can now create other files of programs using these functions without worrying about side effects.

A last use of `static` is as a storage class specifier for function identifiers. This is used to restrict scope. Static function declarations are visible only within the file in which they are declared. Thus, unlike ordinary functions, which can be accessed from other files, a `static` function is available only throughout its own file, and no other. Again, this facility is useful in developing private modules of function definitions.

5.13 SUMMARY

1. Functions are the most general structuring concept in C. They should be used to implement "top-down" problem solving, namely, breaking up a problem into smaller and smaller subproblems until each piece is readily expressed in code.

2. A `return` statement terminates the execution of a function and passes control back to the calling environment. If the `return` statement contains an expression, then the value of the expression is passed back to the calling environment as well.

3. Arguments to functions are passed "call by value."

4. The storage class of a function is always `extern`, and its type specifier is `int` unless otherwise explicitly declared. The `return` statement should return a value compatible with the function type.

5. Collections of functions can be put into files to constitute libraries. These libraries are easy to extend by writing new functions that build on old ones.

6. The principal storage class is automatic. Automatic variables appear and disappear with block entry and exit. They can be hidden when an inner block redeclares an outer block identifier.

7. Scope rules are the visibility constraints associated with identifiers. For example, if in a file we have

```
        .   .    .    .
static f ()
{
        .   .   .   .   .
}           .

static int    a, b, c;
    .    .    .    .
```

then `f ()` will be known throughout this file but in no other, and `a`, `b`, and `c` will be known only in this file and only below the place where they are declared.

8. The external storage class is the default class for all functions and all variables declared outside of functions. These identifiers may be used throughout the program. Such identifiers can be hidden by redeclaration, but their values cannot be destroyed.

9. The storage class `register` is of use for speeding up programs, but is semantically equivalent to automatic.

10. The storage class `static` is used to preserve exit values of variables. It is also used to restrict the scope of external identifiers. This latter use enhances modularization and program security by providing a form of privacy to functions and variables.

5.14 EXERCISES

1. Write a function called `bio()` that will print out your name, address, and phone number on separate lines. Then write a `main()` function to invoke `bio()` three times.

2. Write a function power (x, n) that will compute the *n*th power of x, where x is a double and n is an int.

3. Write a function prn_char (c, n) that will print the char c repeatedly n times. Notice that white space can be printed by invoking prn_char (' ', n). Use prn_char () to write out your initials in large letters on the screen. Each letter should be 12 lines high.

4. Write a function that returns the fourth root of its int argument k. The value returned should be a double. Use the library function sqrt ().

5. What will the following program print?

```
int z;

f (x)
int    x;
{
    x = 2;
    z += x;
}

main ()
{
    z = 5;
    f (z);
    printf ("z = %d\n",  z);
}
```

6. Extend the statistics package to include standard deviation.

7. Write an array of 100 random numbers into a file. Edit the file by adding a line at the top with the number "100" in it. Then use the file as input to the program in this chapter that prints accumulative statistics. Use the function probability () to generate a file containing random floating numbers between 0.0 and 1.0, and test to see if the average of the numbers is 0.5. For truly random numbers between 0.0 and 1.0, we expect the average of a very large number of them to be very close to 0.5.

8. A polynomial of degree 2 in x is given by

$$a x^2 + b x + c$$

Write the code for a function f (x, a, b, c) that will compute the value of an arbitrary polynomial of degree 2. Make use of the identity

$$(a x + b) x + c = a x^2 + b x + c$$

to minimize multiplications.

9. Write the code for a function that will print a table of values for an arbitrary polynomial of degree 2. It should call the function written in exercise 8 at many equally spaced points, say 20, in a closed interval $[p, q]$.

10. Using a character such as *, draw a bar plot on the screen or on a printer for the values computed in exercise 9. Use – as the symbol for the location of the *x*-axis and | for that of the *y*-axis.

11. For the function of exercise 8, pass in the int value 1 for the parameter a. On most C systems you will get a wrong result if you try computing the polynomial where the formal parameter a was declared either float or double. Explain this lack of appropriate conversion for your system.

12. Write a function that returns the *n*th Fibonacci number. Write a second function isprime(n), which returns 1 if n is a prime and 0 if it is not. Write a third function, which calls both of these functions to determine if the *n*th Fibonacci number is a prime and then prints out the result. Finally, write main(), which interactively asks for an integer k and then calls your third function.

13. Take the program written to solve exercise 12 and rewrite it to place key variables and function arguments in registers. Now, time both versions of the program to see how much execution speed is gained with register variables. Do not forget that there are only a small number of registers available on most machines. In the UNIX operating system, to time an executable program that resides in *a.out*, one would use the command

    time a.out

14. Write a function that finds all factors of any particular number. For example,

    $$27 = 3 \times 3 \times 3 \qquad 11 = 11 \text{ (prime)} \qquad 15 = 3 \times 5$$

15. What is printed in the following program? This exercise gives you practice on understanding the scope of identifiers. You should be able to answer the question by hand simulating the program and then running it as a check.

```
main()
{
        int    a = 1, b = 2, c = 3;

        ++a;
        c += ++b;
        printf("\nfirst:%5d%5d%5d", a, b, c);
        {
                float    b = 2.0;
                int      c;

                c = b * 3;
                a += c;
                printf("\nsecond:%5d%5.1f%5d", a, b, c);
        }
        printf("\nthird:%5d%5d%5d\n\n", a, b, c);
}
```

16. What is printed by the following program?

```
main()
{
    int    i, rf1, rf2;

    for (i = 0; i < 5; ++i) {
        rf1 = f1(i);
        rf2 = f2(i);
    }
    printf("\n%s%5d\n\n%s%5d\n\n",
            "f1() last returned", rf1,
            "f2() last returned", rf2);
}

f1(i)
register    i;
{
    int    k = 0;

    for ( ; i > 0; --i)
        ++k;
    return (k);
}

f2(i)
register    i;
{
    static    k;
    for ( ; i > 0; --i)
        ++k;
    return (k);
}
```

17. Variables of storage class extern should be used with care. The following code is meaningless but illustrates the difficulties in writing clear code when side effects are involved. What is printed?

```
int n = 7;

main()
{
    extern int    n;
    printf("\nthe value of  n  is%5d\n\n", (f(++n), n));
}

f(t)
int t;
{
    n = (t + 1) * (n + 1);
}
```

18. Write a coin-tossing program using a random number generator to simulate the toss. If you write your own random number generator, arrange for the output to be either 0 or 1. If you use a system-supplied random number generator (most systems have one), take the returned value modulo 2. Let "heads" be represented by 1 and "tails" by 0. Run the program for 10, 100, 1000, and 10000 tosses and keep track of the longest sequence of heads. If you know some probability theory, see if this simulation is in line with theory.

19. Simulations that involve using repeated calls on random number generators to reproduce a probabilistic event are called Monte Carlo simulations, so-called because Monte Carlo has one of the world's most famous gaming casinos. Let us use this technique to decide the breakeven point in a birthday bet. We wish to find the probability that any two people in a room with k people will have been born in the same month. It is clear that that probability is 0 if there is only 0 or 1 person in the room. For two people, the probability is 1/12. (We assume it is equally likely that a person is born in any of the twelve months. In reality this is only an approximation.) Simulate this by running 100 trials with 3, 4, . . . , 11 people in the room. The random number generator should pick a number between 1 and 12. You should use 12 variables (later we will use arrays; see Chapter 7) that are initially zero, meaning no one in the room was born in that month. When any variable gets to two, that trial is true with two people in the room having the same birthday. The sum of true trials over 100 is the computed simulated probability. What k gives the breakeven point?

20. ("Call by reference," see Chapter 7) We wish to write a function that takes two variables and exchanges their values. This is a frequently needed operation, especially in sorting programs. Explain why the following function will not work:

```
exchange (a, b)      /* wrong */
double    a, b;
{
      double    temp;

      temp = a;
      a = b;
      b = temp;
}
```

Pointers are needed to accomplish this.

```
exchange (p, q)
double    *p, *q;   /* addresses of doubles are expected */
{
      double    temp;

      temp = *p;    /* assign temp the value pointed at by p */
      *p = *q;
      *q = temp;
}
```

To change the values of a and b in a program, we could write

```
exchange (&a,  &b) ;
```

The & operator takes the address of a variable. Use this technique to rewrite the function sum_of_squares() so that the computed sum is an output variable and is not returned.

Branching Statements, Bitwise Expressions, and enum

The first half of this chapter treats a variety of flow of control constructs and bitwise expressions. The goto, break, and continue statements interrupt ordinary sequential or iterative control flow. The switch statement can be considered a generalization of the if-else statement. It can select among several different cases. The conditional operator provides for the selection of alternative expressions. In discussing bitwise expressions, which are explicitly dependent on machine representation of data, we illustrate their usefulness in packing and unpacking data.

The second half of this chapter discusses the enumeration type, which allows the programmer to specify a finite set of unique identifiers as a type. Thus, the seven days of the week could be specified as a programmer-defined type. We will illuminate much of this material by implementing a completely worked out interactive game program.

6.1 THE goto STATEMENT

The goto statement is considered a harmful construct in most accounts of modern programming methodology. It is an unconditional branch to an arbitrary labeled statement somewhere else in the function. Thus, it can undermine all the useful structure provided by other flow of control mechanisms (for, while, do, if, switch).

The syntax of a labeled statement is

label ::= *identifier*
labeled_statement ::= *label* : *statement*

Some examples of labeled statements are

```
spot1:   a = b + c;
label44:   x = sqrt(y);
error_error_error:   printf("error\n");
bug1:   bug2:   bug3:   printf("bug found\n");   /* multiple labels */
```

but not

```
333:   a = b + c;        /*  333  is not an identifier  */
ww + zz:   x = sqrt(y);  /*  ww + zz  is not an identifier  */
a:   a = a + b;          /*  a  is not a unique identifier  */
```

The label identifier must be unique within the smallest enclosing block. The scope of a label is within the function in which it occurs, except for those blocks where the label identifier has been redefined. Control can be unconditionally transferred to a labeled statement by executing a goto statement of the form

        goto *label*;

An example would be

```
{
        .   .   .   .   .
        goto error;
        .   .   .   .
}
error:   printf("\nan error has occurred");
    .   .   .   .   .
```

The goto statement and its corresponding labeled statement both must be in the body of the same function. Here is a more specific piece of code which makes use of a goto.

```
    .   .   .   .   .
while (scanf("%lf", &x) == 1) {
        if (x < 0.0)
                goto negative_alert;
        printf("\n%f   %f", sqrt(x), sqrt(2 * x));
}
negative_alert: printf("\na negative value has occurred");
    .   .   .   .   .
```

Note that this example could have been rewritten in a number of ways without using a goto.

In general the goto should be avoided. The goto is a primitive method of altering flow of control, which in a richly structured language is unnecessary. Labeled statements and goto's are the hallmark of incremental patchwork program design. A programmer who modifies a program by adding goto's to additional code fragments soon makes the program incomprehensible.

When should a goto be used? A simple answer is not at all. Indeed, one cannot go wrong by following this advice. However, in some rare instances, which should be carefully documented, a goto can make the program significantly more efficient. In other cases it can simplify flow of control. This may occur when a special value is tested for in a deeply nested inner loop and, when this value is found, the program control needs to branch to the outermost level of the function.

6.2 THE break AND continue STATEMENTS

Two special statements,

        break;   and   continue;

interrupt the normal flow of control. The break statement causes an exit from the innermost enclosing loop or switch statement. In the following example a test for a negative argument is made, and if the test is true, then a break statement is used to pass control to the statement immediately following the loop.

```
        . . . . .
while (1) {
        scanf ("%lf", &x);
        if (x < 0.0)
            break;        /* exit loop if the value is negative */
        printf ("\n%f", sqrt (x));
        . . . . .
}
            /* break jumps to here */
```

This is a typical use of break. What would otherwise be an infinite loop is made to terminate upon a given condition tested by the if expression.

The continue statement causes the current iteration of a loop to stop and causes the next iteration of the loop to begin immediately. The following code processes all characters except digits.

```
for (i = 0; i < TOTAL; ++i) {
    c = getchar ();
    if ( '0'<= c && c <= '9')
        continue;
        . . . . .        /* process other characters */
/*  continue transfers control to here to begin next iteration */
}
```

The continue statement may occur only inside for, while, and do loops. As the example shows, continue transfers control to the end of the current iteration, whereas break would terminate the loop.

In the presence of a continue statement, a for loop of the form

```
for (expression1; expression2; expression3) {
    . . . . .
    continue;
    . . . . .
}
```

is equivalent to

```
expression1;
while (expression2) {
    . . . . .
    goto next;
    . . . . .
next:
    expression3;
}
```

which is different from

```
expression1;
while (expression2) {
        .  .  .  .  .
     continue;
        .  .  .  .  .
     expression3;
}
```

See the exercises for a convenient way to test this.

6.3 THE switch STATEMENT

The switch is a multi-way conditional statement generalizing the if-else statement.

> *switch_statement* ::= switch (*integral_expression*) *switch_statement_list*
> *switch_statement_list* ::= {*case_label* : }$_{0+}$ *statement*
> | { {*local_declaration_list*}$_{opt}$ {*switch_statement_list*}$_{0+}$ }
> *case_label* ::= default | case *integral_constant_expression*

The following is a typical example of a switch:

```
switch (c) {
case 'a':
     ++a_cnt;
     break;
case 'b':
     ++b_cnt;
     break;
case 'c':
case 'C':
     ++cC_cnt;
     break;
default:
     ++other_cnt;
}
```

Notice that in this example the entire switch statement list is enclosed in braces. This will be so in all but the most degenerate situations. The integral expression following switch is evaluated, with the usual arithmetic conversions taking place. The result must be an int. In this example the expression is just the char variable c. After the expression is evaluated, control then jumps to the appropriate case label. The case labels must all be unique, and each statement may be preceded by zero or more case labels. Typically, the last statement before the next case label is a break statement. If there is no break statement, then execution "falls through" to the next statement in the succeeding case. Missing break statements are a frequent cause of error in switch statements. Finally, there may be a default labeled statement. The keywords case and default cannot occur outside of a switch.

The effect of a `switch`

1. Evaluate the `switch` expression.

2. Execute the `case` with label constant matching the value found in step 1, or, if a match is not found, execute the `default` case, or, if there is no `default` case, terminate the `switch`.

3. Terminate the `switch` when a `break` statement is encountered, or terminate the `switch` by "falling off the end."

Let us review the various forms of branching available to us. The unconditional branch statements include the `goto`, `break`, `continue`, and `return`. The `goto` is unrestricted in its use and should be avoided as a dangerous construct. The `continue` is constrained to use within loops and is often unnecessary. The `break` may be used in loops and is important to the proper structuring of the `switch` statement. The `return` statement must be used in functions that return values.

6.4 THE CONDITIONAL OPERATOR

The conditional operator `?:` is unusual in that it is a ternary operator. It takes three expressions as operands.

   conditional_expression ::= *expression* ? *expression* : *expression*

In a construct such as

   exp1 ? *exp2* : *exp3*

exp1 is evaluated first. If it is nonzero (*true*), then *exp2* is evaluated, and that is the value of the conditional expression as a whole. If *exp1* is zero (*false*), then *exp3* is evaluated, and that is the value of the conditional expression as a whole. Thus, a conditional expression can be used to do the work of an `if-else` statement. Consider, for example, the code

```
if (y < z)
     x = y;
else
     x = z;
```

which assigns to x the minimum of y and z. This also can be accomplished by writing

```
x = (y < z) ? y : z;
```

The parentheses are not necessary because the precedence of the conditional operator is just above =. However, parentheses are usually used to make clear what is being tested for.

The type of the conditional expression

   exp1 ? *exp2* : *exp3*

is determined by *exp2* and *exp3*. If they are of different type, then the usual conversion rules are applied. Note carefully that the type of the conditional expression does not depend on which of the two expressions *exp2* or *exp3* is evaluated. The conditional operator ? : associates "right to left."

Declarations and initializations			

char   a = 'a', b = 'b', c = 'c';   /* a has decimal value 97 */
 int   i = 1, j = 2, k = 3;
 float x = 3.337;			

Expression	Equivalent expression	Value	Type
i == j ? a : b	(i == j) ? a : b	98	int
k % 3 == 0 ? i : x + 1	((k % 3) == 0) ? i : (x + 1)	1.0	double
k % 3 ? i : x + 1	(k % 3) ? i : (x + 1)	4.337	double

Statement	This is printed
printf("\n%d tree%c", k, (k == 1) ? '\0' : 's');	3 trees
printf("\n%d frog%c", i, (i == 1) ? '\0' : 's');	1 frog

6.5 BITWISE OPERATORS AND EXPRESSIONS

The bitwise operators act on integral expressions represented as a string of binary digits. They are explicitly machine dependent. We will restrict our discussion to machines having a two's complement integer representation of 32 bits with 8-bit bytes and ASCII character codes.

Bitwise operators		
logical operators:	(unary) bitwise complement:	~
	bitwise and:	&
	bitwise exclusive or:	∧
	bitwise or:	|
shift operators:	left shift:	<<
	right shift:	>>

Just as with other operators, the bitwise operators have rules of precedence and associativity which determine precisely how expressions involving these operators are evaluated.

Operators	Associativity
~ ! - (unary) ++ -- sizeof (*type*)	right to left
* / %	left to right
+ -	left to right
<< >>	left to right
< <= > >=	left to right
== !=	left to right
&	left to right
^	left to right
|	left to right
&&	left to right
||	left to right
? :	right to left
= += -= *= *etc*	right to left
, (comma operator)	left to right

The ~ operator is unary. All the other bitwise operators are binary. They operate on integral variables. The following table contains 32-bit representations of some integer values. The various bitwise operators act with respect to this binary representation.

Decimal	Octal	Binary
0	0	00000000000000000000000000000000
-1	037777777777	11111111111111111111111111111111
15	017	00000000000000000000000000001111
-16	037777777760	11111111111111111111111111110000
32	040	00000000000000000000000000100000
-33	037777777037	11111111111111111111111111011111
2147483647	017777777777	01111111111111111111111111111111
-2147483648	020000000000	10000000000000000000000000000000

Notice that in two's complement a binary string and its complement add to -1.

Bitwise Complement

The complement operator ~, also called the "one's complement operator," inverts the bit string representation of its argument. The 0s become 1s and the 1s become 0s. For example, if x has the representation

00000000000000000000000001100001

then ~x has the representation

```
11111111111111111111111110011110
```

Bitwise Binary Logical Operators

The two arguments, properly widened, are operated on bit position by bit position. The following table shows the bitwise operators acting on 1-bit fields. The table defines the semantics of the operators.

values of:

x	y	x & y	x $^\wedge$ y	x | y
0	0	0	0	0
1	0	0	1	1
0	1	0	1	1
1	1	1	0	1

The next table contains examples of the bitwise operators acting on int variables.

Declarations and assignments		

int   x, y;
x = 33333;
y = -77777;		

Expression	*Representation*	*Value*
x	00000000000000001000001000110101	33333
y	11111111111111101101000000101111	-77777
x & y	00000000000000001000000000100101	32805
x $^\wedge$ y	11111111111111100101001000011010	-110054
x | y	11111111111111101101001000111111	-77249
~(x | y)	00000000000000010010110111000000	77248

Left and Right Shift Operators

The two operands of a shift operator must be integral expressions. The right operand is converted to an int. The type of the expression as a whole is that of its left operand. The left shift operator << shifts the bit representation of the left operand the number of places specified by the right argument. The low-order bits are replaced by 0s.

Declaration and initialization		
char x = 'Z';		
Expression	*Representation*	*Action*
x	01011010	unshifted
x << 1	10110100	left shifted 1
x << 4	10100000	left shifted 4

The right shift operator >> is not quite symmetric to the left shift operator. On unsigned integral expressions, the right shift operator shifts in 0s. On expressions of type char, short, int, and long, some machines shift in 0s and others shift in sign bits. The VAX shifts in sign bits.

Declarations and assignments		
char x, y; unsigned char u; x = 'Z'; y = 'Z' << 1; u = -1;		
Expression	*Representation*	*Action*
x	01011010	unshifted
x >> 1	00101101	right shifted 1
y	10110100	unshifted
y >> 3	11110110	right shifted 3
u	11111111	unshifted
u >> 5	00000111	right shifted 5

There are two restrictions on the use of the shift operators. The right operand may not be negative, and the value of the right operand may not exceed the number of bits used to represent the left operand. If these restrictions are violated, the shift expression is undefined. The following table illustrates the rules of precedence and associativity with respect to the shift operators:

Declarations and assignments		
char c; int i, j, k; c = 'w'; i = j = k = (3 << 1);		

Expression	*Equivalent expression*	*Type*
c << 1 << 2	(c << 1) << 2	char
c + 1 << 1 << 2	((c + 1) << 1 << 2	int
i < j >> k * 3 && j == k	(i < (j >> (k * 3))) && (j == k)	int

6.6 MASKS

A mask is a constant or variable that is used to extract desired bits in a variable or expression. For example, the int constant 1 has the bit representation

```
00000000000000000000000000000001
```

It can be used to determine the lower order bit of an int expression. The following code makes use of this mask and prints an alternating sequence of 0s and 1s.

```
int   i;

for (i = 0; i < 10; ++i)
     printf("%d", i & 1);
```

If we wish to find the value of a particular bit in an expression, we can use a mask that is 1 in that position and 0 elsewhere. Thus, the hexadecimal constant 0x10 would be a mask for a fifth bit, counting from the right. The expression

```
(v & 0x10) ? 1 : 0
```

is either 1 or 0 depending on the fifth bit in v.

The constant 0xff has the bit representation

```
00000000000000000000000011111111
```

Because only the low-order byte in 0xff is turned on, the expression

```
v & 0xff
```

will yield a value with a representation having all its high-order bytes zero and its low-order byte the same as the low-order byte in v. This is expressed by saying that 0xff is a mask for the low-order byte.

Using these ideas, we can write a function that will print out the bit representation of an int value. It is a useful function to explore how values of expressions are represented in memory.

```
/*** print the bit representation of an int ***/

bit_print(v)
int    v;
{
       int    i, mask;

       mask = 1;           /*  mask = 000 . . . 01  */
       mask <<= 31;        /*  shift the 1 bit to the high-order end  */

       for (i = 1; i <= 32; ++i) {
             putchar(((v & mask) == 0) ? '0' : '1');
             v <<= 1;
       }
}
```

6.7 PACKING AND UNPACKING

The use of bitwise expressions allows for data compression across byte boundaries. This is useful in saving space, but it is even more useful in saving time. On a machine handling 4 bytes per instruction cycle, this is the equivalent of processing 32 bits in parallel. The following program can be used to pack four characters into an int. It uses shift operations to do the packing byte by byte.

```
/*** pack four characters into an int ***/

pack(a, b, c, d)
char    a, b, c, d;
{
       int    p;       /*  p  will be packed with  a, b, c, d  */

       p = a;
       p = (p << 8) | b;
       p = (p << 8) | c;
       p = (p << 8) | d;
       return (p);
}
```

Having written pack(), we now want to be able to retrieve the characters from within the 32-bit int. This is efficiently done using masks.

```
/*** unpack an int into four characters ***/

unpack(p)
int    p;
{
      extern char    a, b, c, d;

      d = p & 0xff;
      c = (p & 0xff00) >> 8;
      b = (p & 0xff0000) >> 16;
      a = (p & 0xff000000) >> 24;
}
```

Imagine wanting to keep an abbreviated employee record in one integer. We will suppose that an "employee identification number" can be stored in 9 bits, and a "job type" can be stored in 6 bits (a maximum of 64 different types). The employee's "gender" can be stored in 1 bit. These three fields will require 16 bits, which on the VAX is a short integer. We can think of the three bit fields as follows:

Identification	*Job type*	*Gender*
bbbbbbbbb	bbbbbb	b

The following function can be used in a program designed to enter employee data into a short. The inverse problem of reading data out of the short would be accomplished by making use of masks.

```
/*** create employee data in a short int ***/

short create_employee_data(id_no, job_type, gender)
char    gender;
int     id_no, job_type;
{
      short    employee = 0;

      employee |= (gender == 'm' || gender == 'M') ? 0 : 1;
      employee |= job_type << 1;
      employee |= id_no << 7;
      return (employee);
}
```

Since a left shift by 1 bit is equivalent to multiplication by 2, programmers sometimes use shift operations to perform arithmetic efficiently. However, as it obscures the meaning of the program, this practice is not recommended.

6.8 ENUMERATION TYPES

The keyword enum is used to declare enumeration types. It provides a means of naming a finite set, and of declaring variables that take on values which are elements of the set. In the example

```
enum day   {sun, mon, tue, wed, thu, fri, sat}   d1, d2;
```

the set consists of the days of the week, and the variables d1 and d2 can take on as values only the elements of the set. Thus

```
d1 = fri;
```

assigns the value fri to d1 and

```
if (d1 == d2)
        .    .    .    .         /*  do something  */
```

tests whether d1 is equal to d2. The type of the variables d1 and d2 is enum day. Note carefully that enum by itself is not a data type. enum day is an example of an enumeration type.

The syntax for the enumeration types follows:

> *enumeration_type_declaration ::= enum_specifier identifier {, identifier}$_{0+}$;*
> *enum_specifier ::=   enum e_tag { e_list }*
> * | enum e_tag*
> * | enum { e_list }*
> *e_tag ::= identifier*
> *e_list ::= enumerator {, enumerator}$_{0+}$*
> *enumerator ::= identifier {= integral_constant_expression}$_{opt}$*

An example is

```
enum day   {sun, mon, tue, wed, thu, fri, sat}   d1, d2;
```

where the construction as a whole is an *enum_type_declaration*, and the following list gives syntactic names to its parts:

enum day {sun, mon, tue, wed, thu, fri, sat}	*enum_specifier*
day	*e_tag*
sun, mon, tue, wed, thur, fri, sat	*e_list*
sun	*enumerator*
mon	*enumerator*
. . . . .	

If we write

```
enum suit {clubs, diamonds, hearts, spades};
```

then no storage is allocated, but a *template* is set up for the type enum suit. This means that the type specifier enum suit is now available for writing declarations. The identifier suit is a tag (*e_tag*), which is associated with the *e_list*

```
clubs, diamonds, hearts, spades
```

To declare variables of type enum suit, we could write

```
enum suit  c1, c2, c3, c4, c5;
```

At this point, space in memory is allocated and the variables c1, c2, c3, c4, c5 can have values from the *e_list* associated with the tag suit.

An *e_tag* need not be present. Consider

```
enum {fir, pine} tree;
```

Since there is no *e_tag*, the type of the variable tree has no name. The situation is described by saying that the variable tree is of the type whose values are taken from the *e_list* fir, pine.

The compiler assigns an int value starting with 0 to each *enumerator* in an *e_list*. In the previous example fir has value 0 and pine has value 1. This implicit representation may be altered by assigning an explicit constant to an *enumerator* in the *e_list*. Further elements in the list are assigned subsequent values. Consider

```
enum {apple = 7, pear, orange = 3, lemon, peach} fruit;
```

The *enumerator* apple has the value 7, and therefore pear has value 8. Similarly, orange has value 3, lemon has value 4, and peach has value 5.

In general one should treat enumerators as programmer-specified constants and use them to aid program clarity. These values can be used with casts. The tags and the enumerators, as well as the variables must all have distinct identifiers. The following function illustrates the use of enumeration types.

```
/***   compute the next day   ***/

enum day   {sun, mon, tue, wed, thu, fri, sat};

enum day    day_after(d)
enum day    d;
{
      enum day    nd;        /*  nd  is  next day  */

      switch (d) {
      case sun:
            nd = mon;
            break;
      case mon:
            nd = tue;
            break;
      case tue:
            nd = wed;
            break;
      case wed:
            nd = thu;
            break;
      case thu:
            nd = fri;
            break;
      case fri:
            nd = sat;
            break;
      case sat:
            nd = sun;
      }
      return (nd);
}
```

Another version of this function makes use of casts to accomplish the same ends.

```
/*** compute the next day with casts ***/

enum day   {sun, mon, tue, wed, thu, fri, sat};

enum day    day_after(d)
enum day    d;
{
    return ((enum day) (((int) d + 1) % 7));
}
```

Enumeration types can be used in ordinary expressions provided type compatibility is maintained. However, if one uses them as a form of integer type and constantly accesses their implicit representation, it is better just to use integer variables instead. The importance of enumeration types is their self-documenting character, where the enumerators are themselves mnemonic, such as the *e_list* values for enum day and enum suit. Furthermore, they force the compiler to provide programmer-defined type checking so that one does not inadvertently mix apples and diamonds.

6.9 AN EXAMPLE: THE GAME OF PAPER, ROCK, SCISSORS

We will illustrate some of the concepts introduced in this chapter by writing a program to play the traditional children's game called "paper, rock, scissors." In this game each child uses her or his hand to represent one of the three objects. A flat hand held in a horizontal position represents "paper," a fist represents "rock," and two extended fingers represent "scissors." The children face each other and at the count of three display their choices. If the choices are the same, then the game is a tie. Otherwise, a win is determined by the rules:

> "Paper covers the rock"
> "Rock breaks the scissors"
> "Scissors cut the paper"

We will assume that the functions making up this game program exist in a single file. The following declaration is external. Since it is used by many of the functions, it is placed at the top of the file.

```
enum p_r_s {
      paper, rock, scissors, game, help, instructions, quit
};
```

The function main() keeps track of wins, losses, and ties, and calls other functions as appropriate.

```
main ()
{
    enum p_r_s   player, machine;
    enum p_r_s   selection_by_player(), selection_by_machine();
    int          win, lose, tie;      /*  keep track of results  */

    win = lose = tie = 0;

    instructions_for_the_player();
    while ((player = selection_by_player()) != quit)
        switch (player) {
        case paper:
        case rock:
        case scissors:
            machine = selection_by_machine();
            if (player == machine) {
                ++tie;
                printf("\n    a tie");
            }
            else if (you_won(player, machine)) {
                ++win;
                printf("\n    you won");
            }
            else {
                ++lose;
                printf("\n    i won");
            }
            break;
        case game:
            game_status(win, lose, tie);
            break;
        case instructions:
            instructions_for_the_player();
            break;
        case help:
            help_for_the_player();
            break;
        }
    game_status(win, lose, tie);
    printf("\n\nBYE\n\n");
}
```

The first function called in main() gives instructions to the player. Embedded in it are some of the design considerations for programming this game.

```
instructions_for_the_player()
{
    printf("\n%s\n\n%s\n\n%s\n%s\n%s\n\n%s\n%s\n%s\n\n%s\n%s\n%s",
        "PAPER, ROCK, SCISSORS",
        "In this game",
        "   p   is for paper,",
        "   r   is for rock,",
        "   s   is for scissors.",
        "Both the player and the machine will choose one",
        "of p, r, or s.  If the two choices are the same,",
        "then the game is a tie.  Otherwise:",
        "   \"paper covers the rock\"     (a win for paper),",
        "   \"rock breaks the scissors\"  (a win for rock),",
        "   \"scissors cut the paper\"    (a win for scissors).");

    printf("\n\n%s\n\n%s\n%s\n%s\n%s\n\n%s\n\n%s",
        "There are other allowable inputs:",
        "   g   for game status   (the number of wins so far),",
        "   h   for help,",
        "   i   for instructions  (reprint these instructions),",
        "   q   for quit          (to quit the game).",
        "This game is played repeatedly until  q  is entered.",
        "Good luck!");
}
```

The next function is used to process the input made by the player. Notice that white space is skipped and that all other characters input at the terminal are processed, most of them through the default case of the switch.

```
enum p_r_s  selection_by_player ()
{
     char          c;
     enum p_r_s    player;

     printf ("\n\ninput p, r, or s:   ");
     while ((c = getchar ()) == ' ' || c == '\n' || c == '\t')
          ;     /*  skip white space  */
     switch (c) {
     case 'p':
          player = paper;
          break;
     case 'r':
          player = rock;
          break;
     case 's':
          player = scissors;
          break;
     case 'g':
          player = game;
          break;
     case 'i':
          player = instructions;
          break;
     case 'q':
          player = quit;
          break;
     default:
          player = help;
     }
     return (player);
}
```

The machine's selection is computed by the next function. The method used is elementary; the program can be improved by using a random number generator.

```
enum p_r_s  selection_by_machine ()
{
     static int  i;

     i = ++i % 3;      /*  random () would be better  */
     return ((i == 0) ? paper : ((i == 1) ? rock : scissors));
}
```

Once the player and the machine have made a selection, and it is determined that the selections are not the same, the outcome has to be determined. Here is the function that does this.

```
you_won(player, machine)
enum p_r_s    player, machine;
{
      int    victory;       /*  true (1) if player wins  */
                            /*  false (0) if player loses  */

      if (player == paper)
           victory = machine == rock;
      else if (player == rock)
           victory = machine == scissors;
      else /*  player == scissors  */
           victory = machine == paper;
      return (victory);
}
```

If the character g is input, then game_status() is invoked; if any character other than
white space or p, r, s, g, i, or q is input, then help_for_the_player() is invoked.

```
game_status(win, lose, tie)
{
      printf("\nGAME STATUS");
      printf("\n\n%7d%s\n%7d%s\n%7d%s\n%7d%s",
           win, "  games won by you",
           lose, "  games won by me",
           tie, "  games tied",
           win + lose + tie, "  games played");
}


help_for_the_player()
{
      printf("\n%s\n\n%s\n%s\n%s\n%s\n%s\n%s\n%s",
           "the following characters can be used for input:",
           "     p    for paper",
           "     r    for rock",
           "     s    for scissors",
           "     g    to find out the game status",
           "     h    to print this list",
           "     i    to reprint the instructions for this game",
           "     q    to quit this game");
}
```

6.10 SUMMARY

1. The four statement types

    return   break   continue   goto

    cause an unconditional transfer of flow of control. Their use should be minimized.

2. goto's are considered harmful to good programming. Avoid them.

3. The switch statement provides a multi-way conditional branch. It is useful when dealing with a large number of special cases.

4. Bitwise expressions allow storage compaction and parallel operations on the machine-dependent bit representation of integral valued expressions.

5. Bitwise operations are machine dependent. On a VAX, integers have two's complement representations. Thus, the sign bit (the high-order bit) is 0 for nonnegative integers and 1 for negative integers. On a VAX, the right shift operator causes the sign bit to be shifted in on integral expressions that are not of an unsigned type. This means that if the sign bit is 0, then 0s are shifted in, and if the sign bit is 1, then 1s are shifted in. For expressions of any unsigned type the C language specifies that the right shift operator will shift in 0s.

6. Masks are particular values used typically with the & operator to extract a given series of bits. Packing is the act of placing a number of distinct values into various subfields of a given variable. Unpacking extracts these values.

7. By means of the enum specifier the programmer can create new data types. These are the enumeration types. Variables of such a data type typically take values from an *e_list* consisting of a set of values called *enumerators*.

8. Enumerators are distinct identifiers chosen for their mnemonic significance. Their use provides a type-checking constraint for the programmer, and self-documentation for the program.

9. Enumerators, and hence variables of an enumeration type, have integer values that can be used in expressions, with type conflicts being resolved by the proper use of casts.

6.11 EXERCISES

1. Rewrite the following two pieces of code to avoid using break or continue.

```
while (c = getchar()){
    if (c == 'E')
        break;
    ++count;
    if (c >= '0' && c <= '9')
        ++digit_count;
}

i = -5;
n = 50;
while (i < n) {
    ++i;
    if (i == 0)
        continue;
    total += i;
    printf("\ni is %d and total is %d", i, total);
}
```

2. Write a program to compute the inverse of a floating point number. The program should interactively ask for x and then compute and print the inverse of x. For example, if 3 is the input, then 0.333333333333333 should be printed. The program should avoid dividing by zero and should continue to ask for data until it receives the sentinel value 1.0 to end the session. Write two versions of the program:

   (a) Write a version using a goto or continue when x == 0.0 is detected.

   (b) Write a version without such a transfer.

3. Show how a while statement can be rewritten as a goto statement and an if statement. Which is the better construct and why?

4. The following code segment illustrates how the overuse of the goto statement makes for incoherent control flow.

```
            d = b * b - 4.0 * a * c;
            if (d == 0.0)
                 goto  L1;
            else if (d > 0.0) {
                 if (a != 0.0) {
                      r1 = (-b + sqrt(d)) / (2.0 * a);
                      r2 = (-b - sqrt(d)) / (2.0 * a);
                      goto L4;
                 }
                 else
                      goto L3;
            }
            else
                 goto L2;
    L1:
            if (a != 0.0)
            r1 = r2 = -b / (2.0 * a);
            else
                 goto L3;
            goto L4;
    L2:
            if (a != 0.0) {
                 printf("\nimaginary roots");
                 goto L4;
            }
    L3:
            printf("\ndegenerate case");
    L4:
            .    .    .    .    .
```

Note how the programmer kept adding different cases and had to repatch the code until the program logic became obscure. Rewrite this code without goto statements.

5. Write the octal, hexadecimal, and binary equivalent of the decimal integers 2, 4, 8, 16, 32, 64, 49, 490, 4900.

6. Suppose that integers have a 16-bit two's complement representation. Write the binary representation for -1, -5, -101, -1023. Recall that the two's complement representation of negative integers is obtained by taking the representation of the corresponding positive integer, complementing it, and adding 1.

7. Alice, Betty, and Carole all vote on 16 separate referendums. Each individual's vote is to be stored bitwise in a 16-bit integer. Write a function called majority(a, b, c), which takes the votes of Alice, Betty, and Carole stored in a, b, and c, respectively, and returns a 16-bit outcome variable that contains the bitwise majority of a, b, and c.

8. Write a function called circular_shift(a, n), which takes a and shifts it left n positions, where the high-order bits are reintroduced as the low-order bits. For example,

```
10000001   circular shift 1 yields   00000011
01101011   circular shift 3 yields   01011011
11110000   circular shift 4 yields   00001111
```

9. Write a function that reverses the bit representation of a byte. For example

```
01110101   reversed yields   10101110
10101111   reversed yields   11110101
```

10. Write a function that will extract every other bit position from a 32-bit expression and store it in a 16-bit variable.

11. Write a function that uses a `switch` to take the representations of decimal digits as `char`'s and converts them to 4-bit binary strings packed into an `int`. If an `int` has 32 bits, then 8 digits can be packed into it. Also write the inverse function that will unpack the 8 decimal digits and change them back to their ASCII code.

12. The mathematical operation `min(x, y)` can be represented by the conditional expression

```
(x < y) ? x : y
```

In a similar fashion, using only conditional expressions, describe the mathematical operations

    `min(x, y, z)`   and   `max(x, y, z, w)`

13. Declare `enum month` with an *e_list* consisting of the enumerators `jan`, `feb`, ... Write a function called `last_month()` which returns the previous month. For example, if `jan` is the input, then `dec` should be returned. Write another function that, when given a variable of type `enum month`, prints its three-letter name. Note that when `printf()` is used, a variable of an enumeration type is printed as its implicit integer value. That is,

```
printf("\n%d", jan);
```

prints 0, not `jan`. Write `main()` so that it calls these functions to produce a table of all twelve months listed next to their predecessor months.

14. Write a next-day program for a particular year. The program should take as input two integers, say 21 and 5, which represent 21 May, and it should print as output 22 May, which is the next day. Use enumeration types in the program, and pay particular attention to the problem of crossing from one month to the next.

15. Incorporate a random number generator in the code that is used to make the machine's selection in the "paper, rock, scissors" game program.

16. Write a roulette program. The roulette (machine) is to select a number between 0 and 35 at random. The player can place an odd/even bet or can place a bet on a particular number. A winning odd/even bet is paid off at 2 to 1, except that all odd/even bets lose if the roulette selects 0. If the player places a bet on a particular number and the roulette selects it, then the player is paid off at 35 to 1.

17. A twentieth-century date can be written as day: month: year, where day has 31 values, month 12 values, and year 100 values. Thus, day can be represented by 5 bits, month by 4 bits, and year by 7 bits. Write a program that packs and unpacks a date into a 16-bit integer. The unpacked date should be represented as the three int variables day, month, and year.

18. For packed data, it is necessary to use bit expressions. Write a program that acts directly on a date (see exercise 17) and produces the next calendar day in packed form. Contrast this to the program written in exercise 14.

19. Compare the two programs written for changing dates. Time both and see which runs faster over a large number of trials. Omit all printing when you make this test.

20. Rewrite the majority function in Chapter 4 in such a way that the five boolean variables b1 to b5 are packed in a single char variable b.

21. Rewrite the program for exercise 20 to take advantage of machine arithmetic. Adding 1 to a binary representation is equivalent to the effect of the nested for statements found in Chapter 4. Therefore, your program should generate the table using a single unnested for statement.

22. (Balanced Meal Program) Use the enum type to define five basic food groups: meats, vegetables, fruits, grains and fish. Use a random number generator to select an item from each food group. Write a function meal(), which picks an item from each of the five groups and prints out this menu. Print 20 menus. How many different menus are available?

23. Write a program that picks out five cards at random. A card should be a suit plus a pip value. The pip value for an ace is 1, for a deuce is 2, . . . , and for a king is 13. Use enumeration types to represent these values. The program should check that all the cards in the hand are distinct, and it should print out the hand in a visually pleasing way.

24. Write a set of routines that test whether the hand generated by exercise 23 is a flush, a straight, or a full house. A flush is where all five cards are the same suit. A straight is where all five cards can be placed in consecutive sequence by pip value. A full house is three of a kind plus a pair. Run your random hand generator and print out any hand that is one of these three kinds. Print out the hand number it is (keep track of all hands produced). Continue to print out hands until one of each of the three kinds has been generated, or you have generated 5000 distinct hands. If the latter happens, there is probably something wrong with your program. Why?

25. Which of the following two statements is legal? First study the syntax for a switch statement to answer this. Then write a test program to see if your compiler complains.

```
switch (1);
switch (1)   switch(1);
```

26. Consider the following code written on a two's complement machine.

```
int        big;
unsigned   k;

k = -1;
k >>= 1;
big = k;
```

Explain why `big` has the largest possible `int` value. Suppose instead, we write

```
big = -1;
big >>= 1;
```

Does `big` still have the largest possible `int` value? Explain.

27. Rewrite the function `you_won()` in the program "paper, rock, scissors" so that a `switch` statement is used.

28. In the game "paper, rock, scissors," an outcome that is not a tie is conveyed to the player by printing `you won` or `i won`. Change the program so that messages of the following type are printed:

```
you chose paper and i chose rock: you won
```

29. Rewrite the function `pack()` given in this chapter so that its body contains only one statement of the form

```
return (expression);
```

30. Rewrite the function `pack()` so that only arithmetic operations are used.

31. Experiment with the second version of the function `day_after()` to see what the compiler does when casts are not used.

32. What gets printed?

```
for (putchar('1'); putchar('2'); putchar('3')) {
        putchar('4');
        continue;
        putchar('5');
}
```

Is the output of the following code the same?

```
putchar('1');
while (putchar('2')) {
        putchar('4');
        continue;
        putchar('5');
        putchar('3');
}
```

To understand the relevance of this problem, read in Chapter 4 about the `for` statement and its equivalence to the `while` statement.

7

Pointers, Arrays, and Strings

A distinguishing characteristic of C is the sophisticated use of pointers and pointer arithmetic. Especially important is the pointer as an array address. Arrays are a data type that use subscripted variables and make possible the representation of a large number of homogeneous values. Another crucial use of pointers is to pass addresses of variables to functions so that the values of the variables can be changed in the calling environment. This is the equivalent of "call by reference" in other languages. Arrays of characters are strings, and they are sufficiently important to be treated as a special topic.

7.1 POINTERS

A simple variable in a program is stored in a certain number of bytes at a particular memory location, or address, in the machine. For example, on our system the compiler assigns four contiguous bytes of memory for an int. The pointer is used in programs that access memory and manipulate addresses. We have already seen, for example, that addresses are used in the argument list to scanf() so that values converted from characters in the input stream can be stored in memory.

If v is a variable, then &v is the location, or address, in memory of its stored value. The address operator & is unary and has the same precedence and "right to left" associativity as the other unary operators. Addresses are a set of values that can be manipulated. Pointer variables can be declared in programs and then used to take addresses as values. The declaration

```
int    *p;
```

declares p to be of type pointer to int. Its legal range of values always includes the special address 0 and a set of positive integers that are interpreted as machine addresses on the given C system. Some examples of assignment to the pointer p are

```
p = 0;
p = NULL;            /*  equivalent to  p = 0;  */
p = &i;
p = (int *) 1501;    /*  an absolute address in memory  */
```

In the third example we think of p as "referring to i" or "pointing to i" or "containing the address of i." In the fourth example the cast is necessary to avoid a compiler warning.

The indirection or dereferencing operator * is unary and has the same precedence and "right to left" associativity as the other unary operators. If p is a pointer, then *p is the value of the variable of which p is the address. The name "indirection" is taken from machine language programming. The direct value of p is a memory location, whereas *p is the indirect value of p, namely, the value at the memory location stored in p. In a certain sense * is the inverse operator to &. Suppose we declare

```
double    x, y, *p;
```

Then the two statements

```
p = &x;
y = *p;
```

are equivalent to

```
y = *&x;
```

which in turn is equivalent to

```
y = x;
```

The following program illustrates the distinction between a pointer value and its dereferenced value.

```
main()
{
    int    i = 7, *p;

    p = &i;
    printf("\nthe value of   i   is   %d", *p);
    printf("\nthe location of   i   is   %d\n\n", p);
}
```

The output of this program on our system is the following:

```
the value of   i   is   7
the location of   i   is   2147479220
```

The actual location of a variable in memory is system dependent. The operator * takes the value of p to be a memory location and returns the value stored in this location, appropriately interpreted according to the type declaration of p. If we had wanted to initialize p rather than assign its value in an assignment statement, we would have written

```
int    i = 7, *p = &i;
```

Note carefully that this is an initialization of p, not *p. The variable p has type int * and its initial value is &i.

The following table illustrates how some pointer expressions are evaluated.

Declarations and initializations

```
int    i = 3, j = 5, k, *p = &i, *q = &j, *r;
double x = 11.7;
```

Expression	Equivalent expression	Value
p == & i	p == (& i)	1
* * & p	* (* (& p))	3
r = & x	r = (& x)	/* illegal pointer combination */
/* a pointer to double should not be assigned to a pointer to int */		
3 * - * p / * q + 7	((3 * (-(* p))) / (* q)) + 7	6
3 * - * p /* q + 7	?	/* "/*" begins a comment */
* (r = & k) = *p * * q	(* (r = & k)) = ((*p) * (*q))	15

Of course, not every value is stored in an accessible memory location. It is useful to keep in mind the following prohibitions.

Constructs not *to be pointed at*

Do not point at constants.

```
&3                     /* illegal */
```

Do not point at arrays—an array name is a constant.

```
int   a[77];
&a                     /* compiler warning */
```

Do not point at ordinary expressions.

```
&(k + 99)        /* illegal */
```

Do not point at register variables.

```
register v;
&v                     /* illegal */
```

The address operator can be applied to variables and array elements. If a is an array, then expressions such as &a[0] and &a[i+j+3] make sense.

7.2 POINTER PARAMETERS IN FUNCTIONS

Pointers have several critical roles in C. As we shall see in Chapters 9 and 10, pointers are used to construct complicated data structures such as lists and trees. In this section we will describe how pointers are used as arguments to functions so as to be able to modify stored values of variables in the calling environment.

All arguments to functions are passed "call by value." This means that the stored values of those arguments in the calling environment cannot be changed by the function. Until now we have used two means of passing values back to the external environment. The first is to use a return statement in the body of the function, and the second is to use a global variable known both to the function and to the external environment. Let us illustrate this with two versions of a function max(), which returns the larger of two values.

```
/* use of a return statement to pass out a value  */

max(a, b)
int    a, b;
{
     return ((a > b) ? a : b);
}
```

This function is invoked by a statement such as

```
v = max(x, y);      /* v is assigned the max of x and y */
```

The second version of this function uses the external variable v to retain the computed maximum.

```
/*  use of an external variable to pass out a value  */

int   v;      /*  external  */

max(a, b)
int   a,b;
{
      v = (a > b) ? a : b;
}
```

In contrast to the first version this function is called without assignment.

```
max(x, y);      /*  v  is assigned the max of  x  and  y  */
```

In modern programming practice, the use of an external or global variable as a means of communication between a function and its calling environment is considered undesirable. A function call that causes a change in a variable not explicitly in its argument list is said to have a "side effect." When the second version of max() is called, the external variable v as a side effect is assigned the maximum value of x and y. Because it communicates with its calling environment by use of a return statement, the first version of max() is preferable to the second. The return mechanism, however, is too limited to be the sole means of communication to the calling environment. Many functions need to output several results. Another means of communication is accomplished by using pointers as parameters and passing in addresses when the function is called.

Call by Reference

The process of declaring a function parameter as a pointer and consistently using the dereferenced parameter in the function body is known as "call by reference." When an address is passed as an argument, the function can be made to change the value of the addressed variable in the calling environment. Here is a version of max() that illustrates "call by reference."

```
/*  use of a pointer variable to pass out a value  */

max(a, b, m_ptr)
int   a, b, *m_ptr;
{
      *m_ptr = (a > b) ? a : b;
}
```

This version of max() would be invoked by a statement such as

```
max(x, y, &v);      /*  v  will contain the max of  x  and  y  */
```

Note that within the body of this version of max () the pointer m_ptr is dereferenced. When invoked with the address &v, the computed maximum value will be assigned to the dereferenced address, which in this case means the variable v. In this manner, the variable m_ptr is made to communicate with the calling environment.

Let us use "call by reference" to produce two output values. We wish to sort two values pointed at by p and q so that they end up in order.

```
order (p,  q)
int    *p,  *q;
{
     int    temp;

     if (*p > *q) {
          temp = *p;
          *p = *q;
          *q = temp;
     }
}
```

Typically this function is called by a statement such as

```
order (&i,  &j);
```

which causes i and j to end up with the appropriate ordered values. Note carefully that the addresses of i and j are passed "call by value," and that these addresses cannot be changed in the calling environment by the function. However, they can be dereferenced, and this provides the mechanism by which the function can change the stored values of i and j in the calling environment.

"Call by reference" is accomplished by

1. Declaring a function parameter to be a pointer
2. Using the dereferenced pointer in the function body
3. Passing in an address as an actual argument when the function is called

7.3 ONE-DIMENSIONAL ARRAYS

Programs often make use of homogeneous data. For example, if we want to manipulate some grades, we might declare

```
int    grade0, grade1, grade2;
```

If the number of grades is large, it will be cumbersome to represent and manipulate the data by means of unique identifiers. Instead, an array, which is a derived type, can be used. An array can be thought of as a simple variable with an index, or subscript, added. The brackets [and] are used to contain the array subscripts. To use `grade[0]`, `grade[1]`, and `grade[2]` in a program, we would declare

```
int    grade[3];
```

where the integer 3 in the declaration represents the number of elements in the array. The indexing of array elements always starts at 0.

A one-dimensional array declaration is a type followed by an identifier with a bracketed constant `int` expression. The value of the expression, which must be positive, is the size of the array. It specifies the number of elements in the array. The array subscripts can range from 0 to *size* − 1. The lower bound of the array subscripts is 0 and the upper bound is *size* − 1. Thus, the following relationships hold:

```
int a[size]; /* space for a[0], a[1], ... , a[size − 1]
               is allocated */
```

lower bound = 0
upper bound = *size* − 1
size = *upper bound* + 1

It is good programming practice to define the size of an array as a symbolic constant. An example of an array declaration illustrating this is

```
#define    SIZE    50

int    a[SIZE];      /* space for  a[0], ... , a[49] is allocated */
```

Initialization

Arrays may be of storage class automatic, external, or static, but not register. External and static arrays can be initialized using an array initializer.

one_dimensional_array_initializer ::= { *initializer_list* }
initializer_list ::= *initializer* {, *initializer*}$_0$+
initializer ::= {*constant_expression*}$_{opt}$

An example is

```
static float   f[5] = {0.0, 1.0, 2.0, 3.0, 4.0};
```

This initializes `f[0]` to `0.0`, `f[1]` to `1.0`, etc. When a list of initializers is shorter than the number of array elements to be initialized, the remaining elements are initialized to zero. If an external or static array is not initialized, then the system initializes all elements to zero automatically. In contrast, automatic arrays cannot be initialized and the elements of such arrays always start with "garbage" values.

If an external or static array is declared without a size and is initialized to a series of values, it is implicitly given the size of the number of initializers. Thus

```
int a[] = {3, 4, 5, −9};      and      int a[4] = {3, 4, 5, −9};
```

are equivalent external declarations. This feature works with character arrays as well. However, the compiler allows an initialization such as

```
static char   s[] = "a  is for apple or alphabet pie";
```

which is taken to be equivalent to

```
static char   s[] = {'a', ' ', ' ', 'i', 's',  .  .  . , 'e','\0'};
```

As with other automatic arrays, automatic character arrays cannot be initialized.

Indexing

If a is an array, we can write a[*expr*], where *expr* is an integral expression, to access an element of the array. We call *expr* a subscript, or index, of a. Assume that the declaration

```
int   i, a[SIZE];
```

has been made. The expression a[i] can be made to refer to any element of the array by assignment of an appropriate value to the subscript i. A single array element a[i] is accessed when i has a value greater than or equal to 0 and less than or equal to SIZE - 1. If i has a value outside this range, a run-time error will occur when a[i] is accessed. This is a common programming error. The effect of the error is system dependent, and can be quite confusing. One frequent result is that the value of some unrelated variable will be returned or modified. It is the programmer's job to ensure that all subscripts to arrays stay within bounds.

The following code illustrates the use of indexing to sum the elements of an array:

```
sum = 0;
for (i = 0;  i < SIZE;  ++i)
    sum += a[i];
```

Another simple example illustrating the use of indexing is the following code, which prints the elements of an array five to a row:

```
for (i = 0;  i < SIZE;  ++i)
    printf("%c%12d",  (i % 5 == 0) ? '\n' : '\0', a[i]);
```

Notice how the various parts of the for statement are neatly tailored to provide a terse notation for dealing with a computation on an array.

7.4 THE RELATIONSHIP OF POINTERS TO ARRAYS

Pointers and arrays are used in almost the exact same way to access memory. However, there are differences between them, and these differences are subtle and important. A pointer is a variable that takes addresses as values. An array name is an address, or pointer, that is fixed. When an array is declared, the compiler must allocate a base address and a sufficient amount of storage to contain all the elements of the array. The base address is the initial location in memory where the array is stored; it is the address of the first element (index 0) of the array. Suppose that we make the declaration

```
#define   SIZE    100

int    a[SIZE], *p;
```

and suppose that the system causes memory bytes numbered 300, 304, 308, . . . , 696 to be the addresses of a[0], a[1], a[2], . . . , a[99], respectively, with location 300 being the base address of a. We are assuming that each byte is addressable and that four bytes are used to store an int. This is system dependent. The two statements

```
    p = a;          and        p = &a[0];
```

are equivalent and would assign 300 to p. Pointer arithmetic provides an alternative to array indexing. The two statements

```
    p = a + 1;        and        p = &a[1];
```

are equivalent and would assign 304 to p. Assuming that the elements of a have been assigned values, we can use the following code to sum the array:

```
sum = 0;
for (p = a; p < &a[SIZE]; ++p)
        sum += *p;
```

In this loop the pointer variable p is initialized to the base address of the array a. Then the successive values of p are equivalent to &a[0], &a[1], ... In general, if i is a variable of type int, then p + i is the *i*th offset from the address p. In a similar manner, a + i is the *i*th offset from the base address of the array a. Here is another way of summing the array:

```
sum = 0;
for (i = 0; i < SIZE; ++i)
        sum += *(a + i);
```

Because a is a constant pointer, expressions such as

```
    a = p              ++a            a += 2
```

are illegal. We cannot change the address of a.

Pointer Arithmetic and Element Size

Pointer arithmetic is one of the powerful features of C. If the variable p is a pointer to a particular type, then the expression p + 1 yields the correct machine address for storing or accessing the next variable of that type. In a similar fashion, pointer expressions such as p + i and ++p and p += i all make sense. If p and q are both pointing to elements of an array, then p – q yields the int value representing the number of array elements between p and q. Even though pointer expressions and arithmetic expressions have a similar appearance, there is a critical difference in interpretation between the two types of expressions. The following program illustrates the difference:

```
/*** pointer arithmetic is not integer arithmetic ***/

main()
{
        char     c, *c_ptr1, *c_ptr2;
        int      i, *i_ptr1, *i_ptr2;
        double   d, *d_ptr1, *d_ptr2;

        c_ptr1 = &c;       /* assign addresses to pointers */
        i_ptr1 = &i;
        d_ptr1 = &d;
        c_ptr2 = c_ptr1 + 1;      /* offset by 1 */
        i_ptr2 = i_ptr1 + 1;
        d_ptr2 = d_ptr1 + 1;

        /* print the value of pointer expressions */
        printf("\n%d    %d    %d",
             c_ptr2 - c_ptr1, i_ptr2 - i_ptr1, d_ptr2 - d_ptr1);

        /* print corresponding expressions using integer arithmetic */
        printf("\n%s%d        %s%d          %s%d\n\n",
            "char offset: ", (int)c_ptr2 - (int)c_ptr1,
            "int offset: ", (int)i_ptr2 - (int)i_ptr1,
            "double offset: ", (int)d_ptr2 - (int)d_ptr1);
}
```

On a VAX a char is stored in 1 byte, an int in 4 bytes, and a double in 8 bytes. Here is the output of this program on our system:

```
1    1    1
char offset: 1        int offset: 4        double offset: 8
```

The number of bytes used to store the various types on a given system can be found by making use of the sizeof operator. We presented such a program in Chapter 3.

7.5 ARRAYS AS FUNCTION ARGUMENTS

A formal parameter that is declared as an array is actually a pointer. When an array is being passed, its base address is passed "call by value." The array elements themselves are not copied. As a notational convenience, the compiler allows array bracket notation to be used in declaring pointers as parameters. This notation reminds the programmer and other readers of the code that the function should be called with an array. To illustrate this we write a function that sums the elements of an array of type double:

```
double sum(a, n)
double    a[];
double    n;      /* n is the size of the array */
{
        int       i;
        double    s = 0.0;

        for (i = 0; i < n; ++i)
            s += a[i];
        return (s);
}
```

As part of the header of a function definition the declaration

    `double a[];`   is equivalent to   `double *a;`

On the other hand, as declarations within the body of a function they are *not* equivalent. The first will create a constant pointer (and no storage), whereas the second will create a pointer variable.

Suppose that in a `main()` function we have an array, or vector, v declared with 100 elements. After the elements have been assigned values, we can use the above function `sum()` to add various of the elements of v. The following table illustrates the possibilities:

Various ways that sum() might be called

Invocation	What gets computed and returned
sum(v, 100)	v[0] + v[1] + · · · · + v[99]
sum(v, 88)	v[0] + v[1] + · · · · + v[87]
sum(v, m)	v[0] + v[1] + · · · · + v[m−1]
sum(&v[5], m − 5)	v[5] + v[6] + · · · · + v[m−1]
sum(v + 7, 2 * k)	v[7] + v[8] + · · · · + v[2*k+]

The last call illustrates again the use of pointer arithmetic. The base address of v is offset by 7 and `sum()` initializes the local pointer variable a to this address. This causes all address calculations inside the function call to be similarly offset.

7.6 AN EXAMPLE: BUBBLE SORT

Although we have already presented a bubble sort in Chapter 1, we will do so again here and illustrate in some detail how the function works on a particular array of integers. We will use the function `order()` written in section 7.2.

```
bubble(a, n)
int    a[], n;        /*  n  is the size of  a[]   */
{
       int   i, j;

       for (i = 0;  i < n - 1;  ++i)
              for (j = n - 1;  i < j;  --j)
                     order(&a[j-1],  &a[j]);
}
```

Suppose we declare

```
static int    a[] = {7, 3, 66, 3, -5, 22, -77, 2};
```

and then invoke `bubble(a, 8)`. The following table shows the elements of a[] after each pass of the outer loop:

unordered data:	7	3	66	3	-5	22	-77	2
first pass:	-77	7	3	66	3	-5	22	2
second pass:	-77	-5	7	3	66	3	2	22
third pass:	-77	-5	2	7	3	66	3	22
fourth pass:	-77	-5	2	3	7	3	66	22
fifth pass:	-77	-5	2	3	3	7	22	66
sixth pass:	-77	-5	2	3	3	7	22	66
seventh pass:	-77	-5	2	3	3	7	22	66

At the start of the first pass a[6] is compared with a[7]. Since the values are in order they are not exchanged. Then a[5] is compared with a[6], and since these values are out of order they are exchanged. Then a[4] is compared with a[5], etc. Adjacent out-of-order values are exchanged. The effect of the first pass is to "bubble" the smallest value in the array into the element a[0]. In the second pass a[0] is left unchanged and a[6] is compared first with a[7], etc. After the second pass the next to the smallest value is in a[1]. Since each pass bubbles the next smallest element to its appropriate array position, the algorithm will, after n - 1 passes, have all the elements ordered. Notice in this example that after the fifth pass all the elements have been ordered. It is possible to modify the algorithm to terminate earlier by adding a variable that detects if no exchanges are made in a given pass. We leave this as an exercise.

A bubble sort is very inefficient. If the size of the array is n, then the number of comparisons performed is proportional to n^2.

7.7 AN EXAMPLE: MERGE AND MERGE SORT

Suppose that we have two ordered arrays of integers, say a[] and b[]. If we want to merge them into another ordered array, say c[], we can use a simple algorithm. First compare a[0] and b[0]. Whichever is smaller, say b[0], put into c[0]. Next compare a[0] and b[1]. Whichever is smaller, say b[1], put into c[1]. Next compare a[0] and b[2]. Whichever is smaller, say a[0], put into c[3]. Next compare a[1] and b[2], and so on. Eventually one of the arrays a[] or b[] will be exhausted. At that point, the remainder of the elements in the other array must be copied into c[]. The function that does this is the following:

```
/***  merge  a[]  and  b[]  into  c[]  ***/

merge(a, b, c, m, n)
int    a[], b[], c[], m, n;    /*  m  and  n  are the
                                   sizes of  a[]  and  b[]  */
{
    int   i = 0, j = 0, k = 0;

    while (i < m && j < n)
        if (a[i] < b[j])
            c[k++] = a[i++];
        else
            c[k++] = b[j++];
    while (i < m)        /*  pick up any remainder  */
        c[k++] = a[i++];
    while (j < n)
        c[k++] = b[j++];
}
```

The array c[] is assumed to contain enough space to hold both a[] and b[]. The programmer must make certain that the bounds on c[] are not overrun.

In contrast to a bubble sort, a merge sort is very efficient. We will write a function called mergesort() to act on an array key[], which has a size that is a power of 2. The "power of 2" requirement will help to make the explanation simpler. In the exercises, we indicate how this restriction is removed. To understand how merge sort works, let us suppose that key[] contains the following 16 integers:

```
    4   3   1   67   55   8   0   4   -5   37   7   4   2   9   1   -1
```

The algorithm will work on the data in a number of passes. The following table shows how we want the data to look after each pass:

unordered data:	4	3	1	67	55	8	0	4	-5	37	7	4	2	9	1	-1
first pass:	3	4	1	67	8	55	0	4	-5	37	4	7	2	9	-1	1
second pass:	1	3	4	67	0	4	8	55	-5	4	7	37	-1	1	2	9
third pass:	0	1	3	4	4	8	55	67	-5	-1	1	2	4	7	9	37
fourth pass:	-5	-1	0	1	1	2	3	4	4	4	7	8	9	37	55	67

After the first pass we want each successive pair of integers to be in order. After the second pass we want each successive quartet of integers to be in order. After the third pass we want each successive octet of integers to be in order. Finally, after the fourth pass we want all 16 of the integers to be in order. At each stage merge() is used to accomplish the desired ordering. For example, after the third pass we have the two subarrays

```
0   1   3   4   4   8   55  67    and    -5  -1  1   2   4   7   9   37
```

which are both in order. When we merge these two subarrays, we obtain the completely ordered array given in the last line of the above table. Surprisingly, the code that accomplishes this is quite short. It illustrates the power of pointer arithmetic.

```
/*** mergesort:  use merge() to sort an array  ***/

#define   MAXSIZE    1024

mergesort(key, n)
int    key[], n;        /* n is the size of key[] */
{
    int   j, k, m, w[MAXSIZE];   /* w provides work space */

    for (m = 1; m < n; m *= 2)
        ;
    if (n == m && n <= MAXSIZE)        /* n  is a power of 2 */
        for (k = 1; k < n; k *= 2) {
            for (j = 0; j < n - k; j += 2 * k)
                merge(key + j, key + j + k, w + j, k, k);
            for (j = 0; j < n; ++j)    /* write w back into key */
                key[j] = w[j];
        }
    else {
        if (n != m)
            printf("error: size of array not a power of 2\n\n");
        if (n > MAXSIZE)
            printf("error: size of array is too big\n\n");
    }
}
```

DISSECTION OF THE *mergesort* PROGRAM

```
for (m = 1; m < n; m *= 2)
    ;
```

After this loop m is the smallest power of 2 that is greater than or equal to n.

```
if (n == m && n <= MAXSIZE)        /* n is a power of 2 */
    .   .   .   .   .
else {
    if (n != m)
        printf("error: size of array not a power of 2\n\n");
    if (n > MAXSIZE)
        printf("error: size of array is too big\n\n");
}
```

We first test to see if n is a power of 2 and less than or equal to MAXSIZE; if not, we exit with the proper warning.

```
for (k = 1; k < n; k *= 2) {
    for (j = 0; j < n - k; j += 2 * k)
        merge(key + j, key + j + k, w + j, k, k);
    for (j = 0; j < n; ++j)    /* write w back into key */
        key[j] = w[j];
}
```

This is the heart of the algorithm. Suppose we start with key[] having the data given as unordered in the above table. In the first pass of the outer loop k is 1. Consider the inner loop

```
    for (j = 0; j < n - k; j += 2 * k)
        merge(key + j, key + j + k, w + j, k, k);
```

The first call to merge() is equivalent to

```
    merge(key + 0, key + 0 + 1, w + 0, 1, 1);
```

The arrays based at key and key + 1, both of size 1, are being merged and put into the array based at w; this will result in w[0] and w[1] being in order. The next call to merge() is equivalent to

```
    merge(key + 2, key + 2 + 1, w + 2, 1, 1);
```

The arrays based at key + 2 and key + 3, both of size 1, are being merged and put into the array based at w+2; this will result in w[2] and w[3] being in order. The next call . . . , and so on. After the first pass of the outer loop, each successive pair of elements in w[] is in order and is as given in the above table. At this point, the array w[] is copied into key[]. In the second pass of the outer loop, k is 2. The next call to merge() is equivalent to

```
    merge(key + 0, key + 0 + 2, w + 0, 2, 2);
```

The arrays based at key and key + 2, both of size 2, are being merged and put into the array based at w. This will result in w[0], w[1], w[2], w[3] being in order. The next call to merge() is equivalent to

```
    merge(key + 4, key + 4 + 2, w + 4, 2, 2);
```

The arrays based at key + 4 and key + 6, both of size 2, are being merged and put into the array based at w + 4; this will result in w[4], w[5], w[6], and w[7] being in order. The next call . . . and so on. After the second pass of the outer loop, each successive quartet of elements in w[] is in order and is as given in the above table, and so on.

Here is a function that can be used to test `mergesort()`. The array `key[]` is `static`, so that we can conveniently initialize the array.

```
#define   KEYSIZE    16

main()
{
     int           i;
     int static    key[] = {
          4,  3,  1,  67,  55,  8,  0,  4,  -5,  37,  7,  4,  2,  9,  1,  -1
     };

     mergesort(key, KEYSIZE);
     for (i = 0; i < KEYSIZE; ++i)
          printf("%d  ", key[i]);
     printf("\n\n");
}
```

The amount of work that a merge sort does when sorting *n* elements is proportional to *n* log *n*. Compared to a bubble sort, this is a very significant improvement. Sorting is critical to the efficient handling of large amounts of stored information. However, it is beyond the scope of this text to discuss the topic in detail; see *The Art of Computer Programming, Vol. 3 (Sorting and Searching)* by Donald Ervin Knuth (Reading, Mass.: Addison-Wesley, 1973).

7.8 STRINGS

Strings are one-dimensional arrays of type `char`. By convention a string in C is terminated by the end-of-string sentinel \0, or null character. Because of this, dealing with strings has its own flavor, and we treat the topic separately. It is useful to think of strings as having a variable length, delimited by \0, but with a maximum length determined by the size of the string. The size of a string must include the storage needed for the end-of-string sentinel. As with all arrays, it is the job of the programmer to make sure that string bounds are not overrun.

String constants are written between double quotes. For example, `"abc"` is a character array of size 4, with the last element being the null character \0. Therefore, a string constant such as `"a"` is not the same thing as the character constant `'a'`. The array `"a"` has two elements, the first with value `'a'` and the second with value `'\0'`. The following program highlights some differences between arrays and pointers, illustrates the difference between initialization and assignment, and shows that string constants can be changed.

```
/***   arrays and pointers are different   ***/

char    s[] = "ABC";
char    *p = "a  is for apple or alphabet pie";

main()
{
        char    *q = "which all get a slice of, come taste it and try";

        printf("\n%s:  %s\n        %s", s, p, q);
        for (p = q; *q != '\0'; ++q)
            *q += 1;
        printf("\n        %s\n\n", p);
}
```

DISSECTION OF THE *change_it* PROGRAM

```
char    s[] = "ABC";
```

This illustrates character array initialization. The compiler treats this as equivalent to

```
char    s[] = {'A', 'B', 'C', '\0'};
```

The size of the array is 4; the array name s is a constant pointer to char. Automatic arrays cannot be initialized. If this line is moved to inside the body of main(), the compiler will complain.

```
char    *p = "a  is for apple or alphabet pie";
```

p is a variable of type pointer to char; its storage class is external. It is being initialized with a pointer value that points to

```
"a  is for apple or alphabet pie"
```

```
char    *q = "which all get a slice of, come taste it and try";
```

q is a variable of type pointer to char; its storage class is automatic. It is being initialized with a pointer value that points to

```
"which all get a slice of, come taste it and try"
```

Pointer variables of any storage class may be initialized.

```
printf("\n%s: %s\n        %s", s, p, q);
```

The following is printed:

```
ABC:  a  is for apple or alphabet pie
        which all get a slice of, come taste it and try
```

```
for (p = q; *q != '\0'; ++q)
    *q += 1;
```

After p is assigned the value q, the original value of p is irretrievably lost; thus, the string constant "a is for . . . " cannot be accessed again. As long as the value of what q is pointing at is not '\0', the variable pointed to by q is indexed by 1, and then q itself is indexed by 1. The indexing of q causes it to point to the next character in the string.

```
printf("\n      %s\n\n", p);
```

The following is printed;

xijdi!bmm!hfu!b!tmjdf!pg-!dpnf!ubtuf!ju!boe!usz

Note that x is one more than w, i is one more than h, and so on. This illustrates the power of pointers and pointer arithmetic in C. Although this mechanism can be used to modify string constants, it is not considered good programming practice to do so.

String Handling Functions in the Standard Library

The standard library contains many useful string handling functions. Although these functions are not part of the C language, they are available on most systems.

A description of string handling functions in the standard library

Functions that return an int

```
strcmp(s1, s2)
```

s1 and s2 are pointers to char. An integer is returned which is less than, equal to, or greater than zero depending on whether s1 is lexicographically less than, equal to, or greater than s2.

```
strncmp(s1, s2, n)
```

Similar to strcmp() except that at most n characters are compared.

```
strlen(s)
```

s is a pointer to char. A count of the number of characters before \0 is returned.

Functions that return a pointer to char

```
index(s, c)
```

s is a pointer to char and c is a char. A pointer to the first occurrence of c in the string s is returned, or NULL is returned if c is not in the string.

`rindex(s, c)`

Similar to `index()` except that the search is from the right.

`strcat(s1, s2)`

s1 and s2 are pointers to `char`. A copy of s2, including the null character, is appended to the end of s1 and the value s1 is returned. It is assumed that s1 has enough space to hold the result.

`strncat(s1, s2, n)`

Similar to `strcat()` except that at most n non-null characters are appended followed by \0.

`strcpy(s1, s2)`

s1 and s2 are pointers to `char`. s2 is copied into s1 until \0 is moved; whatever exists in s1 is overwritten. It is assumed that s1 has enough space to hold the result; the value s1 is returned.

`strncpy(s1, s2, n)`

Similar to `strcpy()` except that exactly n characters are moved. A copy of s2 is truncated or padded with \0 characters, if necessary, and exactly n characters are moved. If the length of s2 is n or more, the string s1 may not be null terminated.

There is nothing special about these functions. They are written in C and are all quite short. Variables in them are often declared to have storage class `register` to make them execute more quickly. Here is one way the function `strlen()` could be written:

```
strlen(s)
register char    *s;
{
      register int    n;

      for (n = 0; *s != '\0'; ++s)
           ++n;
      return (n);
}
```

Another version of this function is the following:

```
strlen(s)
register char    *s;
{
      register int    n = 0;

      while (*s++)
           ++n;
      return (n);
}
```

Notice that when s is pointing to the null character, the value of ∗s is zero, causing the loop to terminate.

The function strcat(), which concatenates two strings, could be written as follows:

```
char *strcat(s1, s2)
register char    *s1, *s2;
{
     register char    *p;

     p = s1;
     while (*p++)
          ;
     --p;
     while (*p++ = *s2++)
          ;
     return (s1);
}
```

It is the programmer's responsibility to allocate sufficient space for strings passed to functions from the standard library.

The following table illustrates the use of some of the string handling functions:

Declarations and assignments	

`char   *p, *s1, *s2, *s3, *s4, t[33];`
`s1 = "how now brown cow";`
`s2 = "jump over the moon";`
`s3 = "jump, cow!";`
`s4 = "?";`
`s5 = "";`
`*t = '\0';`	

Expression	*Value*
`strlen(s1)`	17
`strlen(s1 + 9)`	8
`strlen(p)` `/* p is not null terminated */`	`/* error */`
`strcmp(s1, s2)`	*negative integer*
`strcmp(s2, s1)`	*positive integer*
`strcmp(s5, t)`	0
`strncmp(s2, s3, s4)`	0
`strncmp(s1 + 14, s3 + 6, 3)`	0

The next table also illustrates the use of string handling functions. The declarations and assignments are assumed to be the same as in the previous table.

Declarations and assignments
/* the same as in the previous table */

Statements	What gets printed
`strcpy(t, s1 + 14);` `printf("%s", t);`	cow
`strcpy(t, s1);` `printf("%s", t);`	how now brown cow

`strcpy(t, s1 + 8);`
`strcat(t, s4);`
`strcat(t, " ");`
`strcat(t, s2);`
`strcat(t, s4);`
`printf("%s", t);`
	brown cow? jump over the moon?

`p = index(s1, 'o');` `printf("%s", p);`	ow now brown cow
`p = index(index(p, 'b'), 'w');` `printf("%s", p);`	wn cow
`p = rindex(s3, 'm');` `printf("%s%s%s", p, " ", p + 5);`	mp, cow! ow!

`strcpy(t, s1);`
`strcat(t, s2);`
`printf("%s", t);`
	???

/* the upper bound of the array t has been overrun */	

7.9 AN EXAMPLE: WORD COUNT

To illustrate string processing, we will write a function that counts the number of words in a string. We assume that words in the string are separated by white space.

```
/***  count the number of words in a string  ***/

word_cnt(s)
char    *s;
{
     int    cnt = 0;

     while (*s != '\0') {
          while (*s == ' ' || *s == '\n' || *s == '\t')
               ++s;    /* skip white space */
          if (*s != '\0') {
               ++cnt;   /* found a word */
               while (*s != ' ' && *s != '\n'
                              && *s != '\t' && *s != '\0')
                    ++s;    /* skip the word */
          }
     }
     return (cnt);
}
```

This is a typical string processing function. Pointer arithmetic and dereferencing are used to search for various patterns or characters.

7.10 MULTI-DIMENSIONAL ARRAYS

The C language allows arrays of any type, including arrays of arrays. With two bracket pairs we obtain a two-dimensional array. This idea can be iterated to obtain arrays of higher dimension. With each bracket pair we add another array dimension.

Examples of declarations of arrays	*Remarks*
`int a[100];`	a one-dimensional array
`int b[3][5];`	a two-dimensional array
`int c[7][9][2];`	a three-dimensional array

A k-dimensional array has a size for each of its k dimensions. If we let s_i represent the size of its ith dimension, then the declaration of the array will allocate space for $s_1 \times s_2 \times \cdots \times s_k$ elements. In the above table b has 3×5 elements, and c has $7 \times 9 \times 2$ elements. Starting at the base address of the array, all the array elements are stored contiguously in memory.

Two-dimensional arrays

Even though array elements are stored contiguously one after the other, it is often convenient to think of a two-dimensional array as a rectangular collection of elements with rows and columns. For example, if we declare

```
int    b[3][5];
```

then we can think of the array elements arranged as follows:

	col 1	*col 2*	*col 3*	*col 4*	*col 5*
row 1	b[0][0]	b[0][1]	b[0][2]	b[0][3]	b[0][4]
row 2	b[1][0]	b[1][1]	b[1][2]	b[1][3]	b[1][4]
row 3	b[2][0]	b[2][1]	b[2][2]	b[2][3]	b[2][4]

Because of the relationship of pointers to arrays, there are numerous ways to access elements of a two-dimensional array.

Expressions equivalent to b[i][j]

```
* (b[i] + j)
(*(b + i))[j]
*((*(b + i)) + j)
*(&b[0][0] + 5*i + j)
```

The parentheses are necessary because the brackets [] have higher precedence than the indirection operator *. The base address of the array is &b[0][0], and starting at this address the compiler allocates contiguous space for 15 int's. For any array, the mapping between pointer value and array indices is called "the storage mapping function." For the array b, the storage mapping function is specified by noting that

b[i][j]   is equivalent to   *(&b[0][0] + 5*i + j)

When a multi-dimensional array is a formal parameter in a function definition, all sizes except the first must be specified so the compiler can determine the correct storage mapping function. After the elements of the array b[][] given above have been assigned values, the following function can be used to sum the elements of the array. The column size must be specified.

```
sum(v)
int    v[][5];
{
    int    i, j, s = 0;

    for (i = 0; i < 3; ++i)
        for (j = 0; j < 5; ++j)
            s += v[i][j];
    return (s);
}
```

In the header of the function definition the declaration

```
int  v[] [5];              is equivalent to              int  (*v) [5];
```

Arrays of dimension higher than two work in a similar fashion. If we declare

```
int    c[7] [9] [2];
```

then the compiler will allocate space for 7 × 9 × 2 contiguous int's. The base
address of the array is &c[0] [0] [0] and the storage mapping function is specified by
noting that

```
c[i] [j] [k]     is equivalent to     *(&c[0] [0] [0] + 9*2*i + 2*j + k)
```

A programmer need not make direct use of the storage mapping function. If an expression such as c[i] [j] [k] is used in a program, the compiler uses the storage mapping
function to generate object code to access the correct array element in memory. If a
function is written that uses a multi-dimensional array as a parameter, then all sizes
of the array except the first must be specified so that the compiler can generate the
correct storage mapping function within the function body. Here is a function that will
sum the elements of the array c:

```
sum (v)
int    v[] [9] [2];
{
      int    i, j, k, s = 0;

      for (i = 0; i < 7; ++i)
          for (j = 0; j < 9; ++j)
              for (k = 0; k < 2; ++k)
                  s += v[i] [j] [k];
      return (s);
}
```

In the header of a function definition the parameter declarations

```
int c[] [9] [2];          int c[7] [9] [2];          int (*c) [9] [2];
```

are all equivalent. The constant 7 acts as a reminder to human readers of the code,
but the compiler disregards it. The other two constants are needed by the compiler to
generate the correct storage mapping function.

7.11 ARRAYS OF POINTERS

Arrays of pointers have many uses. In the following program an array of pointers to char is used to sort words into lexicographical order.

```
/***   sort words lexicographically  ***/

#define   MAXWORDS    100
#define   MAXSPACE    3000

main()
{
      char    *p[MAXWORDS], w[MAXSPACE], *q = w;
      int     i, n;

      printf("\nhow many words are to be sorted?   ");
      scanf("%d", &n);
      if (n <= MAXWORDS) {
            printf("\ninput  %d  words:   ", n);
            for (i = 0; i < n; ++i) {
                  scanf("%s", p[i] = q);
                  q += strlen(q) + 1;
            }
            bubble_sort(p, n);
            printf("\n%14s", "sorted list:   ");
            for (i = 0; i < n; ++i)
                  printf("%s\n%14s", p[i], "");
            printf("\n");
      }
      else
            printf("\n\ntoo many words: only %d allowed", MAXWORDS);
}
```

DISSECTION OF THE *sort_words* PROGRAM

```
#define   MAXWORDS    100
#define   MAXSPACE    3000

main()
{
      char    *p[MAXWORDS], w[MAXSPACE], *q = w;
      int     i, n;
```

Because brackets [] have higher precedence than *, the declaration

```
char *p[100];
```
 is equivalent to
```
char *(p[100]);
```

This makes p an array of pointers to char. In contrast to this, note that

```
char (*r) [7];          is equivalent to          char r[] [7];
```

and would make r a pointer to "array of 7 char's". An array of pointers is not the same as a pointer to an array. The character array w will provide work space; the variable q is a pointer to char with initial value w.

```
printf("\nhow many words are to be sorted? ");
scanf("%d", &n);
```

The user is asked how many words are to be sorted; the reply is stored in n.

```
if (n <= MAXWORDS) {
    .   .   .   .   .
}
else
        printf("\n\ntoo many words: only %d allowed", MAXWORDS);
```

If n is too big, the program exits with an appropriate message.

```
printf("\ninput %d words: ", n);
for (i = 0; i < n; ++i) {
    scanf("%s", p[i] + q);
    q += strlen(q) + 1;
}
```

The user is asked to input n words. Suppose that n has the value 18 and that the following words are typed in:

```
a  is for apple or alphabet pie
which all get a slice of, come taste it and try.
```

The format %s in the control string of a scanf() statement causes the next nonwhite sequence of characters in the input stream to be interpreted as a string. In the first call to scanf() the string "a" is placed in memory at the address given by the expression p[i] = q, with i having value 0. Since q has as its value the base address of the array w, that value is assigned to p[0] and that is the value of the expression as a whole. In the next statement, q is incremented by 2. After the first pass of the for loop we may think of w in memory as

with p[0] having the value &w[0] and q having the value &w[2]. After the second pass of the for loop we may think of w in memory as with p[1] having the value &w[2] and q having the value &w[5]. After the third pass of the for loop we may think of w in memory as

a	\0	i	s	\0	f	o	r	\0	...		...	...
0	1	2	3	4	5	6	7	8	9			2999

with p[2] having the value &w[5] and q having the value of &w[9], and so on.

```
bubble_sort(p, n);
```

This function is presented below; it accomplishes the sorting.

```
printf("\n%14s", "sorted list: ");
for (i = 0; i < n; ++i)
    printf("%s\n%14s", p[i], "");
printf("\n");
```

We have chosen to write the sorted list in a column; if the number of words is large, this might not be a convenient format. The following is printed:

```
sorted list:   a
               a
               all
               alphabet
               .   .   .   .   .
               taste
               try.
               which
```

The function bubble_sort() used to sort the words is similar in form to the function bubble() written earlier in this chapter.

```
bubble_sort(p, n)
char    *p[];
int     n;      /*  n  is the size of  p[]  */
{
        char    *temp;
        int     i, j;

        for (i = 0; i < n - 1; ++i)
            for (j = n - 1; i < j; --j)
                if (strcmp(p[j-1], p[j]) > 0) {
                    temp = p[j-1];
                    p[j-1] = p[j];
                    p[j] = temp;
                }
}
```

Although a sorted list of words is printed, the words themselves are not physically reordered in memory. It is the pointer values of the elements of p that are being reordered. Of course, if the *sort_words* program were intended for serious work on a large amount of data, we would use a more efficient sorting algorithm. Here, the inefficiency is magnified because the comparison is made by invoking the function strcmp(), and, in addition to the work done by strcmp() itself, there is the overhead of a function call.

The *sort_words* program as presented is not robust. If 100 words were sorted and each word contained more than 30 characters, an unlikely occurrence, then the work space provided by w would be inadequate. We leave it as an exercise to correct this deficiency.

For certain applications we might want to sort words contained in a file. To use the *sort_words* program to do this, we would have to enter at the beginning of the file, the number of words that the file contains and then give the command

> *sort_words* < *file*

It is inconvenient to have to know ahead of time how many words are to be processed. To circumvent this, we need the list processing tools presented in Chapter 10. Arrays of pointers are extensively used in list processing.

7.12 ARGUMENTS TO main()

Two arguments, conventionally called argc and argv, can be used with main() to communicate with the operating system. Here is a program that prints its command line arguments. It is a variant of the *echo* command in UNIX.

```
main(argc, argv)
int     argc;
char    *argv[];
{
    int    i;

    printf("\nargc = %d%9s", argc, "");
    for (i = 0; i < argc; ++i)
        printf("argv[%d] = %s\n%17s", i, argv[i], "");
    printf("\n");
}
```

The variable argc provides a count of the number of command line arguments. The array argv is an array of pointers to char, and can be thought of as an array of strings. Since the element argv[0] contains the name of the command itself, the value of argc is always 1 or more. Suppose that the above program is in the file *my_echo.c*. If we compile the program with the command

    cc my_echo.c

and then give the command *a.out*, the following is printed on the screen:

    argc = 1   argv[0] = a.out

Now suppose that we move *a.out* to *my_echo*, and then give the command

    my_echo abc: a is for apple and alphabet pie

The following is printed on the screen:

```
argc = 9          argv[0] = my_echo
                  argv[1] = abc:
                  argv[2] = a
                  argv[3] = is
                  argv[4] = for
                  argv[5] = apple
                  argv[6] = or
                  argv[7] = alphabet
                  argv[8] = pie
```

File names are often passed as arguments to main() (see Chapter 11).

7.13 RAGGED ARRAYS

We want to contrast a two-dimensional array of type char with a one-dimensional array of pointers to char. There are both similarities and differences between these two constructs.

```
main()
{
    static char    a[2][32] =
        {"abc:  ", "a  is for apple or alphabet pie"};
    static char    *p[2] =
        {"abc:  ", "a  is for apple or alphabet pie"};

    printf("\n%s%s\n%s%s\n", a[0], a[1], p[0], p[1]);
    printf("%c%c%c", a[0][0], a[0][1], a[0][2]);
    printf("%c%c%c", p[0][0], p[0][1], p[0][2]);
    printf("\n");
}
```

The output of this program is the following:

```
abc:   a   is for apple or alphabet pie
abc:   a   is for apple or alphabet pie
abcabc
```

The program and its output illustrate similarities in the two constructs. Let us consider the program in some detail.

The identifier a is a two-dimensional array, and its declaration causes space for 64 char's to be allocated. Its storage class is static so that the array can be initialized. (Automatic arrays cannot be initialized.) The two-dimensional initializer is equivalent to

```
{{'a', 'b', 'c', ':', ' ', ' ', '\0'}, {'a', . . . }}
```

The identifier a is an array, each of whose elements is an array of 32 char's. Thus a[0] and a[1] are arrays of 32 char's. Since arrays of characters are strings, a[0] and a[1] are strings. The array a[0] is initialized to

```
{'a', 'b', 'c', ':', ' ', ' ', '\0'}
```

and since only seven elements are specified, the rest are initialized to zero (the null character). Even though not all elements are used in this program, space for them has been allocated. The compiler uses a storage mapping function to access a[i][j]. Each access requires one multiply and one addition.

The identifier p is a one-dimensional array of pointers to char. Its declaration causes space for two pointers to be allocated (4 bytes for each pointer on a VAX). The element p[0] is initialized to point at "abc: " and this string requires space for 7 char's. The element p[1] is initialized to point at "a   is. . . " and this string requires space for 33 char's. This includes the null character \0 at the end of the string. Thus, p does its work in less space than a. Moreover, the compiler does not generate code for a storage mapping function to access p[i][j], which means that p does its work faster than a. Note that a[0][31] is a valid expression, but that p[0][31] is not. The expression p[0][31] overruns the bounds of the string pointed to by p[0].

An array of pointers whose elements are used to point to arrays of varying sizes is called a *ragged array*. Since in the above program the rows of p have different lengths, it is an example of a ragged array. If we think of the elements p[i][j] arranged as a "rectangular" collection of elements in rows and columns, the disparate row lengths give the "rectangle" a ragged look. Hence the name "ragged array."

7.14 SUMMARY

1. A pointer variable typically takes as values either NULL or addresses of other variables.

2. The address operator & and the indirection or dereferencing operator * are unary operators with the same precedence and "right to left" associativity as the other unary operators. If v is a variable, then the expression

       *&v   is equivalent to   v

3. Pointers are used as formal parameters in headers to function definitions to effect "call by reference." When addresses of variables are passed as arguments, they can be dereferenced in the function to pass values to the variables in the calling environment.

4. A declaration such as

   ```
   int    a[100];
   ```

   makes a an array of int's. The compiler allocates contiguous space in memory for 100 int's and numbers the elements of a from 0 to 99. The array name a is a constant pointer to the base address of the array. Elements of the array are accessed by expressions such as a[i] or *(a + i) where i is an int.

5. Arrays of any type can be created, including arrays of arrays. For example,

   ```
   double    b[30][50];
   ```

   declares b to be an array of "array of 50 double's"; the elements of b are accessed by expressions such as b[i][j]. The base address of the array is &b[0][0], not b.

6. When an array is passed as an argument to a function, a pointer is actually passed. In the header to a function definition the declaration

       int a[];   is equivalent to   int *a;

   In the header to a function definition the declaration of a multi-dimensional array must have all sizes specified except the first.

7. Strings are one-dimensional arrays of characters. By convention they are terminated with the null character \0, which acts as a sentinel.

8. The standard library contains many useful string handling functions. For example, strlen() returns the length of a string as an int.

9. Arguments to main() are typically called argc and argv. The value of argc is the number of command line arguments. It is also the size of argv, which is an array of pointers to char (strings). The elements of argv address the command line arguments.

10. Ragged arrays are constructed from arrays of pointers. The elements of the array can point to arrays with different sizes.

7.15 EXERCISES

1. If i is an int and p is a pointer to int, what gets printed?

```
i = 3;
p = &i;
printf("%d %d %d %d", p, *p + 7, **&p, p - (p - 2));
```

2. If i and j are int's and p and q are pointers to int, which of the following assignment expressions are illegal?

```
p = & i      p = &*&i      i = (int)p      q = &p
*q = &j      i = (*&)j      i = *&*&j       i = *p++ + *q
```

3. Write a program with the declaration

```
char    a, b, c, d, *p, *q, *r;
```

and print out the locations that are assigned to all these variables by your compiler.

4. What is printed and why?

```
#include    <stdio.h>

main()
{
        char    *pc = NULL;
        int     *pi = NULL;
        double  *pd = NULL;

        printf("\n%d  %d  %d\n%d  %d  %d\n\n",
            (int)(pc + 1), (int)(pi + 1), (int)(pd + 1),
            (int)(pc + 3), (int)(pi + 5), (int)(pd + 7));
}
```

5. The following array declarations have several errors. Identify each of them.

```
#define    SIZE    4

main()
{
        int    a[SIZE] = {0, 2, 2, 3, 4};
        int    b[SIZE - 5];
        int    c[3.0];
```

6. In the following program why does nothing happen when `f ()` is called?

```
main ()
{
    int    a[5], *p = a;

    printf ("\np has the value   %d", (int) p);
    f (a);
    p = a;
    printf ("\np  has the value   %d\n\n", (int) p);
}


f (a)
int    a[];
{
    int    i = 77777, *q = &i;

    a = q;       /*  a  is assigned the address of  i  */
}
```

7. What is wrong with the following program? Correct the program and explain the meaning of its output.

```
int    a[] = {5, 6, 7, 8, 9};

main ()
{
    int    a[5], *p = a + 3;

    printf ("\na[?]  = %d?\na[?+1]  = %d?\n\n", *p, *p + 1);
}
```

8. A real polynomial $p(x)$ of degree n or less is given by

$$p(x) = a_0 + a_1 x + a_2 x^2 + \cdots + a_n x^n$$

with the coefficients $a_0, a_1, \ldots, a_n$ representing real numbers. If $a_n \neq 0$ then the degree of $p(x)$ is n. Polynomials can be represented in a machine by an array such as

```
#define    N    5      /*  N  is the max degree  */

double     p[N + 1];
```

Write a function

```
eval (p, n, x)
double    p[], x;
int       n;           /*  n  is the max degree of  p  */
{
        .   .   .   .   .
```

that returns the value of the polynomial p evaluated at x. Write two versions of the function. The first version should be written from a straightforward naive approach. The second version should incorporate Horner's Rule. For polynomials of degree 5 Horner's Rule is expressed by writing

$$p(x) = a_0 + x(a_1 + x(a_2 + x(a_3 + x(a_4 + x(a_5)))))$$

How many additions and multiplications are used by each of your two versions of the eval () function?

9. Write a function that adds two polynomials of at most degree *n*.

```
add(f, g, h, n)
double    f[], g[], h[];      /*  f = g + h  */
int       n;        /*  n  is the max degree of f, g, and h  */
{
         .   .   .   .   .
```

10. Write an algorithm to multiply two polynomials of at most degree *n*. Use your function add () to sum intermediate results. This is not very efficient. Can you write a routine that is better?

11. Modify bubble () so that it terminates after the first pass in which no two elements are interchanged.

12. Modify mergesort () so that it can be used with an array of any size, not just with a size that is a power of two. Recall that any positive integer can be expressed as a sum of powers of two. For example,

$$27 = 16 + 8 + 2 + 1$$

Consider the array as a collection of subarrays of sizes that are powers of two. Sort the subarrays and then use merge () to produce the final sorted array.

13. Write a program that will test the relative efficiency of bubble () versus your mergesort () written in the previous problem. Generate test data by using a random number generator to fill arrays. Run your program on arrays of various sizes, say with 10, 100, 500, and 1000 elements. Plot the running time for each sort versus the size of the array. For large array sizes you should see the growth indicated by the formulas given in the text. For small array sizes there is too much overhead to detect this growth pattern.

14. A palindrome is a string that reads the same both forward and backward. Some examples are

    "ABCBA"   "123343321"   "otto"   "i am ma i"   "C"

Write a function that takes as a parameter a string and returns the int value 1 if the string is a palindrome and returns 0 otherwise.

15. Modify the palindrome function you wrote for exercise 14 so that blanks and capitals are ignored in the matching process. Under these rules the following are examples of palindromes:

    "Anna"   "A man a plan a canal Panama"   "ott o"

16. Take a foreign language dictionary and write down approximately 50 words and their translation. Use two arrays such as

    ```
    char    *foreign[50], *english[50];
    ```

    to translate from a foreign sentence to English.

17. A simple encryption scheme is to interchange letters of the alphabet on a one-to-one basis. This can be accomplished with a translation table for the 52 lower- and uppercase letters. Write a program that uses such a scheme to encode text. Write another program that will decode text that has been encoded. Do you know why this is a poor scheme? Learn about a more secure system and then program it. If UNIX is available to you, read the on-line manual concerning *crypt* to get the flavor of some of the concerns involved with encryption.

18. What gets printed?

    ```
    int    t[3][3] = {{2, 5, 7}, {0, -1, -2}, {7, 9, 3}};

    main ()
    {
         f(t);
    }

    f(a)
    int    (*a)[3];
    {
         printf("\n%d %d %d %d  . . .    infinity\n\n",
              a[1][0], -a[1][1], a[0][0], a[2][2]);
    }
    ```

19. In exercise 18 change the declaration in the header of the function definition of f() to

    ```
    int    (*a)[2];
    ```

    and leave the rest of the code alone. What gets printed and why? Find run-time errors in the code, if any. (It is a moot question whether there are run-time errors or not.)

20. Choose a character and use a two-dimensional array that matches the size of your screen to graph the functions sin() and cos() from 0 to 2π on your screen. Since on most screens the space in which a character is printed is not square, there is horizontal/vertical distortion. Experiment with your graphs to see if you can remove this distortion.

21. Write out a dissection for the following program. An understanding of the storage mapping function is needed to explain it. A complete explanation of the last `printf()` statement is rather technical and should be attempted only by advanced computer science students.

```
main()
{
    int    b[3][5], i, j, *p = *b;

    for (i = 0; i < 3; ++i)
        for (j = 0; j < 5; ++j)
            b[i][j] = i * 5 + j;
    for (i = 0; printf("\n"), i < 3; ++i)
        for (j = 0; j < 5; ++j)
            printf("%12d", b[i][j]);
    for (i = 0; i < 15; ++i) {
        if (i % 5 == 0)
            printf("\n");
        printf("%12d", *(p + i));
    }
    printf("\n\n%12d%12d\n%12d%12d\n%12d%12d\n%12d%12d",
        **b, **(b + 1),
        *(b[0] + 1), *(*b + 1),
        *(b[1] + 2), *(*(b + 1) + 2),
        *(b[2] + 3), *(*(b + 2) + 3));
    printf("\n\n%-11s%s%12d\n%-11s%s%12d\n%-11s%s%12d\n\n",
        "(int) b", "=", (int) b,
        "(int) *b", "=", (int) *b,
        "(int) **b", "=", (int) **b);
}
```

22. Modify the *sort_words* program so that tests are made to ensure that the work space w is not overrun. Your program should allow for some very long words but the current size of w should not be increased.

23. In UNIX, flags to commands are usually preceded by a minus sign and occur as the second argument on the command line. Modify the *my_echo* program so that it will print out its arguments in capital letters if the flag −c is present. Do not print out the argument that contains the flag.

24. If UNIX is available to you, read about the *echo* command in the on-line manual and then write your own program to accomplish the same thing.

25. Complete the following table.

Declarations and initializations

``char static *p[2][3] = {
    "abc", "defg", "hi",
    "jklmno", "pqrstuvw", "xyz"
};```

Expression	Equivalent expression	Value
***p	p[0][0][0]	'a'
**p[1]		
**(p[1] + 2)		
((p + 1) + 1)[7]		/* error */
(*(*(p + 1) + 1))[7]		
*(p[1][2] + 2)		

26. (Advanced) The following program has an error in it:

```
main()
{
    char    *strcat(), *p1 = "abc", *p2 = "pacific sea";

    printf("\n%s   %s   %s\n\n", p1, p2, strcat(p1, p2));
}
```

When the program runs on our system, it produces the following output:

```
abcpacific sea    acific sea    abcpacific sea
```

This output makes sense and tells us something about our compiler. Explain what is happening.

8

Recursion,
Functions as Arguments,
and the Preprocessor

The more advanced uses of functions are described in this chapter. Especially important is recursion, which occurs whenever a function invokes an instance of itself, either directly or indirectly. Some programming tasks are naturally solved with the use of recursion. Also described in this chapter is the mechanism used to pass functions as arguments. The chapter ends with a detailed discussion of the preprocessor, especially the #define macro facility. Macros can be used to generate in-line code in place of function calls.

8.1 RECURSION

A function is said to be recursive if it calls itself, either directly or indirectly. In C all functions can be used recursively. In its simplest form the idea of recursion is straightforward. Try the following program.

```
main()
{
      printf("   The universe is never ending!   ");
      main();
}
```

Another simple example of a recursive function is the following. It computes the sum of the first *n* positive integers.

```
sum(n)
int   n;
{
      if (n <= 1)
            return (n);
      else
            return (n + sum(n - 1));
}
```

The recursive function `sum()` is analyzed as illustrated in the following table. First the base case is considered. Then, working out from the base case, the other cases are considered.

Function call	Value returned
sum(1)	1
sum(2)	2 + sum(1) or 2 + 1
sum(3)	3 + sum(2) or 3 + 2 + 1
sum(4)	4 + sum(3) or 4 + 3 + 2 + 1
sum(5)	5 + sum(4) or 5 + 4 + 3 + 2 + 1

Simple recursive routines follow a standard template. Typically there is a base case (or cases) that is tested for upon entry to the function. Then there is a general recursive case in which one of the variables, often an integer, is passed as an argument in such a way as to ultimately lead to the base case. In `sum()` the variable n was reduced by 1 each time until the base case with n equal to 1 was reached. Let us write a few more recursive functions to practice this technique.

For a nonnegative integer n the factorial of n, written n !, is defined by

$$0! = 1$$
$$n! = n(n - 1)(n - 2) \cdots 3 \cdot 2 \cdot 1 \qquad \text{for} \qquad n > 0$$

An equivalent recursive definition is given by

$$0! = 1$$
$$n! = n((n - 1)!) \qquad \text{for} \qquad n > 0$$

Let us put this recursive definition into code.

```
factorial(n)        /*  recursive version  */
int    n;
{
    if (n <= 1)
        return (1);
    else
        return (n * factorial(n - 1));
}
```

As in `sum()`, when the integer n is passed to `factorial()`, the recursion activates n nested copies of the function before returning level by level to the original call. This means that n function calls are used in the computation. Most simple recursive functions can be easily rewritten as iterative functions.

```
factorial(n)        /*  iterative version  */
int    n;
{
    int    product;

    for (product = 1; n > 1;  --n)
        product *= n;
    return (product);
}
```

For a given nonnegative input value, both factorial functions return the same value, but the iterative version requires only one function call regardless of the value passed in.

The next example illustrates a recursive function that manipulates characters. It can easily be rewritten as an equivalent iterative function. We leave this as an exercise.

```
/*** reverse the characters between s[j] and s[k] recursively ***/

reverse(s, j, k)
char    *s;
int     j, k;
{
     if (j < k) {
          swap(&s[j], &s[k]);
          reverse(s, ++j, --k);
     }
}


swap(p, q)
char    *p, *q;
{
     char    temp;

     temp = *p;
     *p = *q;
     *q = temp;
}
```

Efficiency Considerations

Many algorithms have an equivalent iterative and recursive formulation. Typically, recursion is more elegant and requires fewer variables to make the same calculation. Recursion takes care of its bookkeeping by stacking for each invocation the relevant arguments. This stacking of arguments, while invisible to the user, is still costly in time and space. On a VAX, a simple recursive call with one integer argument can require eight 32-bit words on the stack. Let us discuss the effect of this with respect to the calculation of the Fibonacci sequence.

The sequence of Fibonacci numbers is defined recursively as

$$x_0 = 0 \,,$$
$$x_1 = 1 \,,$$
$$x_{j+1} = x_j + x_{j-1} \quad \text{for} \quad j = 1, 2, \ldots$$

Except for x_0 and x_1, every element in the sequence is the sum of the previous two elements. The sequence begins 0, 1, 1, 2, 3, 5, ... A program to compute this sequence iteratively was given in Chapter 4. Here is a function that computes Fibonacci numbers recursively:

```
fibonacci (n)
int    n;
{
    if  (n <= 1)
        return  (n);
    else
        return  (fibonacci (n - 1) + fibonacci (n - 2));
}
```

As the following table shows, the number of function calls required to compute fibonacci (n) for even moderate values of n is considerable.

Value of n	Value of fibonacci (n)	Number of function calls required to recursively compute fibonacci (n)
0	0	1
1	1	1
2	1	3
3	2	5
4	3	9
5	5	15
6	8	25
7	13	41
8	21	67
9	34	109
. . .	. . .	. . .
23	28657	92735
24	46368	150049
25	75025	242785
. . .	. . .	. . .
41	165580141	535828591
42	267914296	866988873
43	433494437	1402817465

While it is seductive to use recursion, one must be careful about run-time limitations and inefficiencies. It is sometimes necessary to recode a recursion as an equivalent iteration.

Some programmers feel that because the use of recursion is inefficient, it should not be used. However, for some applications recursive code is easy to write, understand, and maintain. These reasons often prescribe the use of recursion. In the examples that follow we use recursion in those situations where it is the natural organizing principle.

8.2 AN EXAMPLE: QUICKSORT

Quicksort was created by C. Anthony R. Hoare and described in his 1962 paper "Quicksort" *(Computer Journal, Vol. 5, No. 1)*. Of all the various sorting techniques, quicksort is perhaps the most widely used internal sort. An internal sort is one in which all the data to be sorted fits entirely within main memory.

Let us suppose that we want to sort an array of integers of size n. If the values of the elements are randomly distributed, then on average the number of comparisons done by quicksort is proportional to $n \log n$. However, in the worst case, the number of comparisons is proportional to n^2. This is a disadvantage of quicksort. There are other sorts, mergesort for example, which, even in the worst case, do work proportional to $n \log n$. However, of all the $n \log n$ sorting methods known, quicksort is, on average, the fastest by a constant factor. Another advantage of quicksort is that it does its work in place. No additional work space is needed.

Quicksort is usually implemented recursively. The underlying idea is to "divide and conquer." Given an array a[] of integers, we choose one of its elements to be the "pivot element." We then rearrange the array so that the first part consists of elements whose values are all less than the pivot and the remaining part consists of elements whose values are all greater than or equal to the pivot. This is accomplished by the function partition(). In addition, partition() returns the size of the first part of the rearranged array. We call this the "partition break size." Once the array has been rearranged with respect to the pivot, we invoke quicksort() on each subarray.

```
quicksort(a, n)
int    a[], n;       /* n  is the size of a[]  */
{
      int    k, pivot;       /* k  is the partition break size  */

      if (find_pivot(a, n, &pivot) != 0) {
            k = partition(a, n, pivot);
            quicksort(a, k);
            quicksort(a + k, n - k);
      }
}
```

Ideally, the pivot should be chosen so that at each step the array is partitioned into two parts, each with an equal (or nearly equal) number of elements. This would minimize the total amount of work performed by quicksort(). Since we do not know a priori what this value should be, we select for the pivot the first value that will provide a partition. Assuming that the values of the array elements are randomly distributed, this is equivalent to choosing the value of pivot randomly.

```
find_pivot(a, n, pivot_ptr)    /* find the pivot, if there is one */
int   a[], n, *pivot_ptr;      /* n is the size of a[] */
{
       int   i;

       for (i = 1; i < n; ++i)
            if (a[0] != a[i]) {
                *pivot_ptr = (a[0] > a[i]) ? a[0] : a[i];
                return (1);
            }
       return (0);       /* all elements have the same value */
}
```

We successively compare elements to a[0], searching for two distinct values among the elements of the array and assigning the larger value to be the pivot. This guarantees that when partition() is invoked, each part will contain at least one element. If the values of all the array elements are identical, there is no pivot and the array is already in order.

The major work is done by partition(). We will explain in detail how this function works.

```
/***  partition a[] with respect to pivot  ***/

partition(a, n, pivot)
int   a[], n, pivot;       /*  n  is the size of a[]  */
{
       int   i = 0, j = n - 1;

       while (i <= j) {
            while (a[i] < pivot)
                 ++i;
            while (a[j] >= pivot)
                 --j;
            if (i < j)
                 swap(&a[i++], &a[j--]);
       }
       return (i);       /*  partition break size  */
}
```

Suppose that n has value 12 and that a[] is an array of size 12, with its elements having the values

4	7	9	5	2	5	9	2	1	9	-5	-3

When find_pivot(a, n, &pivot_ptr) is invoked, a[0] and a[1] are compared and found to be different. The value 7, the larger of 4 and 7, is assigned to pivot. Now partition(a, n, pivot) is called.

DISSECTION OF partition(a, n, pivot)

```
partition(a, n, pivot)
int    a[], n, pivot;       /*  n  is the size of a[]  */
{
```

```
        int    i = 0, j = n - 1;
```

We think of the index i as starting on the left and the index j as starting on the right.

```
while (i <= j) {
        while (a[i] < pivot)
              ++i;
        while (a[j] >= pivot)
              --j;
        if (i < j)
              swap(&a[i++], &a[j--]);
}
```

This loop will continue to be executed until i is one more than j. In the following table we show how the data looks after each pass of the outer while loop; the elements that were swapped in that pass are boxed.

unordered data:	4	7	9	5	2	5	9	2	1	9	−5	−3
first pass:	4	−3	9	5	2	5	9	2	1	9	−5	7
second pass:	4	−3	−5	5	2	5	9	2	1	9	9	7
third pass:	4	−3	−5	5	2	5	1	2	9	9	9	7
fourth pass:	4	−3	−5	5	2	5	1	2	9	9	9	7

When the loop exits, i has value 8, which corresponds to the 9th element of the array.

```
return (i); /* partition break size */
```

The value 8 is returned. This means that the first 8 elements of the rearranged, or partitioned, array have values less than pivot, or 7, and the remainder of the elements have values greater than or equal to pivot.

When quicksort() is invoked on arrays with randomly distributed elements, it does its work efficiently. Surprisingly, if an array is already in order, either ascending or descending, quicksort() is very inefficient. In these cases, if the array has size n, the amount of work done is proportional to n^2. The reason is that the pivot chosen at each step gives rise to an inefficient partition break size. We want to rewrite find_ pivot() so that quicksort() will work efficiently, even on arrays that are in order, or that are largely in order. The idea is to compare the first, middle, and last elements of the array, and from these three values choose the middle value to be the pivot. This improves the likelihood that the chosen pivot will break the array into subarrays with nearly equal sizes.

```
find_pivot(a, n, pivot_ptr)   /* find the pivot, if there is one */
int    a[], n, *pivot_ptr;    /* n is the size of a[] */
{
    int    b[3], i;

    if (n > 3) {       /* a carefully chosen inequality */
        b[0] = a[0];
        b[1] = a[n/2];
        b[2] = a[n-1];
        quicksort(b, 3);
        if (b[0] != b[2]) {
            *pivot_ptr = (b[0] < b[1]) ? b[1] : b[2];
            return (1);
        }
    }
    for (i = 1; i < n; ++i)
        if (a[0] != a[i]) {
            *pivot_ptr = (a[0] > a[i]) ? a[0] : a[i];
            return (1);
        }
    return (0);        /* all elements have the same value */
}
```

Notice that `find_pivot()` is now a recursive function. It invokes itself indirectly through the call to `quicksort()`. More efficient is a series of `if-else` statements used to directly reorder the elements of an array of size 3. We leave this as an exercise.

8.3 AN EXAMPLE: FINDING THE *k*TH RANK ORDER ELEMENT

If we want to find the *k*th rank order element of an array, we could first sort it and then find the value of its *k*th element. However, this is overkill. The following code, which makes use of `partition()` and `find_pivot()` written above, is much more efficient:

```
/*** find the kth rank order element in a[]  ***/

rank_order(a, n, k)
int   a[], n;      /* n is the size of a[]  */
int   k;           /* k  must satisfy  1 <= k  and  k <= n  */
{
      int   pivot, b;     /* b  is the partition break size  */

      if (find_pivot(a, n, &pivot) != 0) {
          b = partition(a, n, pivot);
          if (b == k - 1)
              return (pivot);
          else if (b > k - 1)
              return (rank_order(a, b, k));
          else if (b < k - 1)
              return (rank_order(a + b, n - b, k - b));
      }
      return (a[0]);     /* all elements are the same  */
}
```

As an example, suppose that we create an array with randomly distributed integers, and then find the median value.

```
#define   N   1000

main()
{
      int   a[N], i;

      for (i = 0; i < N; ++i)
          a[i] = rand();
      printf("\nthe median of  %d  random numbers is  %d\n\n",
          N, rank_order(a, N, (N + 1)/2));
}
```

The output of this program is system dependent. On our system it is

```
the median of  1000  random numbers is  1113125436
```

Since rand() on our system generates integers between 0 and $2^{31} - 1$, we expect the median value to be in the neighborhood of 2^{30}, and it is.

8.4 FUNCTIONS AS ARGUMENTS

Since all functions have external scope and are at the same level, one cannot be defined within another. However, C allows pointers to functions, which can then be passed as arguments.

Suppose that we want to compute

$$\sum_{k=m}^{n} f^{2}(k)$$

for a variety of functions f. For example, in one instance f might be the sin function and in another f might be given by

$$f(k) = \frac{1}{k}$$

Here is a routine that can be used to accomplish the task.

```
double sum_square(f, m, n)
double    (*f) (), m, n;
{
    double    k, sum = 0.0;

    for (k = m; k <= n; ++k)
        sum += (*f) (k) * (*f) (k);
    return (sum);
}
```

The declaration

```
double    (*f) ();
```

tells the compiler that f is a pointer to a function, which returns a double. The parentheses are necessary because () binds tighter than *. In contrast

```
double    *g ();
```

would declare the identifier g to be a function that returns a pointer to double. In the body of the function definition we think of

f	the pointer to a function
*f	the function itself
(*f) (k)	the call to the function

To illustrate the use of sum_square (), we next write f () and main ().

```
double f (x)
double    x;
{
    return (1.0 / x);
}

main ()
{
    double    f (), sin (), sum_square ();

    printf ("\n%. 7f    %. 7f \n\n",
        sum_square (f, 1.0, 10000.0), sum_square (sin, 0.0, 7.0));
}
```

The output of this program is

```
1.6448341    3.5568003
```

Mathematically the sum of $1/k^2$ from 1 to infinity is $\pi^2/6$, and the first number in the output of the program approximates this.

8.5 AN EXAMPLE: USING BISECTION TO FIND THE ROOT OF A FUNCTION

An important problem that arises in engineering, mathematics, and other disciplines is to find the root of a given real valued function. A real number x that satisfies the equation $f(x) = 0$ is called a root of f. In simple cases, for example if f is a quadratic

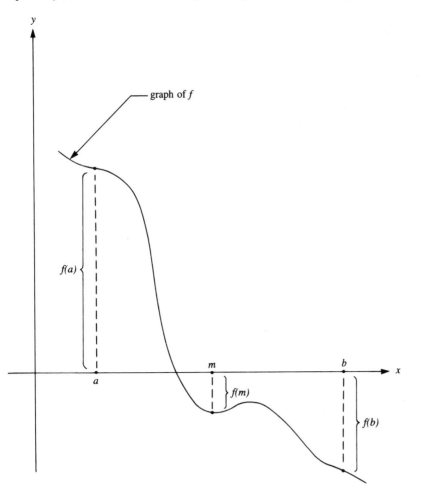

polynomial, a formula for the roots is known. However, in general there is no formula and a root must be found by numerical methods.

Suppose that *f* is a real valued function and is continuous on the interval [*a, b*]. If *f(a)* and *f(b)* are of opposite sign, then the continuity of the function guarantees that it has a root in the interval [*a, b*].

Notice that the condition that *f(a)* and *f(b)* have opposite sign is equivalent to the product *f(a) f(b)* being negative. The method of bisection proceeds as follows. Let *m* be the midpoint of the interval. If *f(m)* is zero, we have found a root. If not, then either *f(a)* and *f(m)* are of opposite sign or *f(m)* and *f(b)* are of opposite sign. Suppose that the first case holds. We then know that *f* has a root in the interval [*a, m*], and we now start the process over again. After each iteration we obtain an interval that is half the length of the previous interval. When the interval is sufficiently small, we take its midpoint as an approximation to a root of *f*. In general, we cannot hope to find the exact root. For most functions the precise mathematical root will not have an exact machine representation.

```
/***   find a root of f() by bisection   ***/

double root(f, a, b, eps)
double    (*f)();
double    a, b;        /*  find a root in the interval [a, b]  */
double    eps;         /*  epsilon:  the desired precision  */
{
    double    m;

    m = (a + b) / 2.0;    /*  midpoint of the interval [a, b]  */
    if (f(m) == 0.0 || b - a < eps)
        return (m);
    else if ((*f)(a) * (*f)(m) < 0.0)
        return (root(f, a, m, eps));
    else
        return (root(f, m, b, eps));
}
```

As a test we write the code for a fifth-degree polynomial p() and then write main() to invoke root().

```
double p(x)
double    x;
{
    return (x * x * x * x * x  +  x  +  3.0);
}

main()
{
    double    p(), root(), x;

    x = root(p, -2.0, 0.0, 1e-7);
    printf("\n%17s%25.16f\n%17s%25.16f\n\n",
        "approximate root:", x, "function value:", p(x));
}
```

The output of the program is

```
approximate root:      -1.1329975426197052
 function value:        0.0000002149536893
```

The Kepler Equation

In the early 1600s Johannes Kepler wanted to solve the equation

$$m = x - e \sin x$$

for various values of the parameters m and e. One way to view the problem is to graph

$$y = x \qquad \text{and} \qquad y = m + e \sin x$$

together. A solution to the Kepler equation then corresponds to the point where the two graphs intersect.

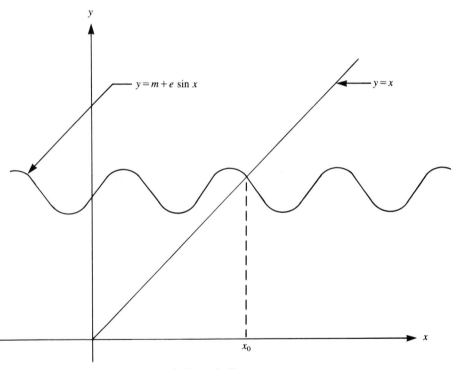

A solution to the Kepler equation

Let us solve the problem with *m* = 2.2 and *e* = 0.5.

```
#define    M      2.2
#define    E      0.5

double kepler(x)
double    x;
{
    double    sin();

    return (M  -  x  +  E * sin(x));
}

main()
{
    double    kepler(), root(), x;

    x = root(kepler, 0.0, 7.0, 1e-12);
    printf("\n%17s%25.16f\n%17s%25.16f\n\n",
        "approximate root:", x, "function value:", kepler(x));
}
```

Here is the output of this program.

```
approximate root:        2.4994545281637670
    function value:       -0.0000000000003729
```

8.6 THE PREPROCESSOR

The C language relies to a great degree on the preprocessor to extend its power and notation. Lines that begin with a # in column 1 are called *control lines*, and these lines communicate with the preprocessor. The syntax for control lines is independent of the rest of the C language. A control line has an effect that continues from its place in a file until the end of that file.

A control line of the form

```
#include "filename"
```

causes the preprocessor to replace the line with a copy of the contents of the named file. A search for the file is made first in the current directory and then in standard places. With a control line of the form

```
#include <filename>
```

the preprocessor looks for the file only in the standard places and not in the current directory. There is no restriction on what an included file can contain. In particular, it can contain other control lines, which will be expanded by the preprocessor in turn.

Control lines with #define occur in two forms:

#define *identifier token_string*_{opt}
#define *identifier* (*identifier,* . . . , *identifier*) *token_string*_{opt}

A long definition of either form can be continued to the next line by placing a \ at the end of the current line. If a simple #define of the first form occurs in a file, the processor replaces every occurrence of *identifier* by *token_string* in the remainder of the file, except in quoted strings. Consider the example

```
#define    SECONDS_PER_DAY    (60 * 60 * 24)
```

In this example the token string is (60 * 60 * 24) and the preprocessor will replace every occurrence of SECONDS_PER_DAY by that string in the remainder of the file. A common mistake is to end a #define line with a semicolon, making it part of the replacement string when it is not wanted.

There are many important uses of simple #define's that improve program clarity and portability. For example, if special constants such as π or e or the speed of light c are used in a program, they should be defined:

```
#define    PI    3.14159
#define    E     2.71828          /*  base for natural logarithms  */
#define    C     299792.4562      /*  speed of light in km/sec  */
```

Other special constants that are often used in programs are also best coded as symbolic constants:

```
#define    EOF      (-1)          /*  typical end of file value  */
#define    TRUE     1
#define    FALSE    0
#define    MAXINT   2147483647    /*  largest 4-byte integer  */
```

Program limits that are programmer decisions can also be specified symbolically:

```
#define    ITERS    50            /*  number of iterations  */
#define    SIZE     250           /*  array size  */
#define    EPS      1.0e-9        /*  a numerical limit  */
```

In general, symbolic constants aid documentation by replacing what might otherwise be a mysterious constant with a mnemonic identifier. They aid portability by allowing constants that may be system dependent to be altered once. They aid reliability by restricting to one place the check on the actual representation of the constant.

Suppose that the file *program.c* has preprocessor control lines in it. The UNIX command

cc −E program.c

causes the preprocessor to expand *program.c* and print on the screen. No compilation takes place. This allows the programmer to check the results of the preprocessor. It is always helpful to keep in mind that the preprocessor does not "know C."

By convention, capital letters are used for the identifiers in simple #define's. Although any identifier can be used, the use of capitals allows the reader of a program to readily identify text that will be expanded by the preprocessor.

Syntactic Sugar

It is possible to alter the syntax of C toward some user preference. A frequent programming error is to use the token = in place of the token == in logical expressions. A programmer could use

```
#define   EQ    ==
```

to defend against such a mistake. This superficial alteration of the programming syntax is called syntactic sugar. Another example of this is to change the while statement by introducing "do," which is an ALGOL-style construction.

```
#define   do   /*  blank  */
```

With these two #define lines at the top of the file, the code

```
while (i EQ 1) do
{
        .   .   .   .          /*  do something  */
```

after the preprocessor pass will become

```
while (i == 1)
{
        .   .   .   .   .
```

One must keep in mind that since do will disappear from anywhere in the file, the do-while statement cannot be used.

There are two rules that one must keep in mind when using a simple #define. The first is that text inside a string or character constant does not get replaced by the preprocessor. The second is that the identifier in a #define with a nonempty replacement string gets expanded with implied space around it. This means that some syntax in C cannot be redefined through the #define mechanism. Suppose that we have the following lines at the beginning of a file:

```
#define   BLANK
#define   SLASH        /
#define   ASTERISK   *
```

Since the preprocessor does not make changes in quoted strings, a string such as "alphabetBLANKpie" will be left unchanged, but the sequence

"alphabet"BLANK"pie"   will be expanded to   "alphabet""pie"

However, the phrase SLASH ASTERISK becomes / * rather than /*. This observation is further discussed in the exercises.

The Use of Macros with Arguments

We now want to consider control lines of the form

> #define   *identifier* (*identifier* , . . . , *identifier*) *token_string*$_{opt}$

These are macro definitions with parameters. There can be no space between the first identifier and the left parenthesis, and zero or more identifiers can occur in the parameter list. A simple example of a macro definition with a parameter is

> #define   SQ(x)   ((x) * (x))

The identifier x in the #define is a parameter that is substituted for in later text. The substitution is one of string replacement without consideration of syntactic correctness. For example,

> SQ(7 + w)   expands to   ((7 + w) * (7 + w))

and

> SQ(SQ(*p))   expands to   (((((*p) * (*p))) * (((*p) * (*p)))))

The seemingly extravagant use of parentheses is to protect against the macro expanding an expression that would then lead to an unanticipated order of evaluation. Suppose instead we had defined the macro as

> #define   SQ(x)   x * x

With this definition

> SQ(a + b)   expands to   a + b * a + b

which, because of operator precedence, is not the same as

> ((a + b) * (a + b))

Now suppose that we had defined the macro as

> #define   SQ(x)   (x) * (x)

With this definition

> 4 / SQ(2)   expands to   4 / (2) * (2)

which, because of operator precedence, is not the same as

> 4 / ((2) * (2))

Finally, let us suppose that we had defined the macro as

> #define   SQ (x)   ((x) * (x))

With this definition

> SQ(7)   expands to   (x)   ((x) * (x)) (7)

which is not even close to what was intended. In a macro definition with parameters, there can be no space between the first identifier and the following left parenthesis.

Macros are frequently used to replace function calls by in-line code, which is more efficient. For example, a macro `MIN()` could be used in a program instead of a function `min()`, where the macro definition is given by

```
#define   MIN(x, y)    (((x) < (y)) ? (x) : (y))
```

After this definition an expression such as

```
m = MIN(u, v)
```

gets expanded by the preprocessor to

```
m = (((u) < (v)) ? (u) : (v))
```

The arguments of `MIN()` can be arbitrary expressions of compatible type.

A macro can be defined using another macro. A simple example is

```
#define   SQ(x)      ((x) * (x))
#define   CUBE(x)    (SQ(x) * (x))
#define   FIFTH(x)   (CUBE(x) * SQ(x))
```

The preprocessor expands each `#define` identifier until no more appear in the text. Indeed, the preprocessor can get stuck in an infinite loop by a control line such as

```
#define   ENDLESS   ENDLESS stop me
```

This macro would be continuously expanded into the string `stop me stop me stop me . . .` until the exhaustion of some system resource. Our reference compiler can detect this form of macro recursion and issue an error message.

A control line of the form

```
#undef    identifier
```

will undefine a macro. It causes the previous definition of a macro to be forgotten. In most applications this is not used.

Conditional Compilation

Control lines of the form

```
#if       restricted_constant_expression
#ifdef    identifier
#ifndef   identifier
```

initiate conditional compilation of following text until the control line

```
#endif
```

is reached. A restricted constant expression may not contain `sizeof`, casts, or an enumeration constant. It is tested for being nonzero. After `#ifdef`, the named identifier must be currently defined by an active `#define`. After `#ifndef`, the named identifier must be currently undefined. So, writing

```
#define   DEBUG   1

#if   DEBUG
printf("debug:  x  is  %d\n", x);
#endif
```

will compile the `printf()` statement. We could place such lines throughout the program and trace the values of the variable x. When the token string following DEBUG is changed to 0, these `printf()` statements will be omitted from compilation.

Just as C has an `if-else` statement, so does the preprocessor. Each of the three forms of `#if` can be followed by any number of lines, possibly containing control lines of the form

    #elif   *restricted_constant_expression*

possibly followed by the control line

    #else

and finally followed by the control line

    #endif

The flow of control for conditional compilation is analogous to that of the `if-else` statement in C. Here is an example:

```
#define   FIRST

#ifdef    FIRST
f(a, b, c)      /* first version */
{
      .  .   .   .   .
}
#else
f(a, b, c)      /* second version */
{
      .  .   .   .   .
}
#endif
```

Making compilation conditional on whether certain identifiers are defined or undefined, or whether a constant is zero or nonzero can be useful in a debugging and testing phase of the program development cycle. Debugging statements can be turned on or off based on a single `#define`. Also, alternative pieces of code can be compiled and used based on different requirements.

On our reference UNIX system it is possible to set `#define`'s or `#undef`'s as part of the *cc* command line. The flag −*D* is used to set `#define`'s. Thus the command line

    cc −DFIRST program.c

will compile the file *program.c* with FIRST defined. Likewise, *−UFIRST* is equivalent to placing the control line `#undef FIRST` at the top of the file.

Line Numbers

The compiler maintains a source text line number for use in error and warning messages. This number is usually incremented for each line of text. A control line of the form

    #line   *constant*   *"filename"*

causes the line number to become the specified constant. If a file name is given, this file name will be used, instead of the actual file name, in messages to the user.

8.7 AN EXAMPLE: THE USE OF `qsort()`

In some C systems the function `qsort()` is provided in the standard library. We want to write a program that will illustrate how `qsort()` might be used, and in so doing we will make use of a macro with arguments. In addition, our program will illustrate once again how functions can be passed as arguments.

The on-line manual of our UNIX system describes the function `qsort()` as "an implementation of the quicker-sort algorithm," but gives no details concerning the algorithm. The header to the function definition is described as

```
qsort(base, nel, width, compar)
char    *base;
int     nel, width, (*compar)();
```

When this function is called, the first argument is a pointer to the base of the data, the second argument is the number of elements to be sorted, the third argument is the number of bytes in an element, and the fourth argument is the name of the comparison function to be used. The comparison function is to be called with two arguments that are pointers to the elements that are being compared. It must return an `int` value that is less than, equal to, or greater than zero, depending on whether the first argument is to be considered less than, equal to, or greater than the second argument. Here are the two comparison functions we will use.

```
lexico(p, q)
char    *p, *q;
{
    return (*p - *q);
}


compare_decimal_part(p, q)
double    *p, *q;
{
    double    x;

    x = (*p - (int) *p)  -  (*q - (int) *q);
    return ((x == 0.0) ? 0 : (x < 0.0) ? -1 : 1);
}
```

For the purpose of our test we will create two arrays with randomly distributed elements: an array of characters and an array of floating point numbers. We will then invoke qsort() to put the arrays in desired order.

```
#define    M    30
#define    N    10

#define    PRN(a, lim, cntrl)    printf("\n");                    \
                                 for (i = 0; i < lim; ++i)        \
                                     printf(cntrl, a[i])

main()
{
        int      i, lexico(), compare_decimal_part();
        char     a[M];
        double   b[N];

        for (i = 0; i < M; ++i)                /*  fill a[] and b[]  */
            a[i] = rand() % 26 + 'a';
        for (i = 0; i < N; ++i)
            b[i] = (rand() % 100) / 10.0;
        PRN(a, M, "%2c");
        PRN(b, N, "%6.1f");
        qsort(a, M, 1, lexico);                /*  sort a[] and b[]  */
        qsort((char *) b, N, sizeof(double), compare_decimal_part);
        PRN(a, M, "%2c");
        PRN(b, N, "%6.1f");
        printf("\n\n");
}
```

Notice that the cast (char *) was used to prevent a warning from *lint*. Here is the output of the program:

```
w f a z y z a z o h s n g h c x s f u b s n s n w f u j e l
  5.2   8.1   2.2   1.5   4.0   8.5   2.2   7.9   0.4   6.5
a a b c e f f f g h h j l n n n o s s s s u u w w x y z z z
  4.0   8.1   5.2   2.2   2.2   0.4   1.5   8.5   6.5   7.9
```

8.8 SUMMARY

1. A function is said to be recursive if it calls itself, either directly or indirectly. Recursion is an advanced form of flow of control.

2. Recursion typically consists of a base case or cases and a general case. It is important to make sure that the function will terminate.

3. Any recursive function can be written in an equivalent iterative form. Due to system overhead in calling functions, a recursive function may be less efficient than an equivalent iterative one. However, the difference is often very slight. When a

recursive function is easier to code and maintain than an equivalent iterative one, and the penalty for using it is slight, the recursive form is preferable.

4. To pass a function as an argument, one declares it as pointer to function in the parameter declaration list. Within the body of the function definition it is invoked using the dereferencing operator, as in the example `(*f)()`.

5. The preprocessor provides facilities for file inclusion and macros. Files may be included with source text passed to the compiler by use of control lines of the form

```
#include    "filename"
#include    <filename>
```

6. A `#define` control line can be used to give a symbolic name to a token string. The preprocessor substitutes the string for the symbolic name in the source text before compilation.

7. The use of the `#define` facility to define symbolic constants enhances program readability and portability.

8. The preprocessor provides a general macro facility with argument substitution. A macro with parameters is defined by a control line of the form

$$\#define \quad identifier(\ identifier, \ . \ . \ . \ , \quad identifier \ ) \quad token\_string_{opt}$$

For example,

```
#define    SWAP(x, y)    {int t; t = x; x = y; y = t;}
```

allows for in-line code to perform the swap of two values. It is not a function call.

9. The preprocessor provides for conditional compilation to aid in program testing. To make use of this facility, one can use control lines beginning with `#if`, `#ifdef`, `#ifndef`, `#elif`, `#else`, and `#endif`.

8.9 EXERCISES

1. Rewrite "The universe is never ending!" recursion so that it terminates after seven calls. The program should consist of a single `main()` function that calls itself recursively.

2. Try the following program. If it gives wrong values on your system, explain why.

```
factorial(n)      /*  wrong  */
int   n;
{
    if (n == 0 || n == 1)
        return (1);
    else
        return (n * factorial(--n));
}
```

3. A function that calls another function, which, in turn, calls the original function, is sometimes called *corecursive*. Write a program that counts the number of alphabetic characters in a string and sums the digits in the string. For example, the string `"A0is444apple7"` has eight alphabetic characters, and the digits in the string sum to 19. Write a corecursive function `count_alph()` to count the alphabetic characters. Make it call a second function `sum_digit()` for summing the digits. *Hint:* if necessary use `static` variables.

4. Write a recursive function that, when passed two vectors, returns their scalar product. Use arrays of type `double`.

5. Write a recursive function that returns the length of a string.

6. Write a recursive function that copies a string.

7. Write a recursive function that tests whether a string is a palindrome. A palindrome is a string like `"abcba"` that reads the same in both directions.

8. Write a function `graph_it()` that plots a function passed as an argument on your screen. Since the space in which a character is printed usually is not square, there is vertical/horizontal distortion. Try to compensate for this.

9. Suppose in a program that x, y, and z have the values 1.1, 2.2, and 3.3, respectively. The statement

```
PRN3 (x, y, z);
```

should cause the line

```
x has value 1.1 and y has value 2.2 and z has value 3.3
```

to be printed. Write the macro definition for PRN3 ().

10. Suppose we have

In file a_b_c.h:

```
#define    TRUE    1
#define    A_B_C   main()    \
                   {printf("\nA Big Cheery  \"hello\"\n\n");}
```

In file a_b_c.c:

```
#if        TRUE
#include   "a_b_c.h"
A_B_C
#endif
```

When we give the command

cc a_b_c.c

the compiler complains. Why? Can you permute the lines in one of the files so that the program compiles and runs?

11. A comment in ALGOL starts with the token `comment` and ends with a ";". Try to use preprocessor control lines in a C program so that lines such as

```
comment    all golly gosh - trouble!    ;
```

become comments.

12. Compare `quicksort()` with `mergesort()` (see Chapter 7). Time both functions, using arrays with 10, 100, and 1000 elements. For a small amount of data, run-time overhead dominates. That is, setting up the functions, initializing values, and other miscellaneous steps dominate the actual work required to perform the sorting.

13. Defines are not always as safe as functions, even when all the arguments are enclosed in parentheses. Define a macro `MAX(x, y, z)`, which produces a value corresponding to the largest of its three arguments. Construct some expressions to use in `MAX()` that produce unanticipated results.

14. The definite integral of a continuous real valued function f defined on an interval $[a, b]$ can be approximated by Riemann sums. For a given positive integer n, partition the interval into n subintervals each of length h, where h is defined as $(b - a) / n$. A Riemann sum is given by

$$\sum_{i=0}^{n-1} hf(a + h\,i)$$

Each summand $h\,f(a + h\,i)$ can be viewed geometrically as the signed area of a rectangle where h is the base of the rectangle and $f(a + h\,i)$ is its height. As n gets large, or equivalently, as h gets small, the Riemann sum tends to the definite integral of f on the interval $[a, b]$. First write a function `riemann()` to carry out the above computation in a straightforward way. Use the following header in the function definition.

```
double riemann (f, a, b, n)
double    (*f) ();
double    a, b;        /* integrate f() from a to b */
int       n;           /* n is the number of partitions */
```

Test your function by numerically integrating $\sin x$ from 0 to 2π and the polynomial x^2 from 0 to 2.

Now write a recursive function `r_riemann()` to carry out a related computation. Use the following header in the function definition:

```
double r_riemann (f, a, b, eps)
double    (*f) ();
double    a, b;        /* integrate f() from a to b */
double    eps;         /* a small number such as 1.0e-7 */
```

If the values of riemann(f, a, b, 1) and riemann(f, a, b, 2) differ by less than eps, then r_riemann() will return the average of the two values. If not, return the following sum:

```
r_riemann(f, a, (a + b) / 2.0, eps)   +
    r_riemann(f, (a + b) / 2.0, b, eps)
```

Compare the results of r_riemann() with those obtained from riemann().

15. For low values of n verify by hand that the number of calls needed to recursively compute fibonacci(n) are correct as given in this chapter.

16. Run the following program on your system where fibonacci() is the recursive version presented in this chapter:

```
#define   N   26

main()
{
      int   n;

      for (n = 0; n < N; ++n)
            printf("\n%12d", fibonacci(n));
}
```

No matter how fast a machine you are running this program on, you will see that it slows down as the computation progresses. Time the execution of this program, and do not try this experiment for larger values of N. Suppose that you have a machine with unlimited memory and that each function call takes 20 microseconds. For what value of N (approximately) will it require more than a century for the above program to run to completion?

17. Write an iterative version of the string reversal function.

18. Write a version of partition() that prints out the values of the original array and the values of the array after each pass of the outer while loop. The elements that were swapped in that pass should be distinguished by printing the numbers in quotes.

19. Use a random number generator to fill an array of size 100. Invoke find_pivot() and partition() to find the partition break size for the array. Do this repeatedly, say 100 times, and keep track of the running average of the break size. One expects that the average break size should correspond to the middle of the array. Does this seem to be true from your experimentation?

20. The optimal break size for an array of size n is $n/2$. This identifies two subarrays of equal size, or nearly so, for further processing. For example, given an array of size 100, a break size of 50 is optimal. Notice that a break size of 49 identifies subarrays of sizes 49 and 51, and that a break size of 51 identifies subarrays of sizes 51 and 49. Thus, the break sizes 49 and 51 are both of equal merit. Modify

your program in exercise 19 so that you keep track of the running average of the absolute value of the difference $k - 50$, where k is the break size returned by `partition()`. This number corresponds inversely to how good the break size is. More generally, define

$$m = \frac{|k - (n/2)|}{n}$$

where k is the partition break size returned by `partition()` acting on an array of size n. Fill arrays randomly and run some machine experiments to see what, if anything, can be said about m.

21. Suppose that `a[]` is an array of integers of size 100, and that for each `i` the element `a[i]` has value `i`. If `quicksort(a, 100)` is invoked, how many function calls to `quicksort()` are made? Compute this number for each version of `find_pivot()`.

22. In the second version of `find_pivot()` change the line

         if (n > 3) {   /* a carefully chosen inequality */

    to be the following:

         if (n >= 3) {

    Now when `quicksort()` is invoked, it does not run properly. Why?

23. Explain in detail how the following program works.

```
main()
{
    printf("\nwhat is your favorite line?  ");
    try_me();
    printf("\n\n");
}

try_me()
{
    char   c;

    if ((c = getchar()) != '\n')
        try_me();
    putchar(c);
}
```

24. Suppose that in the function `root()` we change the line

         if (f(m) == 0.0 || b - a < eps)

    to

         if (b - a < eps)

    Will the function still work properly? Explain.

25. Find the points of intersection of the graphs

    $y = m\,x$ and $y = \tan x$

    for *m* having the values 0.1, 0.2, 0.3, . . . , 5.0 .

26. What is the largest floating point constant available on your system? *Hint:* Create a file called *look.c* with the line

    ```
    #include   <stdio.h>
    ```

    in it, and then give the command

    cc −E look.c

27. The following recursive function computes the greatest common divisor of two positive integers. Write an equivalent iterative function.

    ```
    gcd(p, q)
    int    p, q;
    {
          int   r;

          if ((r = p % q)  == 0)
               return (q);
          else
               return (gcd(q, r));
    }
    ```

28. Use a random number generator to fill arrays of varying sizes. Show empirically that the median value approaches a limiting value as the size of the array gets larger.

29. Write a version of `find_pivot()` with a series of `if-else` statements that will order `b[0]`, `b[1]`, and `b[2]`.

30. A knight is a chess piece that moves in the pattern of an ell (L). The chessboard has 64 squares; the knight can make two legal moves if placed at a corner square of the chessboard and can make eight legal moves if placed in a middle square of the board. Write a function that computes the number of legal moves that a knight can make when starting at a specific square on the board. Associate that number with the square. It is called the *connectivity* of the square as viewed by the knight. Write a program that finds and prints the number of legal moves associated with each square on the board. The numbers should be printed as an 8 × 8 array corresponding to the 64 squares on a chessboard, with each number representing the connectivity of its square. This array is the connectivity of the chessboard as viewed by the knight.

31. (Advanced—see "A Method for Finding Hamiltonian Paths and Knight's Tours" by Ira Pohl, in *Communications of the ACM, Vol* 10, *No* 7, *July* 1967.) A knight's tour is a path the knight takes covering all 64 squares without revisiting any square. Warnsdorf's rule states that to find a knight's tour one starts from a corner

square and goes to a square that has not yet been reached and has smallest connectivity. An "adjacent" square is one the knight can immediately move to. When a square is visited, all of the connectivity numbers of adjacent squares are decremented. Employ Warnsdorf's rule to find a knight's tour. Print out an 8 × 8 array corresponding to the chessboard, and in each position print the number of moves it took the knight to reach that square.

32. (Advanced) Pohl's improvement to Warnsdorf's rule was to suggest that ties be broken recursively. Warnsdorf's rule is called a heuristic. It is not guaranteed to work. Still, it is very efficient for a combinatorially difficult problem. Sometimes two squares have the same smallest connectivity. To break the tie, compute recursively which square leads to a further smallest connectivity and choose that square. From any starting square on the ordinary 8 × 8 chessboard, the Pohl-Warnsdorf rule was always found to work. Implement this heuristic algorithm and run it for five different starting squares, printing each tour.

9

Structures, Unions, and typedef

C is an easily extensible language. It can be extended by providing #define's and functions that are stored in user or standard libraries for future use. It can also be extended by defining data types that are constructed from the standard types. The type array of char is a derived type that is used to represent string variables. Arrays are used to represent homogeneous data. The principal mechanism for constructing types whose components are nonhomogeneous aggregates of already defined types is the struct declaration. We will first explain the typedef mechanism, which allows the naming of new types, and then struct and union.

9.1 THE USE OF typedef

C provides a number of fundamental types such as char and int, and a number of derived types such as arrays and pointers. The language also provides the typedef declaration, which allows a type to be explicitly associated with an identifier. Some examples are

```
typedef    int    INCHES, FEET, YARDS;
typedef    int    vector[10];
typedef    char   *string;
```

In each of these type definitions the named identifiers can be used later to declare variables or functions in the same way ordinary types can be used. For example,

```
INCHES    length, width;
```

declares the variables length and width to be of type INCHES, which is equivalent to type int. Thus, INCHES can be used as a type declaration synonymous with int.

What is gained by allowing the programmer to create a new nomenclature for the existing type declarations? One gain is that it allows abbreviations of long declarations. A second advantage comes from having the typedef in one place, which makes it easier to document the program. Furthermore, if there are system sensitive declarations, such as an int that is 4 bytes on one system and 2 bytes on a second system, and these differences are critical to the program, then using typedef allows easier porting of the software. The changes can all occur in specifically localized places; indeed, frequently these would be collected in a header file and appended with an #include control line.

A further possible advantage is that in the future some compilers or *lint* will be written to enforce type checking for the named typedef. Thus, while INCHES and YARDS in the example are both int, a compiler that indicated when these occurred in mixed expressions would provide additional safety.

We illustrate the use of typedef by defining a small number of functions to operate on vectors and matrices.

```
#define    N    3       /* the size of all vectors and matrices */
typedef    double   scalar;
typedef    scalar   vector[N];
typedef    scalar   matrix[N][N];

add(a, b, c)       /*  a =  b + c  */
vector    a, b, c;
{
     int i;

     for (i = 0;  i < N;  ++i)
          a[i] = b[i] + c[i];
}
```

The use of typedef in this example has created the types scalar, vector, and matrix, which is both self-documenting and conceptually appropriate. The programming language has been extended in a natural way to incorporate these new types as a domain. Notice how typedef can be used to build hierarchies of types. For example, we could have written

```
typedef    vector    matrix[N]
```

in place of

```
typedef    scalar    matrix[N][N]
```

Now we create functions that provide operations over these domains.

```
scalar dot_product(a, b)     /*  the dot product of  a   and  b  */
vector    a, b;
{
     int       i;
     scalar    s = 0;

     for (i = 0;  i < N;  ++i)
          s += a[i] * b[i];
     return(s);
}
```

```
multiply(a, b, c)      /*  matrix multiplication:   a = b * c  */
matrix    a, b, c;
{
        int    i, j, k;

        for (i = 0; i < N; ++i)
                for (j = 0; j < N; ++j)
                        for (c[i][j] = 0, k = 0; k < N; ++k)
                                c[i][j] += a[i][k] * b[k][j];
}
```

The use of typedef to define scalar, vector, and matrix allows the programmer to think in terms of the application rather than the C representation. In this way, a language appropriate to vector and matrix problems can be built up.

9.2 STRUCTURES

Structures are a means of aggregating a collection of data items of possibly different types. As a simple example, let us define a structure that will describe a playing card. A playing card such as the three of spades has a pip value, 3, and a suit value, spades. We can declare two variables

```
int    pips;
char   suit;
```

which capture the information. The variable pips will take values from 1 to 13, representing ace to king; and the variable suit will take values from 'c', 'd', 'h', and 's', representing the suits clubs, diamonds, hearts, and spades. Structures allow us to group variables together. Thus

```
struct card {
        int    pips;
        char   suit;
};
```

creates the derived data type struct card, where card is the structure tag name. The tag name can then be used to declare variables of this type. The declaration

```
struct card    c1, c2;
```

allocates storage for the identifiers c1 and c2, which are of type struct card. The identifiers suit and pips are called *members* of struct card. To access the values of the members, we use the structure member operator ".".

Let us assign to c1 the values representing the three of spades and to c2 the values representing the king of diamonds.

```
c1.pips = 3;
c1.suit = 's';
c2.pips = 13;
c2.suit = 'd';
```

A construct of the form

> *structure_variable . member_name*

is used as a variable in the same way a simple variable or an element of an array is used. The member name must be unique within the specified structure. Since the member must always be prefaced or accessed through a unique structure variable identifier, there is no confusion between two members having the same name in different structures. An example is

```
struct s1 {
      char    c;
      int     i;
};

struct s2 {
      char    c;
      float   x;
};

struct s1    a;
struct s2    b;
```

We can access a.c and b.c without ambiguity.

The syntax for structure declarations is as follows:

structure_declaration ::= struct *tag_name declarator_list* ;

structure_type ::= struct *tag_name member_specification*
         | struct *tag_name*
         | struct *member_specification*

tag_name ::= *identifier*

member_specification ::= { { *type_specifier declarator_list* ;}$_{1+}$ }

declarator_list ::= {*declarator*}$_{opt}$ {, *declarator*}$_{0+}$

declarator ::= *identifier*
         | *declarator*
         | *declarator* [{*constant _expression*}$_{opt}$]
         | (*declarator*)
         | *declarator* ()

An example is

```
struct card {
      int     pips;
      char    suit;
} deck[52];
```

The identifier card is the structure tag name. The identifier deck is declared as an array of struct card.

Writing

```
struct {
        char    *last_name;
        int     student_id;
        char    grade;
} s1, s2, s3;
```

declares s1, s2, and s3 to represent three student records, but does not include a tag name for later use in further declarations. The declaration

```
struct student {
        char    *last_name;
        int     student_id;
        char    grade;
};
```

has student as a structure tag name, but no variables are declared of this type. We can now write

```
struct student   temp, class[100];
```

which declares temp and class[100] as type struct student. Only at this point will storage be allocated for these variables.

It is usually good programming practice to associate a tag name with a structure type. It is both convenient for further declarations and for documentation. When using typedef to name a structure type, the tag name is unimportant. An example is

```
typedef struct {
        float   re;
        float   im;
} complex;

complex    a, b, c[100];
```

The type complex now serves in place of the structure type. The programmer achieves a high degree of modularity and portability by using typedef to name such derived types and by storing them in header files.

9.3 ACCESSING A MEMBER

This section will discuss methods for accessing member components of a structure. We have already seen the use of the member operator. For example

```
temp.grade = 'a';
temp.last_name = "Casanova";    ·
temp.student_id = 170017;
```

will assign values to the members of the structure variable `temp`. Here is a function that counts the number of `'f'` grades in `class[]`.

```
fail(class)
struct  student     class[];
{
        int    i,  count = 0;

        for (i = 0;  i < SIZE;  ++i)
             count += class[i].grade == 'f';
        return (count);
}
```

Let us use the structure representation for complex numbers to illustrate the precedence of the member operator.

```
add(a,  b,  c);         /*  *a = b + c  */
complex    *a, b,  c;
{
        (*a).re = b.re + c.re;
        (*a).im = b.im + c.im;
}
```

This function adds two complex numbers. We must write `(*a).re` because `*a.re` would mean `*(a.re)`. The member operator has higher precedence than the dereferencing operator.

The frequency of accessing a structure member indirectly by pointer makes it desirable to have a special notation for this construct. This is done by the structure pointer operator `->` (a minus sign followed by a greater than sign). With this operator, a member is accessed as

pointer_to_structure_variable -> member_name

The body of `add()` can be rewritten in this notation as

```
a -> re = b.re + c.re;
a -> im = b.im + c.im;
```

The structure pointer operator `->`, the member operator ".", along with parentheses `()` and array brackets `[]` have highest precedence and associate left to right. The various accessing modes can be combined in complicated ways.

Declarations and assignments

```
struct student   temp, *p = &temp;

temp.grade = 'a';
temp.last_name = "Casanova";
temp.student_id = 170017;
```

Expression	**Equivalent expression**	**Value**
temp.last_name	p -> last_name	Casanova
temp.grade	p -> grade	a
temp.student_id	p -> student_id	170017
(*p) -> last_name + 2	*((*p) -> last_name) + 2	/* error */
*p -> last_name + 2	*(p -> last_name) + 2	E
* (p -> last_name + 2)	p -> last_name[2]	s

9.4 STRUCTURES AND FUNCTIONS

We will discuss structures as arguments to functions and as values returned from functions. On most systems, structures as arguments are allowed, and our discussion will be for this unrestricted environment. Some systems may require that arguments and returned values all be handled by pointers.

To illustrate the use of structures with functions, we will use the structure card and the structure complex. We will write a set of routines to manipulate both data types. For the remainder of this chapter assume the file *local.h* contains the typedef's for these structures.

In local.h :

```
typedef struct {
     int     pips;
     char    suit;
} card;

typedef struct {
     float   re;
     float   im;
} complex;
```

Pointer-based Functions

Let us write functions that will assign a value to a card, extract the member values of a card, and print the value of a card. The first version of these routines will be restricted to pointer-based argument handling.

```
#include    "local.h"

assign_values(c_ptr, p, s)
card    *c_ptr;
int     p;
char    s;
{
      c_ptr -> pips = p;
      c_ptr -> suit = s;
}

extract_values(c_ptr, p_ptr, s_ptr)
card    *c_ptr;
int     *p_ptr;
char    *s_ptr;
{
      *p_ptr = c_ptr -> pips;
      *s_ptr = c_ptr -> suit;
}
```

The above functions access a card by using a pointer to a variable of type card. The structure pointer operator -> is used throughout to access the required member. We write a card-printing routine that takes a pointer to card and prints its values using extract_values().

```
prn_values(c_ptr)
card    *c_ptr;
{
      int     p;
      char    s, *name;

      extract_values(c_ptr, &p, &s);
      name = (s == 'c') ? "clubs" : (s == 'd') ? "diamonds" :
            (s == 'h') ? "hearts" : (s == 's') ? "spades" : "error";
      printf("\ncard: %d of  %s", p, name);
}
```

Next we illustrate how these functions can be used to assign values to a deck of cards.

```
main()
{
      card    deck[52];
      int     i;

      for (i = 0; i < 13; ++i) {
            assign_values(deck + i, i + 1, 'c');
            assign_values(deck + i + 13, i + 1, 'd');
            assign_values(deck + i + 26, i + 1, 'h');
            assign_values(deck + i + 39, i + 1, 's');
      }
      for (i = 0; i < 13; ++i)          /* print out the hearts */
            prn_values(deck + i + 26);
}
```

This program prints out the heart suit to show that the assignment has been done properly.

Structure-based Functions

On our reference system, structures can be passed as arguments, returned as values, and assigned in expressions. So, if variable a and variable b refer to the same type of structure, the assignment a = b is allowed. This is equivalent to assigning all the individual member fields of b to a. When structures are arguments to functions, they are passed by value. A local copy of the structure is made, and all changes and access is to the local copy. When such a function is exited, the actual structure passed is unchanged. This implies that arrays can be passed call by value by making them a member of a structure. In contrast to the previous code, which uses pointer to card, the following functions pass and return type card:

```
#include  "local.h"

card assign_values(p, s)
int     p;
char    s;
{
      card    c;

      c.pips = p;
      c.suit = s;
      return (c);
}
```

```
extract_values(c, p_ptr, s_ptr)
card    c;
int     *p_ptr;
char    *s_ptr;
{
    *s_ptr = c.suit;
    *p_ptr = c.pips;
}
```

The function `assign_values()` uses the local variable c of type `card`. This is explicitly returned and can be assigned to a variable of type `card`. The function `extract_values()` passes the structure `card` c by value.

9.5 OPERATOR PRECEDENCE AND ASSOCIATIVITY: A FINAL LOOK

We are now in a position to display the entire precedence hierarchy for C operators. The additional operators seen in this chapter are the operators . and ->. These operators, together with [] and (), have the highest precedence. The following table gives the complete list of operators in C:

Operators	*Associativity*
() [] -> .	left to right
~ ! ++ -- sizeof (*type*) – (unary) * (indirection) & (address)	right to left
* / %	left to right
+ –	left to right
<< >>	left to right
< <= > >=	left to right
== !=	left to right
&	left to right
^	left to right
|	left to right
&&	left to right
||	left to right
?:	right to left
= += -= *= etc.	right to left
, (comma operator)	left to right

Several points are worth repeating. Expressions involving just one of the commutative binary operators

```
*     +     &     ^     |
```

are subject to reordering by the compiler for its own convenience, even where they are parenthesized. To guarantee order of evaluation, one must use assignment statements to evaluate intermediate results. The unary operator `sizeof` can be applied to either an expression or a type. In this latter case, the type name must be parenthesized. Some examples are

```
sizeof x;
sizeof (x);
sizeof (x + y);
sizeof (double);
sizeof (card);
```

but not

```
sizeof double;
```

While this table is extensive, some simple rules apply. The primary operators, which include the addressing primitives, member access and subscripting, along with parentheses, are of highest precedence. Unary operators come next. Arithmetic operators follow the usual convention, namely multiplicative operators have higher precedence than additive operators. Assignments of all kinds are of lowest precedence, with the exception of the still lowlier comma operator. When unsure of precedence or associativity rules, either look them up or use parentheses.

9.6 AN EXAMPLE: COMPLEX ARITHMETIC

Engineers and scientists frequently need to calculate with complex numbers. We will write code to accomplish this by using functions that pass and return structures of type `complex`. It is important to observe the ease with which `struct` and `typedef` allow the C language to incorporate user-defined data types.

```
/***   complex arithmetic   ***/

#include    <math.h>
#include    "local.h"

complex assign_values(real_part, imaginary_part)
double   real_part, imaginary_part;
{
    complex   x;

    x.re = real_part;
    x.im = imaginary_part;
    return (x);
}
```

```
complex add(x, y)
complex    x, y;
{
      complex    z;

      z.re = x.re + y.re;
      z.im = x.im + y.im;
      return (z);
}

complex multiply(x, y)
complex    x, y;
{
      complex    z;

      z.re = x.re * y.re - x.im * y.im;
      z.im = x.re * y.im + x.im * y.re;
      return (z);
}
```

The following function returns the conjugate of a complex number:

```
complex conjugate(x)
complex    x;
{
      complex    z;

      z.re = x.re;
      z.im = -x.im;
      return (z);
}
```

The function conjugate() is now used by absolute() to produce the absolute value of a complex number and by length() to produce the length of a complex vector.

```
double absolute(x)
complex    x;
{
      complex    z;

      z = multiply(x, conjugate(x));
      return (sqrt(z.re));
}
```

```
double length(v, n)
complex    v[];
int        n;        /*  n  is the size of  v  */
{
     int      i;
     double   s;
     complex  z;

     for (s = 0.0, i = 0; i < n; ++i) {
          z = multiply(v[i], conjugate(v[i]));
          s +=  z.re;
     }
     return (sqrt(s));
}
```

Notice that whenever `multiply()` is used, its value is first assigned to a variable of type `complex`. Then the real part can be extracted. The following code tests that these functions work:

```
#define   N   5

main()
{
     static double   a[N] = {1.0, 2.0, 3.0, 4.0, 5.0};
     static double   b[N] = {1.0, 2.0, 3.0, 4.0, 5.0};
     complex         c[N];
     int             i;

     for (i = 0; i < N; ++i)
          c[i] = assign_values(a[i], b[i]);
     printf("\nlength is %e", length(c, N));
}
```

9.7 AN EXAMPLE: STUDENT RECORDS

The variations available in C to define complicated data structures involve all meaningful combinations of structure, pointer, and array. We will start with our previous example of a `struct` student and develop it into a more comprehensive data structure for a student record. We will use these specifications to write programs that convert student records from short to long form. We will define the various needed types as follows:

In student.h :

```
#define    COURSES       10
#define    CLASS_SIZE    50

struct student {
      char    *last_name;
      int     student_id;
      char    grade;
};

typedef struct {
      char    month[10];
      short   day;
      short   year;
} date;

typedef struct {
      char    name[20];
      date    birthday;
} personal;

typedef struct {
      personal   p;
      int        student_id;
      char       grade[COURSES];
} student_data;
```

The type `student_data` is constructed with nested structures. One of its members is the structure `p`, which has as one of its members the structure `birthday`. Suppose that `temp` is declared to be of type `student_data`. Then the expression

```
temp.p.birthday.month[0]
```

has, as its value, the first letter of the month of the birthday of the student whose data is in `temp`. Structures such as `date` and `personal` are used in data base applications.

As an example of a function using this representation to input dates we write `read_date()`.

```
#include    "student.h"

read_date(d)
date    *d;
{
      printf("\nenter    month(string)    day(int)    year(int):\n\n    ");
      scanf("%s%hd%hd", d -> month, &d -> day, &d -> year);
}
```

This function prompts the user for information. The expression

```
d -> month
```

is an address by virtue of pointing at an array name. The expressions

```
&d -> day              and              &d -> year
```

are addresses of variables of type `short`. Because `&` is of lower precedence than `->`, an expression such as

```
&d -> day        is equivalent to        &(d -> day)
```

Here is a function to enter grades.

```
read_grades (g)
char     g[];
{
        int    i;

        printf ("\nenter %d grades:   ", COURSES);
        for (i = 0;  i < COURSES;  ++i)
              scanf ("%1s",  &g[i]);
}
```

Basically, understanding structures comes down to understanding how to access their members. We will extract and then output in short form students with particular grades in a given course.

```
#include    "student.h"

struct student extract (s_data, g, n)
student_data    s_data;
char            g;
int             n;
{
        struct student   t;
        int              i;

        if (s_data.grade [n]  == g) {
              t.student_id = s_data.student_id;
              t.last_name = s_data.p.name;
              t.grade = s_data.grade [n];
              return (t);
        }
}
```

9.8 UNIONS

A union, like a structure, is a derived type. Unions follow the same syntax as structures but have members that share storage. A union variable defines a set of alternative values that may be stored in a shared portion of memory.

```
union  int_or_float {
      int     n;
      float   x;
} temp;
```

The compiler allocates a piece of storage that can accommodate the largest of the specified members. The notation used to access a member of a union is identical to that used to access a member of a structure. We can test how the above union might be used as follows:

```
typedef union int_or_float {
      int     n;
      float   x;
} number;

main ()
{
      number    temp;

      temp.n = 4444;
      printf("i: %15.10d     f: %15.10e\n", temp.n, temp.x);
      temp.x = 4444.0;
      printf("i: %15.10d     f: %15.10e\n", temp.n, temp.x);
}
```

This little experiment will demonstrate how your system overlays an int and a float. Here is the output of this program on our system:

```
i:       0000004444    f:  4.3387349787e-29
i:      -0536852854    f:  4.4440000000e+03
```

The point is that the system will interpret the same stored values according to which member component is selected. It is the programmer's responsibility to choose the right one.

Unions are used to conserve storage by allowing the same storage to be used for a variety of types. Consider the problem of extending our previous student record example to include the student's address. Let us assume that some students are on campus and live in a college dormitory and others live off campus. These will be mutually exclusive for each student, and we might store each in a union defined as follows:

```
struct off_campus {
      int      strnum;
      char     strname[20];
      char     city[10];
};

struct on_campus {
      char     coll[10];
      char     dorm[10];
      int      roomnum;
};

union address {
      struct off_campus   town;
      struct on_campus    gown;
};
```

Now we could create a new student record structure by adding two members. One would be the type union address and the other would be a variable to tell which of the two types are stored.

```
typedef struct {
      personal         p;
      int              student_id;
      char             grade[NCOURSES];
      char             on_off;   /* t for an on campus address
                                    f for an off campus address */
      union address    a;
} student_record;
```

Let us write a piece of code that, depending on the member variable on_off, will retrieve from the variable s declared as student_record, either the street number or the room number.

```
(s.on_off == 't') ? s.a.gown.roomnum : s.a.town.strnum;
```

9.9 FIELDS

A *field* is a member with a bit length. Its length is specified by a nonnegative constant expression following a colon. Typically, fields are declared as consecutive members of a structure. An example is

```
struct pcard {      /*  a packed representation  */
      unsigned   pips : 4;
      unsigned   suit : 2;
};
```

The structure `pcard` has a 4-bit field called `pips` capable of storing the 16 values 0 to 15; and a 2-bit field called `suit` capable of storing values 0, 1, 2, and 3 meaning, respectively, clubs, diamonds, hearts, and spades. Thus, the 13 `pips` values and the 4 `suit` values are compactly represented as 6 bits. Access is once again with the member operator. So, if we declare

```
struct pcard   t;
```

then,

```
t.pips = 9;
t.suit = 2;
```

assigns the nine of hearts to the variable `t`.

The syntax for a field member within a structure is

field_member ::= *type_specifier* { *identifier* }$_{opt}$: *constant_expression*

The compiler assigns in either a left-to-right or right-to-left order the bits of a machine word needed to store fields within a single word. On the VAX where a word is 32 bits, consecutive fields may sum to less than or equal 32 bits before a next word is required. If a field straddles this boundary, it is forced to start in a new word. Thus, on the VAX the declaration

```
struct x {
      int    f1 : 1;
      int    f2 : 17;
      int    f3 : 18;
   } a;
```

will require two words to store `a`, where the fields `f1` and `f2` will be in word 1 and field `f3` will be in word 2. A field is not allowed to be wider than a word. The chief purpose of using fields is storage conservation. Using 32-bit words, 32 one-bit variables can be stored in a single word, as opposed to using 32 integers. We have already seen the use of bitwise operators and bit manipulation in earlier chapters. This new facility allows us the ability to name sequences of bits within a structure.

Field members are not restricted in type, but implementations need only support `unsigned int`. Arrays of fields are not allowed. Also, fields cannot be addressed directly by pointers, and the address operator & cannot be applied to a field member.

For a 32-bit word `int` representation, the following structure and union definitions allow you to tell what representation is in use. Our first structure divides the word into four 8-bit bytes, and our second structure divides the word into bit fields.

```
struct word_bytes {
    unsigned   byte0 : 8, byte1 : 8, byte2 : 8, byte3 : 8;
};

struct word_bits {
    unsigned   bit0  : 1, bit1  : 1, bit2  : 1, bit3  : 1,
               bit4  : 1, bit5  : 1, bit6  : 1, bit7  : 1,
               bit8  : 1, bit9  : 1, bit10 : 1, bit11 : 1,
               bit12 : 1, bit13 : 1, bit14 : 1, bit15 : 1,
               bit16 : 1, bit17 : 1, bit18 : 1, bit19 : 1,
               bit20 : 1, bit21 : 1, bit22 : 1, bit23 : 1,
               bit24 : 1, bit25 : 1, bit26 : 1, bit27 : 1,
               bit28 : 1, bit29 : 1, bit30 : 1, bit31 : 1;
};

union word {
    int                 x;
    struct word_bytes   y;
    struct word_bits    z;
}  temp;
```

These field representations allow us to get at the machine word in different modes. Using the above, some examples are

```
temp.x = 0;
temp.y.byte3 = 'w';
temp.z.bit5 = 1;
```

The reader should use `bit_print()` from Chapter 6 to see how each of these assignments affects the machine word.

One last point, fields can be unnamed and be used for padding and alignment purposes. If one wished to have a structure for storing 10 decimal digits across two words aligned five to a word, this could be specified as

```
struct ten_digits {
    unsigned   d1 : 4, d2 : 4, d3 : 4, d4 : 4, d5 : 4,
                  : 12;      /* align to the next word */
    unsigned   d6 : 4, d7 : 4, d8 : 4, d9 : 4, d10 : 4;
};
```

An alternate means of alignment to a next word is to use a field with width 0.

9.10 INITIALIZATION OF STRUCTURES

As with other variables, external and static structures can be initialized. The syntax is the same as for initialization of arrays. When declared external or static, a structure variable can be followed by an assignment symbol = and a list of constants contained within braces. If not enough values are used to assign all members of the structure, the remaining members are assigned the default value zero. Automatic structure variables cannot be so initialized, and therefore explicit assignment must be used. Some examples are

```
card   c = {12, 's'};   /* initialize to the queen of spades */

complex   m[3][3] = {
       {{1.0, -0.5}, {2.5, 1.0}, {0.7, 0.7}}
       {{7.0, -6.5}, {-0.5, 1.0}, {45.7, 8.0}},
};      /* m[2][] is assigned zeros */
```

9.11 AN EXAMPLE: PLAYING POKER

Let us use the concepts within this chapter to write the beginnings of a program to play poker. This program will use the system random number generator `rand()` to shuffle a deck specified as an array of type `struct card`. The program will compute the probability that a pat flush is dealt, meaning that exactly five cards of the same suit occur.

We again use a structure to represent a card, and the deck will be represented by an external initialized array.

```
struct card {
       int    pips;   /* 1 to 13 with 1 an ace and 13 a king  */
       char   suit;   /* c d h s  */
};

struct card   deck[52] = {   /* initialize deck */
       {1, 'c'}, {2, 'c'}, {3, 'c'}, {4, 'c'}, {5, 'c'},
       {6, 'c'}, {7, 'c'}, {8, 'c'}, {9, 'c'}, {10, 'c'},
       {11, 'c'}, {12, 'c'}, {13, 'c'},
       {1, 'd'}, {2, 'd'}, {3, 'd'}, {4, 'd'}, {5, 'd'},
       {6, 'd'}, {7, 'd'}, {8, 'd'}, {9, 'd'}, {10, 'd'},
       {11, 'd'}, {12, 'd'}, {13, 'd'},
       {1, 'h'}, {2, 'h'}, {3, 'h'}, {4, 'h'}, {5, 'h'},
       {6, 'h'}, {7, 'h'}, {8, 'h'}, {9, 'h'}, {10, 'h'},
       {11, 'h'}, {12, 'h'}, {13, 'h'},
       {1, 's'}, {2, 's'}, {3, 's'}, {4, 's'}, {5, 's'},
       {6, 's'}, {7, 's'}, {8, 's'}, {9, 's'}, {10, 's'},
       {11, 's'}, {12, 's'}, {13, 's'}
};
```

The card values will be interchanged randomly to obtain a shuffle. Each deck position will be changed once per shuffle.

```
rand52 ()
{
      return  (rand()  %  52);
}
```

This function returns a pseudo random number between 0 and 51. It will be used to shuffle the deck.

```
shuffle (deck)
struct card    deck[];
{
      int    i, j;

      for  (i = 0;  i < 52;  ++i)  {
            j = rand52 ();
            swap (&deck[i],  &deck[j]);
      }
}

swap (p,  q)
struct card    *p, *q;
{
      struct card    temp;

      temp = *p;
      *p = *q;
      *q = temp;
}
```

The *i*th card in the deck is interchanged with a deck location selected at random. This is done for each deck location and simulates a thorough shuffle of the cards.

```
deal_a_hand (deck, h, ncard)       /*  deals the next hand  */
struct card    h[], deck[];
int            ncard;     /*  the deck position of the next card  */
{
      int    i;

      for  (i = 0;  i < 5;  ++i)
            h[i] = deck[ncard + i];       /*  h[] is a 5 card hand  */
}
```

```
is_flush(h)        /*  return 1 for a flush, 0 otherwise  */
struct card    h[];
{
    int    i;
    char   t;          /*  suit  */

    t = h[0].suit;
    /*  test that the other four cards are the same suit as t  */
    for (i = 1; i < 5; ++i)
        if (h[i].suit != t)
            return (0);
    return (1);
}
```

The calling routine will deal out hands and test them for flushes. The probability of a player being dealt a flush is empirically computed. We imagine six players at the table, each being dealt five-card hands.

```
/***  probability of flushing  ***/

#define    DEALS      1000
#define    PLAYERS    6

main()
{
    int            nc;        /*  card number in deck  */
    int            nh = 0;    /*  hand number  */
    int            nf = 0;    /*  flush number  */
    int            i, n;
    struct card    hands[PLAYERS][5];

    for (n = 0; n < DEALS; ++n) {
        shuffle(deck);
        nc = 0;
        for (i = 0; i < PLAYERS; ++i) {    /*  deal out six hands  */
            deal_a_hand(deck, hands[i], nc);
            nc += 5;
            ++nh;
            if (is_flush(hands[i])) {
                ++nf;
                printf("\n\nhand number: %d", nh);
                printf("\nflush number: %d", nf);
                printf("\nflush probability: %f",
                    (double) nf / (double) nh);
            }
        }
    }
    printf("\n\n");
}
```

Each time a flush is found, the hand number and flush number are printed out. These are then divided to give the observed probability of flushing.

9.12 SUMMARY

1. Structures and unions are a principal method for the programmer to define new types.

2. The `typedef` specification can be used to name or rename types.

3. A structure is an aggregation of subparts treated as a single variable. The subparts of the structure are called members.

4. Structure members are accessed by the member operator " . ". If s is a structure variable with a member named m, then s.m refers to the value of the member m within s. An alternate means of accessing members is using the structure pointer operator ->. If p is a pointer pointing at s, then p -> m also refers to s.m. Both " . " and -> have highest precedence among C operators.

5. In most systems, if a and b are structure variables of the same type, then the assignment expression a = b is allowed. Also, a structure variable can be passed as an argument to a function and returned from a function. All systems allow pointers to structures to be arguments or variables. When used as an argument to a function, a pointer to a structure has the advantage of not creating a local copy.

6. Structures can be members of other structures. Considerable complexity is possible when nesting structures, pointers, and arrays within each other. Care should be taken that the proper variables are being accessed.

7. Unions conform to the structure syntax. However, union members are overlaid; in other words, they share the same storage. Unions are a means for conserving storage. The allocated storage can be used to hold a variety of types. It is the programmer's responsibility to know which representation is currently stored in a union variable.

8. Fields are members of a structure that allow different variables to share contiguous bits within a word.

9. Fields can be unnamed, in which case they are used for padding or word alignment purposes. Fields are machine dependent and are not addressable by pointers.

9.13 EXERCISES

1. Write a function add(a, b, c) where the variables a, b, and c are of type matrix.

2. Rewrite matrix multiply(a, b, c) so that a is M by N, b is M by R, and c is R by N. Use typedef to define these rectangular matrices.

3. Write a function that computes the linear combination of two matrices. Namely, linear_combination(a, b, c, s, t) should produce a matrix a, which is the linear combination of matrices b and c multiplied by the scalars s and t, respectively. Thus, an appropriate comment in the program would be

```
/*   a = s * b + t * c   */
```

4. The following two programs illustrate why a typedef can be preferable to the use of a #define:

```
typedef    int    DOLLARS;       /*  first program  */

main()
{
    DOLLARS    a, b, c;
         .   .   .   .

    {                            /*  new block  */
         float    DOLLARS;
              .   .   .   .

    }
}


#define   DOLLARS    int         /*  second program  */

main()
{
    DOLLARS    a, b, c;
         .   .   .   .

    {                            /*  new block  */
         float    DOLLARS;
              .   .   .   .

    }
}
```

What goes wrong in the second program? Can you correct this with another preprocessor command?

5. The following two functions act on arguments of type card, but do not work as expected. Describe what goes wrong.

```
#include    "local.h"

assign_value2(c, p, s)
card    c;      /*  card to be assigned  */
int     p;      /*  pips value assigned  */
char    s;      /*  suit value assigned  */
{
    c.pips = p;
    c.suit = s;
}
```

```
card *passign_value2 (p, s)
int    p;      /* pips value assigned  */
char   s;      /* suit value assigned  */
{
      card    *c;

      c -> pips = p;
      c -> suit = s;
      return (c);    /* return a pointer to card  */
}
```

6. Within the structure type card, change the specification of suit from char to

    typedef enum   suits {club, diamond, heart, spade} suit;

   Now rewrite the functions assign_values() and extract_values() to use this representation.

7. Write a collection of vector and matrix functions that all use complex numbers. Write a routine to print such vectors and matrices on your screen.

8. Create a structure that can describe a restaurant. It should have members that include the name, address, average cost, and type of food. Write a routine that prints out all restaurants of a given food type in order of cost, least costly first.

9. When playing poker or other card games, it is usual to arrange the hand to reflect its values. Write a program that arranges and prints out a hand in sorted order by pips value.

10. Write a function is_straight(), which tests whether a poker hand is a straight. Write a function is_fullhouse(), which tests whether a poker hand is a full house.

11. (Advanced) Write a function hand_value(), which returns the poker value of the hand. The best possible hand is a straight flush, and the worst possible hand is no pair. Extend this function so that it compares two hands to see which is best.

12. Write a function to do complex subtraction. Write two versions, one that returns a pointer to complex, and one that returns a value of type complex.

13. Using the student record example in the text, write a function that prints the average for each student in a class. Let an "a" grade have value 4, a "b" grade have value 3, etc.

14. Write a routine that prints out students in order of their date of birth, oldest first. The original set of student records need not be in this order.

15. Write a function print_student_data(), which prints in a nice format all the information in a structure of type student_data.

16. Write a program that prints all students in short form, clustered by grade. For a given course, first print students whose grade is "a", then students whose grade is "b", etc.

17. What is wrong with the following examples:

(a)
```
union every {
        int     a;
        char    b;
        float   a;
    } a, b;
```

(b)
```
main()
    {
        struct fex {
                int    f1 : 5;
                int    f2 : 15;
            } a;
        int    *pi;

        a.f1 = 14;
        a.f2 = 277;
        pi = &a.f1;
    }
```

(c)
```
main()
    {
        struct {
            float    re;
            float    im;
        } a = {1.0, -2.0};

        printf("\n%e  %e", a.re, a.im);
    }
```

18. Write a typedef for a union of float and complex. The resulting structure should have a "flag" member that tells which domain is being used. Write functions that can add and multiply over both domains. Your functions should decide on appropriate conversions when mixing arguments from both domains.

19. Rewrite the boolean majority function program of Chapter 4 using fields. Represent each boolean variable as a 1-bit field.

20. In commercial applications, it is sometimes useful to use binary coded decimal codes (BCD), where 4 bits are used to represent a decimal digit. A 32-bit word can be used to represent an 8-digit decimal number. Use fields to implement this code. Write two conversion routines, one from binary to BCD and the second from BCD to binary.

21. (Sieve of Eratosthenes) Use an array of structures that is divided into bit fields to implement the sieve algorithm for primes. Do this on 1000 words in order to find all primes less than 32000. Initially all bits will be zero. Each bit is to represent an integer. The idea is to cross out all the multiples of a given prime.

A bit that is 1 will represent a composite number. Start with the prime 2. Every second bit is made 1 starting with bit 4. Then bit 3 is still 0. Every third bit is made 1, starting with bit 6. Bit 4 is 1, so it is skipped. Bit 5 is the next bit with value 0. Every fifth bit is made 1, starting with bit 10. At the end of this process only those bits that are still zero represent primes. Compare the running time of this algorithm with the algorithm found in Chapter 4.

22. Write a program that uses fields that can display the bit representation of other simple types such as char, int, or float. Make use of both fields and unions. The program should take a float and print out on your screen its bit representation. Do this printout in a visually pleasing way. For example, you might print out each nibble in a separate box; for example

```
***** ***** ***** *****
* 1 * * 0 * * 0 * * 1 *
***** ***** ***** *****
```

23. Define a structure that contains the name of a food, its calories per serving, its food type such as meat or fruit, and its costs. Write a program that is able to produce a balanced meal. The foods should be stored as an array of structures. The program should construct a meal so as to come from four different food types and to meet calorie and cost constraints. It should be capable of producing a large number of different menus.

24. Explain the program found in the exercise for Chapter 0.

```
main()
{
    union {
        char    what[16];
        int     cipher[4];
    } mystery, *s;

    s = &mystery;
    s -> cipher[0]  = 0x6c6c6568;
    s -> cipher[1]  = 0x77202c6f;
    s -> cipher[2]  = 0x646c726f;
    s -> cipher[3]  = 0x0000000a;
    printf("%s", s -> what);
}
```

Remember that on the VAX, byte 0 is the least significant. Therefore, when what[0] is overlaid on cipher[0], its value is hexadecimal 68. If your system works differently, try to reprogram this code to output the same message as the reference system does.

10
Structures and
List Processing

This chapter will explain self-referential structures. We will define structures with pointer members that refer to the structure containing them. Such data structures are called *dynamic data structures*. Unlike arrays or simple variables that are normally allocated at block entry, dynamic data structures often require storage management routines to explicitly obtain and release memory.

10.1 SELF-REFERENTIAL STRUCTURES

Let us define a structure with a member field that points at the same structure type. We wish to do this in order to have an unspecified number of such structures nested together.

```
struct list {
      int          data;
      struct list  *next;
} a;
```

This declaration of list can be stored in two words of memory. One word stores the member data and the second word stores the member next. The pointer variable next is called a *link*. Each structure is linked to a succeeding structure by way of the member next. These structures are conveniently displayed pictorially with links shown as arrows.

The structure list

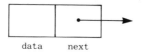

data   next

The pointer variable `next` contains an address of either the location in memory of the successor `list` element or the special value NULL defined as 0. NULL is used to denote the end of the list. Let us see how all this works by manipulating

```
struct list    a, b, c;
```

We will perform some assignments on these structures.

```
a.data = 1;
b.data = 2;
c.data = 3;
a.next = b.next = c.next = NULL;
```

The result of this code is pictorially the following.

Let us chain these together.

```
a.next = &b;
b.next = &c;
```

These pointer assignments result in linking a to b to c.

And now the links allow us to retrieve data from successive elements. Thus

```
a.next -> data
```

has value 2 and

```
a.next -> next -> data
```

has value 3.

10.2 LINEAR LINKED LISTS

A *linear linked list* is like a clothesline on which the data structures hang sequentially. There is a head pointer addressing the first element of the list, and each element points at a successor element, with the last element having a link value NULL. This discussion will use the following header file:

In file list.h :

```
#define   NULL   0            /*  linear list header file  */
typedef   char   DATA;        /*  will use char in examples  */

struct linked_list {
      DATA                   d;
      struct linked_list     *next;
};


typedef   struct linked_list   ELEMENT;
typedef   ELEMENT              *LINK;
```

Storage Allocation

The above specifications do not allocate storage. The system can allocate storage by declaring variables and arrays of type ELEMENT. But what makes these structures especially useful is that utility programs exist to allocate storage dynamically. The standard library function malloc() when called as

```
malloc(size);
```

returns a pointer to enough storage for an object of size bytes. The argument to malloc() is unsigned and the value returned is pointer to char. If head is a variable of type LINK, then

```
head = (LINK) malloc(sizeof(ELEMENT));
```

obtains a piece of memory from the system adequate to store an ELEMENT and assigns its address to the pointer head. As in the above example, it is used with a cast and the sizeof operator. Without the cast a type mismatch warning would occur, because head is not a pointer to char. The sizeof operator calculates the required number of bytes for the particular data structure.

The following code will dynamically create a linear linked list storing the three characters n, e, w:

```
head = (LINK) malloc(sizeof(ELEMENT));
head -> d = 'n';
head -> next = NULL;
```

creates a single element list.

Creating a list dynamically

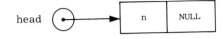

A second element is added by the assignments

```
head -> next = (LINK) malloc(sizeof(ELEMENT));
head -> next -> d = 'e';
head -> next -> next = NULL;
```

There is now a two-element list.

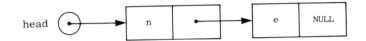

Finally we add a last element.

```
head -> next -> next = (LINK) malloc(sizeof(ELEMENT));
head -> next -> next -> d = 'w';
head -> next -> next -> next = NULL;
```

We have a three-element list pointed at by head and ended with the sentinel value
NULL.

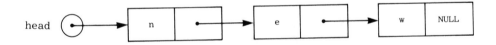

10.3 LIST OPERATIONS

Some of the basic operations on linear lists include:

1. creating a list

2. counting the elements

3. looking up an element

4. concatenating two lists

5. inserting an element

6. deleting an element

We will demonstrate the techniques for programming such operations on lists using both recursion and iteration. The use of recursive functions is natural since lists are a recursively defined construct. Each routine will require the specifications in file *list.h*. Observe that d in these examples could be redefined as an arbitrarily complicated data structure.

As a first example, we will write a function that will produce a list from a string. The function will return a pointer to the head of the resulting list. The heart of the function creates a list element by allocating storage and assigning member values.

```
/***  list creation by recursion  ***/

#include    "list.h"

LINK string_to_list(s)
char    s[];
{
    LINK    head;

    if (s[0] == '\0')        /*  base case  */
        return (NULL);
    else {
        head =   (LINK) malloc(sizeof(ELEMENT));
        head -> d = s[0];
        head -> next = string_to_list(s + 1);
        return (head);
    }
}
```

Notice once more how recursion has a base case, the creation of the empty list, and a general case, the creation of the remainder of the list. The general recursive call returns as its value a LINK pointer to the remaining sublist.

This function can also be written as an iterative routine with the help of the additional auxiliary pointer tail. We will name the iterative version s_to_l() to distinguish it from the recursive version string_to_list().

```
/***  list creation by iteration  ***/

#include   "list.h"

LINK s_to_l(s)
char   s[];
{
     LINK    head = NULL, tail;
     int     i;

     if (s[0] != '\0') {      /*  first element  */
          head =  (LINK) malloc(sizeof(ELEMENT));
          head -> d = s[0];
          tail = head;
          for (i = 1; s[i] != '\0'; ++i) {   /*  add to tail */
               tail -> next = (LINK) malloc(sizeof(ELEMENT));
               tail = tail -> next;
               tail -> d = s[i];
          }
          tail -> next = NULL;      /*  end of list  */
     }
     return (head);
}
```

Functions operating on lists will often require local pointer variables such as head and tail. One should freely use such auxiliary pointers to simplify code. It is also important to hand simulate these routines. It is useful to try your program on the empty list, the unit or single element list, and the two-element list. Frequently, the empty list and the unit list are special cases.

Passing a null string to s_to_l() creates the empty list by having the routine return with value NULL. Creating the one element is done by the first part of the code. The one-element list created from the string "A" is shown in the following diagram. This is the state of the computation before the member next is assigned the value NULL.

One-element list

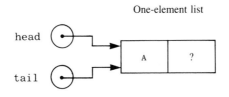

For the two-element case, say "AB", list creation is as pictured. First, the one-element list containing 'A' is created. The `for` statement is then executed, with `i` having value 1 and `s[1]` having value 'B'. A new element is then allocated to the list.

A second element

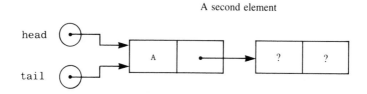

The statement `tail = tail -> next;` advances `tail` to the new element. Then its d member is assigned 'B'.

Updating the tail

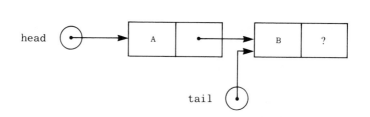

Now `s[2]` has value `\0`, and the `for` statement is exited with a two-element list. Finally, the end of the list is marked with a NULL.

Assigning NULL

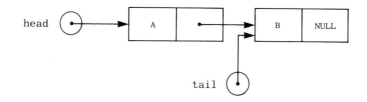

The undefined member values are because `malloc()` is not required to initialize memory to zero.

10.4 SOME LIST PROCESSING FUNCTIONS

We will write two additional functions recursively. The first will count the elements in a list and the second will print the elements of a list. Both will involve recurring down the list and terminating when the NULL pointer is found. All these functions use the header file *list.h*.

The function count () will return 0 if the list is empty, and otherwise will return the number of elements in the list.

```
/***   count a list recursively   ***/

count (head)
LINK    head;
{
     if  (head == NULL)
          return (0);
     else
          return (1 + count (head -> next));
}
```

Similarly, the routine print_list () recursively marches down a list printing the value of member variable d.

```
/***   print a list recursively   ***/

print_list (head)
LINK    head;
{
     if  (head == NULL)
          printf ("NULL");
     else {
          printf ("%c --> ", head -> d);
          print_list (head -> next);
     }
}
```

To illustrate the use of these functions, we will write a calling program that will convert the string "ABC" to a list and print it.

```
main ()
{
     LINK    h;

     h = string_to_list ("ABC");
     printf ("\nthe resulting list is\n");
     print_list (h);
     printf ("\nthis list has %d elements", count (h));
}
```

The program produces the following output:

```
the resulting list is
A --> B --> C --> NULL
this list has 3 elements
```

Often one wishes to take two lists and return a single combined list. The concatenation of list a and b, where a is assumed to be nonempty, will be the list b added to the end of list a. A function to concatenate will march down list a looking for its end as marked by the null pointer. It will keep track of its last non-null pointer and will attach the b list to the next link in this last element of list a.

```
/*** concatenate list   a   and   b  with   a   as head   ***/

concatenate(a, b)
LINK    a, b;         /*  a   must not be NULL   */
{
      if (a -> next == NULL)
          a -> next = b;
      else
          concatenate(a -> next, b);
}
```

Recursion allows us to avoid using any auxiliary pointers to march down the a list. In general, the self-referential character of list processing makes recursion natural to use. The form of these recursive functions is as follows:

```
generic_recursion(head)
LINK    head;
{
      if (head == NULL)
          do the base case
      else
          do the general case and recur with
          generic_recursion(head -> next)
}
```

Insertion

One of the most useful properties of lists is that insertion takes a fixed amount of time once the position in the list is found. In contrast, if one wished to place a value in a large array, retaining all other array values in the same sequential order, the insertion would take, on average, time proportional to the length of the array. The values of all elements of the array that came after the newly inserted value would have to be moved over one element.

Let us illustrate insertion into a list by having two adjacent elements pointed at by p1 and p2, and inserting between them an element pointed at by q.

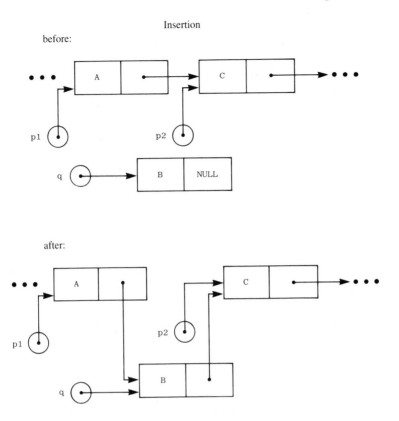

The following function insert() places the element pointed at by q in between the elements pointed at by p1 and p2.

```
/***   inserting an element in a linked list   ***/

insert (p1, p2, q)
LINK    p1, p2, q;
{
        p1 -> next = q;      /*   insert   */
        q -> next = p2;
}
```

Deletion

Deleting an element is very simple in a linked linear list. The predecessor of the element to be deleted has its link member assigned the address of the successor to the deleted element. Again, let us first illustrate graphically the delete operation.

Deletion

before:

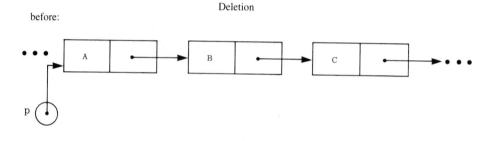

Now executing the code

```
p -> next = p -> next -> next;
```

after:

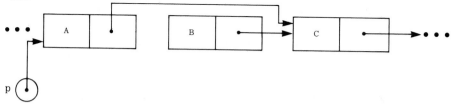

As the diagram shows, the element containing 'B' is no longer accessible and is of no use. Such an inaccessible element is called *garbage*. Since memory is frequently a critical resource, it is desirable that this storage be returned to the system for later use. This may be done with the standard library function free(). When called as follows:

```
free (p) ;
```

makes previously allocated storage for the object pointed at by p available to the system. The argument to free() is pointer to char.

Using free() we will write a deletion routine that returns allocated list storage to the system.

```
/*** recursive deletion of a list ***/

delete_list (head)
LINK    head;
{
    if (head != NULL) {
        delete_list (head -> next) ;
        free (head) ;     /* release storage */
    }
}
```

While it is possible to cast the pointer argument to free(), conventionally we do not do so because no warning results from this omission and the routine works properly.

10.5 STACKS

A stack is a particular form of data abstraction that we will implement with a linear linked list. A stack has access restricted to the head of the list, which is called its *top*. Furthermore, insertion and deletion occur only at the top, and under these restrictions the operations are known as *push* and *pop*, respectively.

A stack can be visualized as a pile of trays. A tray is always picked up from the top and a tray is always returned to the top. Graphically, stacks are drawn vertically.

A stack

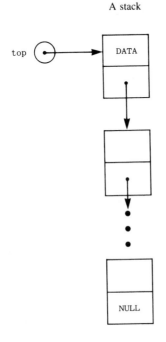

We want to implement the following four standard stack operations.

Function	Action
isempty(t)	return 1 if stack is empty, otherwise 0
vtop(t)	return the value of the top element
pop(t, d)	return the value of the top element and remove it
push(t, d)	place the value d onto the top of the stack

The following header file will be used:

In file stack.h :

```
#define    NULL    0              /*  stack header file  */
typedef    char    DATA;

struct stack {
     DATA              d;
     struct stack   *next;
};

typedef    struct stack   ELEMENT;
typedef    ELEMENT        *TOP;
```

We now define the basic four operations as functions.

```
/***  basic stack routines  ***/

#include    "stack.h"

isempty(t)
TOP    t;
{
     return (t == NULL);
}

DATA vtop(t)
TOP    t;
{
     return (t -> d);
}

pop(t, x)
TOP     *t;
DATA    *x;
{
     TOP    t1 = *t;

     if (! isempty(t1)) {
          *x = t1 -> d;
          *t = t1 -> next;
          free(t1);
     }
     else
          printf("\nempty  stack");
}
```

```
push(t, x)
TOP     *t;
DATA    x;
{
     TOP     temp;

     temp = (TOP) malloc(sizeof(ELEMENT));
     temp -> d = x;
     temp -> next = *t;
     *t = temp;
}
```

The push() routine uses the storage allocator to create a new stack element, and the pop() routine returns the freed up storage back to the system.

A stack is a *last in first out* (LIFO) regime. The last item to be pushed onto the stack is the first to be popped off. So if we were to push first 'a' and second 'b' onto a stack, then pop() would first pop 'b'. We can use this property in a program to reverse a sequence of characters.

```
/***  reversing a string using a stack  ***/

reverse(s)
DATA    s[];
{
     int    i;
     TOP    t = NULL;

     for (i = 0; s[i] != '\0'; ++i)
          push(&t, s[i]);
     for (i = 0; s[i] != '\0'; ++i)
          pop(&t, &s[i]);
}
```

The algorithm builds up a stack local to reverse() until the end of string character is detected. Then the stack is popped back into the array, reversing the original order in which the char values were stored.

10.6 AN EXAMPLE: POLISH NOTATION AND STACK EVALUATION

Ordinary notation for writing expressions is called *infix*, where operators separate arguments. There is another notation for expressions that is very useful for stack-oriented evaluation; this is called *Polish* or parenthesis-free notation. The operator comes after the arguments; for example:

3, 7, +   is equivalent to the infix expression   3 + 7

A more complicated Polish expression would be

    17, 5, *, 2, +

which in infix would be equivalent to

    (17 * 5) + 2

In Polish, the operator is executed as soon as it is encountered left to right. Thus

    17, 5, 2, *, +

is equivalent to the infix

    17 + (5 * 2)

A Polish expression can be evaluated by an algorithm using two stacks. One stack will contain the Polish expression and the other will store the intermediate values during execution. The following algorithm involving a Polish stack and an evaluation stack evaluates Polish expressions where all operators are binary.

A stack algorithm to evaluate Polish expressions

1. If the Polish stack is empty, halt with the top of the evaluation stack as the answer.
2. Pop the Polish stack into x.
3. If x is an operator, pop the evaluation stack twice, into arg1 and arg2. Compute arg1 and arg2 operated on by x, and push the result onto the evaluation stack.
4. If x is a value, then push x onto the evaluation stack; then go to step 1.

We illustrate this algorithm in the following diagram, where the expression

    13, 4, -, 2, 3, *, +

is evaluated.

Stack Algorithm for Evaluating Polish

	E								
	v								
	a								
	l	13							
P	u	4	4						
o	a	-	-	-					
l	t	2	2	2	2				
i	i	3	3	3	3	3		3	
s	o	*	*	* 4	*	* 2	* 2		6
h	n	+	+ 13	+ 13	+ 9	+ 9	+ 9	+ 9	15

Let us write the function `evaluate()`, which uses the stack algorithm just described. The definition of DATA will be changed so that it can store either a value in the form of an int or an operator in the form of a char. Also, a flag will be added that will indicate which kind of data is being stored.

```
typedef struct {
      enum {operator, value}   kind;
      union {
            int    val;
            char   op;
      }                         u;
} DATA;
```

The previous `push()` and `pop()` functions need not be changed.

```
/***  stack evaluation of Polish  ***/

evaluate(polish)
TOP    *polish;
{
      TOP    eval = NULL;        /*  empty evaluation stack  */
      DATA   temp;
      char   bin_op;
      int    arg1, arg2;

      while (!isempty(*polish)) {
            pop(polish, &temp);
            if (temp.kind == operator) {
                  bin_op = temp.u.op;
                  pop(&eval, &temp);
                  arg2 = temp.u.val;
                  pop(&eval, &temp);
                  arg1 = temp.u.val;
                  temp.kind = value;
                  switch(bin_op) {
                  case '+':
                        temp.u.val = arg1 + arg2;
                        break;
                  case '-':
                        temp.u.val = arg1 - arg2;
                        break;
                  case '*':
                        temp.u.val = arg1 * arg2;
                  }
                  push(&eval, temp);
            }
            else      /*  temp.kind == value  */
                  push(&eval, temp);
      }
      pop(&eval, &temp);
      return (temp.u.val);
}
```

This routine is readily extendable to other operations by adding more cases to the switch statement.

10.7 BINARY TREES

A *tree* is a finite set of elements called *nodes*. A tree has a unique node called the *root* node, where the remaining nodes are a disjoint collection of subtrees $T_1, T_2, \ldots, T_n$. If node r has as subtrees $T_1, T_2, \ldots, T_n$, then $r_1, r_2, \ldots, r_n$, roots of these subtrees, are the offspring of r. A node with no offspring is called a *leaf* node.

A general tree

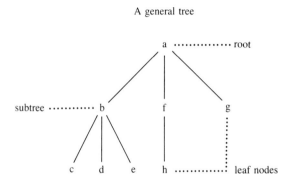

A *binary tree* is a tree whose elements have two offspring. A binary tree considered as a data structure is an object made up of elements that are characterized by two link fields, called left offspring and right offspring. Each link must point at a new object not already pointed at or be NULL. In this representation, a leaf node has both left and right offspring as the value NULL. The following structures and type specifications will be used to define binary trees.

In file tree.h :

```
#define   NULL   0          /*  binary tree header file  */
typedef   char   DATA;

struct node {
      DATA           d;
      struct node    *left_off;
      struct node    *right_off;
};


typedef   struct node    NODE;
typedef   NODE           *BTREE;
```

The file *tree.h* must be included with all binary tree functions defined in this section.

A key advantage of a binary tree over a linear list is that elements are normally reached, on average, in a logarithmic number of link traversals. This gain in time efficiency for retrieving information is at the expense of the space needed to store the extra link field per element. We illustrate this advantage in the exercises.

Binary Tree Traversal

There is one way to march down a linear list, namely from head to tail. There are several natural ways to visit the elements of a binary tree. The three commonest are:

Inorder:	left subtree
	root
	right subtree
Preorder:	root
	left subtree
	right subtree
Postorder:	left subtree
	right subtree
	root

These standard methods of visitation are the basis for recursive algorithms that manipulate binary trees.

```
/***  inorder binary tree traversal  ***/

inorder (root)
BTREE    root;
{
     if (root != NULL) {
          inorder (root -> left_off);      /*  recur left  */
          printf ("%c ", root -> d);
          inorder (root -> right_off);     /*  recur right  */
     }
}
```

The function inorder() will print the values of each node in the binary tree pointed at by root. The pictured binary tree would be traversed by inorder(), printing

A B C D E F G H I J

A binary tree

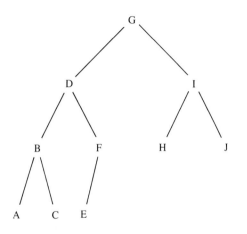

The corresponding preorder and postorder functions are:

```
/***  preorder and postorder traversal  ***/

preorder(root)
BTREE    root;
{
    if (root != NULL) {
        printf("%c ", root -> d);
        preorder(root -> left_off);
        preorder(root -> right_off);
    }
}


postorder(root)
BTREE    root;
{
    if (root != NULL) {
        postorder(root -> left_off);
        postorder(root -> right_off);
        printf("%c ", root -> d);
    }
}
```

Preorder visitation of the binary tree shown above would print

```
G   D   B   A   C   F   E   I   H   J
```

Postorder visitation would print

```
A   C   B   E   F   D   H   J   I   G
```

The reader unfamiliar with these methods should carefully verify these results by hand. Visitation is at the heart of most tree algorithms.

Creating Trees

We will create a binary tree from data values stored as an array. As with lists, we will use the dynamic storage allocator `malloc()` properly cast to avoid type warnings.

```
/***  creating a binary tree  ***/

BTREE  new_node( )
{
    return ((BTREE) malloc(sizeof(NODE)));
}
```

```
BTREE  init_node(d1, p1, p2)
DATA     d1;
BTREE    p1, p2;
{
     BTREE    t;

     t = new_node();
     t -> d = d1;
     t -> left_off = p1;
     t -> right_off = p2;
     return (t);
}
```

We will use these routines as primitives to create a binary tree from data values stored in an array. There is a very nice mapping from the indices of a linear array into nodes of a binary tree. This is done by taking the value a[i] and letting it have as offspring values a[2*i+1] and a[2*i+2]. Then a[0] will be mapped into the unique root node of the resulting binary tree. Its left offspring will be a[1] and its right offspring will be a[2]. The function create_tree() embodies this mapping. The formal parameter size is the number of nodes in the binary tree.

```
/***  create a linked binary tree from an array  ***/

BTREE create_tree(a, i, size)
int    i, size;
DATA   a[];
{
     if (i >= size)
          return (NULL);
     else
          return (
               init_node(a[i],
                    create_tree(a, 2 * i + 1, size),
                    create_tree(a, 2 * i + 2, size)));
}
```

10.8 GENERAL LINKED LISTS

For some data structures, we wish to combine the use of arrays with the use of lists. The arrays provide random accessing and the lists provide sequential accessing. We will show one such example in this section, an implementation of a general tree. In a general tree, a node can have an arbitrary number of offspring. It would be very wasteful to specify a structure using the maximum number of links for each node.

We will represent a general tree as a number of linear linked lists, one for each node in the tree. Each list will be the offspring of a single node. The lists will have an array that will point at the first offspring of the corresponding node. The base element of the array will point at the root node. The following diagram shows such a representation, for the general tree shown at the beginning of section 10.7.

A general tree and associated list structure

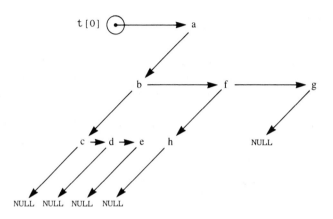

Such trees can be represented using the following header file.

In file gtree.h:

```
#define    NULL    0            /*  general tree header file  */
typedef    char    DATA;

struct node {
      int            ofs_no;
      DATA           d;
      struct node    *sib;
};

typedef    struct node    NODE;
typedef    NODE           *GTREE;
```

We will use an array of type GTREE, say t, where t[0] points to the root element represented as type NODE. Siblings will be reached by linear list chaining, and offspring by array indexing. Let us examine the creation of a particular such tree. We first write routines to create a single node.

```
/***   create a new node   ***/

GTREE new_gnode()
{
      return ((GTREE) malloc(sizeof(NODE)));
}

GTREE init_gnode(d1, num, sibs)
DATA     d1;
int      num;
GTREE    sibs;
{
      GTREE    temp;

      temp = new_gnode();
      temp -> d = d1;
      temp -> ofs_no = num;
      temp -> sib = sibs;
      return (temp);
}
```

Let us use these routines to create the tree of the previous diagram. Since it contains eight nodes, we need an array t[9] of type NODE, where t[0] is the pointer to the root node.

```
t[0] = init_gnode('a', 1, NULL);
t[1] = init_gnode('b', 2, NULL);
t[1] -> sib = init_gnode('f', 6, NULL);
t[1] -> sib -> sib = init_gnode('g', 7, NULL);
t[2] = init_gnode('c', 3, NULL);
t[2] -> sib = init_gnode('d', 4, NULL);
t[2] -> sib -> sib = init_gnode('e', 5, NULL);
t[3] = t[4] = t[5] = NULL;
t[6] = init_gnode('h', 8, NULL);
t[7] = t[8] = NULL;
```

It is easy to detect certain properties in this representation such as whether a node is a leaf node or how many offspring a node has. For node n, if t[n] points at NULL, then the node is a leaf.

Traversal

Traversal becomes a combination of (1) moving along lists and (2) indexing into array elements that point at the lists. It is straightforward to generalize the traversal ordering of preorder, postorder, and inorder to these structures. Once again these algorithms are prototypes for more complicated functions that can be done on a tree, because they guarantee that in linear time each element will be reached.

```
/***  preorder traversal of general trees  ***/

preorder_g(t, ind)
GTREE    t[];
int      ind;      /* t[ind] is the root node  */
{
     GTREE    temp;      /*  temp traverses the sibling list  */

     temp = t[ind];      /*  point at header  */
     while (temp != NULL) {
          printf("%c  %d\n", temp -> d, temp -> ofs_no);
          preorder_g(t, temp -> ofs_no);
          temp = temp -> sib;
     }
}
```

The function `preorder_g()` differs from the corresponding binary tree function in that a `while` loop is necessary to move along the linear list of siblings. Notice that recursion allows each subtree to be handled cleanly.

The Use of `calloc()` and Building Trees

The standard library function `calloc()` provides contiguous allocation of storage for arrays. This function `calloc()`, when called as follows,

```
calloc(n, size);
```

returns a pointer to enough contiguous storage for n objects, each of `size` bytes. This storage is initialized to all zeros. The arguments to `calloc()` are `unsigned`, and the value returned is pointer to `char`. This function can dynamically allocate sufficient storage to contain a run-time defined array. Thus the user need not modify for each run the size of the array or define a large enough size to include all cases of interest.

We will want a routine that can build a general tree from a list of edges and an array of type DATA. For example, if we wish to have an array of size ten to store the tree headers, we can write:

```
t = (GTREE *) calloc(10, sizeof(GTREE));
```

Now we can pass the dynamically allocated array t of type pointer to GTREE to a function buildtree() to construct a general tree. This function will take an edge list representation of a tree and compute its general list structure representation.

```
/*** buildtree constructs a tree from an array of edges ***/

typedef struct {        /* pair represents an edge in a tree */
        int     out;
        int     in;
} PAIR;

buildtree(edges, d, n, t)
DATA     d[];
PAIR     edges[];       /* n - 1 */
int      n;             /* number of nodes */
GTREE    t[];
{
        int     i;
        int     x, y;       /* points of edge */

        t[0] = init_gnode(d[1], 1, NULL); /* takes node 1 as root */
        for (i = 1; i <= n; ++i)
                t[i] = NULL;
        for (i = 0; i < n - 1; ++i) {
                x = edges[i].out;
                y = edges[i].in;
                t[x] = init_gnode(d[y], y, t[x]);
        }
}
```

Similar data structures and functions can be used to develop representations of general graphs, sparse matrices, and complicated networks.

10.9 SUMMARY

1. Self-referential structures use pointers to address identically specified elements.

2. The simplest self-referential structure is the linear linked list. Each element points to its next element, with the last element pointing at NULL defined as 0.

3. The function malloc() is used to dynamically allocate storage. It takes an argument of type unsigned and returns a pointer to char that is the address of the allocated storage.

4. The function `free()` is a storage management routine that returns to available storage the block of memory pointed at by its argument.

5. Standard algorithms for list processing are naturally implemented recursively. Frequently, the base case is the detection of the NULL link. The general case recurs by moving one link over in the list structure.

6. When algorithms are implemented iteratively, one uses an iterative loop that terminates when NULL is detected. Iterative algorithms trade the use of auxiliary pointers for recursion.

7. A stack is implementable as a list, with access restricted to its front end, which is called the top. The stack has a LIFO (last in first out) discipline implemented by the routines `push()` and `pop()`.

8. Binary trees are represented as structures with two link members. They combine the dynamic qualities of linear lists with, on average, significantly shorter access paths to each element. These distances to elements of binary trees are usually logarithmic.

9. Binary trees are traversed most often in one of three major patterns: preorder, inorder, or postorder. Each ordering is determined by when the root is visited. Preorder visits the root first; inorder, after the left subtree; and postorder, last. These traversal patterns are readily implemented as recursions chaining down both left and right subtrees.

10. Data structures of formidable complexity, involving both lists and arrays can be specified. One example of their use is for implementing a general tree where a node has an arbitrary number of offspring. The offspring of a node are represented as a list pointed at by an array of header elements.

10.10 EXERCISES

1. Fix the following so that it compiles correctly.

```
struct husband {
        int             age;
        char            name[10];
        struct wife     spouse;
} a;

struct wife {
        int             age;
        char            name[10];
        struct husband  spouse;
} b;
```

2. Change the `typedef` DATA in file *list.h* to

```
typedef struct {
       char    name[10];
       int     age;
       int     weight;
} DATA;
```

   and write a function `create_l()` that transforms an array of such data into a linear list. Write another routine, one that will count the number of people above a given weight and age.

3. Given a linear list of the type found in exercise 2, write a routine `sort_age()` that will sort the list according to its age values. Write a function `sort_name()` that will sort in lexicographic order based on name values.

4. Try to combine the sorting functions in exercise 3, so that they share the most code. This is best done by defining a routine called `compare()`, which returns a value of either 0 or 1 depending on which element is larger. Use this function as a parameter to a linear list sorting function.

5. Draw the list that would result from `concatenate(a, a)`, where a points at a list of two elements. What happens if the resulting list pointed at by a is passed to `print_list(a)`?

6. Exercise 5 was used to construct a cycle. A cycle is a pointer chain that points back to itself. Cycles are particularly nasty run-time bugs that can be hard to recognize. Write a program `iscycle(head)` that returns 1 if a cycle is detected and 0 otherwise. *Hint:* Mark the initial position of the list and move around until either NULL is reached or the initial address encountered.

7. Write an iterative version of the function `count()`.

8. Modify `concatenate()` so that it returns the address of the head of the resulting list. Also, if the first list is NULL, it should return the second list. Have it tested to see if both lists are the same. If they are, a cycle will result (see exercise 5) and the program should return a warning to that effect.

9. Write `copy_cat(a, b)`, which returns a concatenated copy of the lists a and b. The original lists a and b should remain undisturbed.

10. Write an iterative version of the function `concatenate()`.

11. Write an insertion function that inserts an element at the head of the list.

12. Write an insertion function that inserts an element at the tail of the list.

13. Write an insertion function that inserts an element at the first position in the list following an element storing a particular DATA item.

14. Generalize the previous two exercises. Write an insertion function that inserts an element in the *n*th position in a list, where 0 means the element is placed at the head of the list. If *n* is larger than the length of the list, insert the element at the tail of the list.

15. An element of a doubly linked linear list can be defined as

```
typedef struct dllist {
    DATA              d;
    struct dllist    *last;
    struct dllist    *next;
} ELEMENT;
```

This adds an extra member, but allows easier traversal along the list.

A doubly linked list

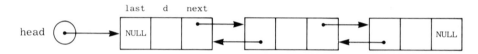

Write iterative routines to perform insertion and deletion.

16. Write a routine `del_dupl()` that deletes duplicate valued elements in a doubly linked list.

17. Evaluate the following Polish expressions:

  (a) 7, 6, -, 3, *
  (b) 9, 2, 3, *, 4, -, +
  (c) 1, 2, +, 3, 4, +, *

18. Write as Polish:

  (a) (7 + 8 + 9) * 4
  (b) (6 - 2) * (5 + 15 * 2)
  (c) 6 - 2 * 5 + 15 * 2

19. Code the programs given in the stack section to evaluate the six Polish expressions given or derived in exercises 17 and 18.

20. Write a routine that allows you to interactively initialize the contents of the stack for Polish expressions. The resulting program will allow you to evaluate expressions interactively until terminated by a program specified termination sequence or control-c.

21. Extend the function `evaluate()` so that it can be used with expressions having unary minus.

22. Write routines that for binary trees:

    (a) count the number of nodes
    (b) count the number of nodes having a particular value, say 'b'
    (c) print out the value of only leaf nodes

23. Create a binary tree from an array of int such that a left offspring has value less than its roots value, and a right offspring has value greater than or equal to the value of its root. Such a tree is displayed in the following diagram.

A binary tree with ordered values

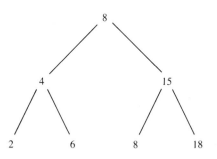

Insert a new element by comparing its value to the root and recurring down the proper subtree until NULL is reached.

24. For the tree of exercise 23, write a function that uses inorder traversal to place the values of the nodes in sorted order in an array key []．

25. Write a program that deletes the root node of a binary tree and replaces the root with the rightmost leaf node.

Deleting the root node with replacement

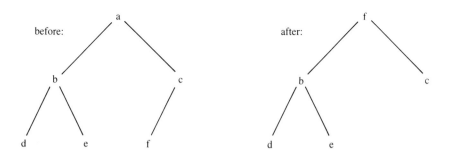

26. (Advanced) Write heapsort. This is a sorting routine based on an ordered binary tree. A heap is a binary tree in which a node has value smaller than any of its offspring. This property guarantees that the root is the smallest element in the tree. We wish to take an unordered array of values and create a heap with these values as data entries. Given a heap,

> First, delete the root, placing it in an output array as the smallest element.
> Second, take the rightmost leaf node and make it the new root.
> Third, compare the root value to the value of both offspring and exchange with the smaller of the two values.
> Fourth, continue to exchange values until the current node is smaller in value than its offspring.

Now the tree is once again a heap. Repeat these steps until the tree is empty and the array has the original tree values in sorted order. You must figure out how to get the tree in heap order to begin with. [See Aho, Hopcroft, and Ullman, *Data Structures and Algorithms* (Reading, Mass.: Addison-Wesley, 1983).]

27. Print out the nodes of a binary tree in level order. The root node is at level zero. The next level of nodes are the offspring of the previous level. First, print the root node. Then print the left offspring and right offspring that are at level one. Continue printing the nodes from left to right, level by level. This is also called breadth-first traversal.

28. Write a routine that computes the maximum level leaf node of a general tree.

29. Write a function that converts a binary tree into a general tree representation.

30. Add a field called weight to our general tree structure. Write functions to:

    (a) compute the sum of all node weights
    (b) compute the maximum weighted path, where the weighted path of node i is the weights of the nodes from the root to node i

    It can be proved that the maximum weighted path occurs at a leaf, given that all weights are nonnegative.

31. Use a general linked list structure to program sparse matrix addition. A sparse matrix is one in which most of its values are zero. A nonzero element of a sparse matrix will be represented by the triple ($i, j, value$). For each row i the triples will be linked as a linear list headed by an array of pointers row[i]. Similarly, for each column j the triples will be linked as a linear list headed by an array of pointers col[j]. To add matrix A to matrix B, we take each row and merge them into a matrix C. If both rows have a triple with the same column value, then the output row element c[i,j] is the sum of the a[i,j] + b[i,j]. Otherwise the element with the smallest column number is added as the next element of the output row.

32. (Advanced) The representation in exercise 31 can also be used to do sparse matrix multiplication. For this, both row and column linked lists are necessary. Program sparse matrix multiplication.

11

Input/Output and the
UNIX Environment

C resides on a machine and uses the facilities of an operating system. We have been using a VAX with the Berkeley 4.2 UNIX operating system as our reference standard; other systems include comparable facilities. C systems include libraries. For example, basic mathematical functions are usually in a mathematical library, and input/output functions are in the standard library. This chapter will explain in detail how to use some of the standard input/output functions, including `printf()` and `scanf()`. Other operating systems provide a comparable set of library functions.

Certain UNIX tools have been provided to aid the programmer in developing C software. A number of the most important UNIX tools that are directly of use to the C programmer will be explained. These include the options available with the *cc* compiler, and the use of *lint*, *cb*, and *make*. The chapter will finish with a brief critique of C and its future use and development.

11.1 THE OUTPUT FUNCTION `printf()`

Throughout this book the workhorse output function has been `printf()`. It has two nice properties that allow flexible use at a high level. First, an arbitrary length list of arguments can be printed, and second, the printing is controlled by simple formats that hide the efforts of conversion from the user. The function `printf()` delivers its character stream to the standard output file, `stdout`. The `printf()` parameter list has two parts:

   control_string   and   *argument_list*

In the example

   `printf("she sells  %d  %s  for  $%f", 99, "sea shells", 3.77);`

we have

   control_string: `"she sells %d %s for$%f"`
   argument_list: `99, "sea shells", 3.77`

A list of expressions separated by commas comprises the argument list. These expressions are evaluated and converted according to the formats in the control string and then placed in the output stream. Characters in the control string that are not part of a format are considered ordinary text and are placed directly in the output stream. The % symbol introduces a format, or conversion specification. A single conversion specification is a string that begins with % and ends with a conversion character.

Conversion character	Meaning	Example
d	decimal integer	45
o	octal integer without a leading 0	55
x	hexadecimal integer without a leading 0x	2d
u	unsigned decimal integer	45
e	floating point number with an exponent	-7.001100e+03
f	floating point number without an exponent	-7001.100000
g	the shorter of e or f is selected	-7001.1
c	single character	k
s	string	Pacific

In the example

```
printf("she sells  %d  %s  for  $%f", 99, "sea shells", 3.77);
```

we can match the formats in the control string with their corresponding arguments in the argument list.

Format	Corresponding argument
%d	99
%s	"sea shells"
%f	3.77

Explicit formatting information may be included in a conversion specification. If it is not included, then certain defaults occur. For example, the format %f with corresponding argument 3.77 will result in 3.770000 being printed. The number is printed with six digits to the right of the decimal point by default. Explicit formatting information is specified as follows. Between the % sign and the conversion character there may be

A minus sign, which means that the converted argument is to be *left adjusted* in its field; if there is no minus sign, then the converted argument is to be *right adjusted* in its field; the place where an argument is printed is called its *field*, and the number of spaces used to print an argument is called its *field width*.

A digit string, which defines the *field width* of the converted argument; if the converted argument has fewer characters than the specified field width, then it will be padded with blanks on the left or right, depending on whether the converted argument is right or left adjusted; if the converted argument has more characters than the specified field width, then the field width will be extended to "whatever is required"; if the field width begins with zero, then zeros will be used for padding rather than blanks.

A period, which separates *field width* from *precision*.

A digit string, which defines the *precision* of the converted argument; for an e or f conversion, this is the number of digits to the right of the decimal point; for an s conversion, it is the maximum number of characters to be printed from a string.

The character 1 or L, which specifies that the conversion character d, o, x, or u that follows corresponds to an argument of type long.

Instead of a digit string, the field width or precision or both may be a *, which indicates that the value is to be obtained from an argument in the argument list.

These formats, or conversion specifications, interact in predictable ways. The field width is the minimum number of spaces that must be there. The default is whatever is required to properly display the argument. Thus the integer value 102 (decimal) will require three spaces for decimal conversion d or octal conversion o, but only two spaces for hexadecimal conversion x. These digits will appear right adjusted unless the minus sign is present. If the field width is too short to properly display the value of the corresponding argument, the field width will be increased to the default. If the entire field is unneeded to display the converted argument, then the remaining part of the field is padded with blanks on the left or right, depending on whether the converted argument is right or left adjusted. The padding character can be made o by specifying the field width with a leading zero.

The digit string representing precision occurs to the right of the period. For string conversions this is the maximum number of characters to be printed from the string. For e and f conversions this is the number of digits to be printed to the right of the decimal point. The following three tables illustrate the effect of various specifications on integral types, floating types, and strings.

Declarations and assignments

```
char   c;
int    i,j,k;

c = 'w';    i = 1;    j = 29;    k = 230551777;
```

Format	Expression	How it is printed in its field	Remarks
		/* quote marks are used to delimit the field */ /* they are not part of what is printed */	
%c	c	"w"	field width 1 by default
%2c	c	" w"	right adjusted
%-3c	c	"w "	left adjusted
%d	c	"119"	field width 3 by default
%5d	c	" 119"	right adjusted
%-5d	c	"119 "	left adjusted
%d	i	"1"	field width 1 by default
%d	-j	"-29"	field width 3 by default
%10d	i	" 1"	right adjusted
%010d	i	"0000000001"	padded with zeros
%010d	-i	"-000000001"	padded with zeros
%-12d	j	"29 "	left adjusted
%12o	j	" 35"	octal—right adjusted
%-12x	j	"1d "	hexadecimal—left adjusted
%d	k	"230551777"	field width 9 by default
%5d	k	"230551777"	9 spaces are needed
%17d	-k	" -230551777"	right adjusted

In the preceding discussion, "precision" refers to how many digits are printed to the right of the decimal point, or to how many characters are printed from a string. Normally, precision refers to the accuracy with which floating numbers are stored in a machine. Although a number with many digits to the right of the decimal place can be assigned to a variable of type float, only 6 (approximately) significant digits are stored. Similarly, only 16 (approximately) significant digits are stored for a double. When a request is made via printf() to print a double with precision greater than 16, what actually gets printed is system dependent. There can be no meaning attached to the digits printed beyond the 16 or so significant digits actually stored in the machine.

The following table illustrates the use of the floating point conversion specifications, and examples occur where the printed precision is more than the number of significant digits stored. The comments in the table about significant figures are in reference to a VAX, or typically any machine that stores a float in 4 bytes and a double in 8 bytes.

Declarations and assignments			

float x;
double y, z;
 	
x = y = 333.12345678901234567890;
z = -555.11111111111111111e-9;			

Format	*Expression*	*How it is printed in its field*	*Remarks*
	/* quote marks are used to delimit the field */ /* they are not part of what is printed */		
%f	x	"333.123444"	precision 6 by default
	/* approximately 6 digits are significant for a float */		
%.1f	x	"333.1"	precision 1
%.9f	x	"333.123443603"	precision 9
%20.3f	x	" 333.123"	right adjusted
%-20.3f	x	"333.123 "	left adjusted
%.9f	y	"333.123456789"	precision 9
%.20f	y	"333.12345678901234000000"	precision 20
	/* approximately 16 digits are significant for a double */		
%20.3e	y	" 3.331e+02"	right adjusted
%-20.3e	y	"3.331e+02 "	left adjusted
%f	z	"-0.000001"	precision 6 by default
%e	z	"-5.551111e-07"	precision 6 by default
%.1e	z	"-5.6e-07"	precision 1
%.3e	z	"-5.551e-07"	precision 3
%20.9e	z	" -5.551111111e-07"	right adjusted
%-20.9e	z	"-5.551111111e-07 "	left adjusted
%2e	z	"-5.551111e-07"	more space needed

The next table illustrates the use of the string conversion specifications.

Declarations and initializations			
| ```
char      c = 'w';
static char s1[] = "she sells sea shells";
static char s2[] = "by the sea shore";
``` | | | |
Format	***Expression***	***How it is printed in its field***	***Remarks***
		`/*` quote marks are used to delimit the field `*/` `/*` they are not part of what is printed `*/`	
`%s`	`c`	`/*  error  */`	a char is not a string
`%s`	`s1`	`"she sells sea shells"`	field width 20 by default
`%7s`	`s1`	`"she sells sea shells"`	more space needed
`%20s`	`s2`	`"    by the sea shore"`	right adjusted
`%-20s`	`s2`	`"by the sea shore    "`	left adjusted
`%.5s`	`s2`	`"by th"`	precision 5
`%.12s`	`s2`	`"by the sea s"`	precision 12
`%15.12s`	`s2`	`"   by the sea s"`	precision 12, right adjusted
`%-15.12s`	`s2`	`"by the sea s   "`	precision 12, left adjusted
`%3.12s`	`s2`	`"by the sea s"`	more space needed

To print the character % in the output stream, one can use the conversion specification %%, which prints a single percent symbol. Of course, the expression '%' can be in the argument list to be printed under the conversion specification %c.

11.2 THE INPUT FUNCTION scanf()

The function scanf() has two nice properties that allow flexible use at a high level. The first is that an arbitrary length list of arguments can be scanned, and the second is that the input is controlled by simple formats that hide the effort at conversion from the user. The scanf() parameter list has two parts:

  control_string   and   *argument_list*

In the example

```
char      c, s1[81], s2[81];
int       n;
double    x;

scanf("%s%d%s%c%lf", s1, &n, s2, &c, &x);
```
```

we have

> *control_string*: "%s%d%s%c%lf"
> *argument_list*: s1, &n, s2, &c, &x

The argument list consists of a list of pointer expressions separated by commas. The standard input file stdin provides the character stream from which scanf () receives its input. The control string may contain

White space, which matches optional white space in the input stream.

An ordinary nonwhite character, other than %, which must match the next character in the input stream.

Conversion specifications, which begin with a % and end with a conversion character; between the % and the conversion character there may be an optional *, which indicates assignment suppression, followed by an optional integer, which defines a maximum field width.

The modifiers 1 or h to the specification character (see below).

The characters in the input stream are converted to values according to the conversion specifications in the control string, and placed at the address given by the corresponding pointer expression in the argument list. Conversion specifications begin with a % character and end with a conversion character.

Conversion character	*How the input stream is interpreted*
d	decimal integer
o	octal integer
x	hexadecimal integer
u	unsigned decimal integer
e	floating point number
f	e and f are equivalent
c	single character
s	string
[*string*]	special string

The conversion characters d, o, x, e, f may be preceded by an 1 to indicate that conversion to a long int or long float is to occur. Alternatively, the conversion characters D, O, X, E, F may be used. In a similar fashion, the conversion characters d, o, x may be preceded by an h to indicate that conversion to a short is to occur.

Except for character input, an input field consists of contiguous nonwhite characters that are appropriate to the specified conversion. The input field ends when a nonappropriate character is reached, or the field width, if specified, is exhausted, whichever comes first. When a string is read in, it is presumed that enough space has been allocated in memory to hold the string and an end-of-string sentinel \0, which will be appended. When one or more characters are read in, white space is not skipped. The format %1s can be used to read in the next nonwhite character. A value of type float can be read in with a %e or %f format. The conversion characters e and f are equivalent. A %le or %lf can be used to read in a double (long float). Floating numbers are formatted in the input stream as an optional sign followed by a digit string, which may contain a decimal point, followed by an optional exponent part consisting of e or E followed by an optional sign followed by a digit string. The specification %[*string*] is used to indicate that a special string is to be read in. If the first character in *string* is not a circumflex ∧, then the string is to be made up only of the characters in *string*. On the other hand, if the first character in *string* is a circumflex, then the string is to be made up of all characters other than those in *string*. Thus the format %[abc] will input a string containing only the letters a, b, c, and will stop if any other character appears in the input stream, including a blank. The format %[∧abc] will input a string terminated by any of a, b, or c, but not by white space. The statement

```
scanf ("%[ab \n\t]", s);
```

will read into the character array s a string containing a's, b's, and the white space characters blank, newline, and tab.

These conversion specifications interact in predictable ways. The field width is the number of spaces that are scanned to retrieve the argument value. The default is whatever is in the input stream. Thus the specification %5s skips white space and then reads only the next five characters in the input stream, but the specification %s reads an arbitrary length white space terminated string.

Characters other than % that appear in the control string are searched for in the input stream. White space is ignored in the control string. To ignore the character % in the input stream, one can use %%, which ignores a single percent character. Of course, the character % can be input to a character variable by using the conversion specification %c.

The function scanf() returns the number of successful conversions performed. The value EOF is returned when the end-of-file mark is reached. Typically, this value is −1. The value 0 is returned when no successful conversions are performed, and this value is always different from EOF. An inappropriate character in the input stream can frustrate expected conversions, causing the value 0 to be returned. As long as the input stream can be matched to the control string, the input stream is scanned and values are converted and assigned. The process stops if the input is inappropriate for the next conversion specification. The value returned by scanf() can be used to test that input occurred as expected, or to test that the end of the file was reached. An example is

```
int      i;
char     c;
char     string[15];

scanf ("%d , %*s %% %c %5s %s", &i, &c, string, &string[5]);
```

With the following characters in the input stream

```
45 , ignore_this  %  C  read_in_this**
```

the value 45 is placed in i, the comma is matched, the string ignore_this is ignored, the % is matched, the character c is placed in the variable c, the string read_ is placed in string[0] through string[4], the character \0 is placed in string[5], and finally the string in_this** is placed in string[5] through string[14], with string[14] containing \0. Since four conversions were successfully made, the value 4 is returned by scanf().

11.3 RELATED FUNCTIONS fprintf(), sprintf(), fscanf(), AND sscanf()

The function printf() writes to the file stdout. The related function fprintf() must have a file pointer specified as its first argument, but the remaining arguments are like those of printf(). In particular,

```
fprintf(stdout, . . . );        and        printf( . . . );
```

are equivalent statements. We shall see in the following section that stdout is a predefined identifier of type pointer to FILE. The user can use other file pointers as well. In a similar fashion the function sprintf(s, . . .) writes to the string s instead of to the file stdout. The programmer must ensure that this string is large enough to store the output.

The function fscanf() corresponds to scanf(), but has as its first argument a file pointer that indicates which file is to be read. Thus a statement of the form

```
fscanf (file_ptr, control_string, argument_list);
```

requires *file_ptr* to be a pointer to FILE and *control_string* and *argument_list* to conform to the conventions required for scanf(). Similarly, sscanf() is the string form of scanf(). Its first argument is a string from which the function takes its input.

11.4 FILES

A file is accessed via a pointer to a structure that is defined in the standard header file *stdio.h* as FILE. This structure contains members that describe the current state of the file. Abstractly, a file is to be thought of as a stream of characters that is processed sequentially. The system provides three standard files.

Written in C	Name	Remark
stdin	standard input file	connected to the keyboard
stdout	standard output file	connected to the screen
stderr	standard error file	connected to the screen

The library function `fopen()` can be used to open a file. It returns a pointer to
FILE. One could write, for example,

```
#include    <stdio.h>

main()
{
    int     c;
    FILE    *fp, *fopen();

    fp = fopen("my_file", "r");
    .  .  .  .  .
```

to open the file named *my_file*. After a file has been opened, the file pointer is used
exclusively in all references to the file. The function `fopen()` is described in some
detail in the following list, which contains descriptions of some useful library functions.
It is not a complete list; the reader should consult manuals to find other available
functions in the standard library. There may be slight variations from system to system.
In the remainder of this chapter, other functions in the list will be illustrated, and the
reader should consult the list as necessary to understand how these functions are used.

A description of some of the functions in the standard library

`fopen(file_name, file_mode)`

> Performs the necessary housekeeping to open a buffered file and returns a pointer
> to FILE. The pointer value NULL is returned if `file_name` cannot be accessed;
> both `file_name` and `file_mode` are strings. The file modes are "r", "w", and
> "a" corresponding to read, write, and append, respectively. The file pointer is
> positioned at the beginning of the file if the file mode is "r" or "w", and it is
> positioned at the end of the file if the file mode is "a"; if the file mode is "w"
> or "a" and the file does not exist, it is created.

`fclose(file_pointer)`

> `file_pointer` is a pointer to FILE. The function `fclose()` performs the nec-
> essary housekeeping to empty buffers and breaks all connections to the indicated
> file. EOF is returned if `file_pointer` is not associated with a file. Open files
> are a limited resource (20 files can be open simultaneously on the VAX); system
> efficiency is improved by keeping only needed files open.

`getc(file_pointer)`

> Retrieves the next character from the file pointed to by `file_pointer`. The value
> of the character is returned as an int; it returns EOF if an end-of-file is encountered
> or if there is an error. This function may be implemented as a macro if <stdio.h>
> is included.

`getchar ()`

> This is equivalent to `getc (stdin)`; it may be implemented as a macro if `<stdio.h>` is included.

`fgetc (file_pointer)`

> Acts similarly to `getc ()`, but it is a function and not a macro.

`ungetc (c, file_pointer)`

> Pushes the character value of c back onto the file pointed to by `file_pointer` and returns the int value of c. If the file is buffered and one or more characters have been read, then at least one character can be pushed back. EOF is returned if it is not possible to push back a character.

`putc (c, file_pointer)`

> Places the character value of c in the output file pointed to by `file_pointer`. It returns the int value of the character written; it may be implemented as a macro if `<stdio.h>` is included.

`putchar (c)`

> This is equivalent to `putc (c, stdout)`; it may be implemented as a macro if `<stdio.h>` is included.

`fput (c, file_pointer)`

> This is similar to `putc (c, file_pointer)` except that it is a function, not a macro.

`gets (s)`

> s is a string variable (pointer to char); `gets (s)` reads a string into s from `stdin`. Characters are placed in s until a newline character is read, at which point the newline character is changed to a null character and is used to terminate s. The value of s (pointer to char) is returned.

`fgets (s, n, file_pointer)`

> Characters are read from the file pointed to by `file_pointer` and placed into the string s until n − 1 characters have been read or a newline character is read, whichever comes first. Unlike `gets ()`, if a newline character is read, it is placed in s. In both cases s is terminated with a null character. The value of s (pointer to char) is returned.

`puts (s)`

> The null terminated string s is copied to `stdout`, except that the terminating null character itself is not copied; a newline character is appended.

`fputs(s, file_pointer)`

The null terminated string s is copied to the file pointed to by `file_pointer`, except that the terminating null character itself is not copied. Unlike `puts()`, a newline character is not appended.

`fseek(file_pointer, offset, place)`

The position of the next input or output operation is set. `offset` is a variable of type `long` and `place` is a variable of type `int`; `place` can take one of the three values 0, 1, or 2, corresponding to the beginning of the file, the current position, or the end of the file, respectively. The file pointer is moved `offset` bytes from `place`. Any effects of `ungetc()` are undone by `fseek()`.

`rewind(file_pointer)`

This is equivalent to `fseek(file_pointer, 0L, 0)`.

`ftell(file_pointer)`

The current `offset` from the beginning of the file pointed to by `file_pointer` is returned as a `long`; in UNIX the offset is measured in bytes.

`unlink(file_name)`

The named file is removed from the directory. If there are no other links to the file in other directories, the space is returned to the operating system and the file is destroyed. This function returns −1 if the file does not exist or cannot be accessed, and 0 is returned otherwise.

`exit(status)`

This function terminates a program when it is called; all buffers are flushed and files are closed. The function returns the value of `status` to the calling process; `status` is an expression of type `int`. By convention 0 is returned to indicate that the program ran properly; a nonzero value is returned otherwise.

`system(command)`

`command` is a string (pointer to `char`) that is executed by the UNIX command interpreter (the shell); for example, the line of code

```
system("cal 1987");
```

will cause the UNIX command *cal 1987* to be executed by the shell, and that in turn will cause a calendar for the year 1987 to be printed on the file `stdout`.

We will write a number of programs that illustrate the use of these standard library functions. The first program capitalizes the letters in a file and writes to stdout.

```
/*** capitalize all the letters in a file ***/

#include    <stdio.h>

main(argc, argv)
int     argc;
char    *argv[];
{
    int     c;
    FILE    *fp, *fopen();

    fp = fopen(argv[1], "r");
    while ((c = getc(fp)) != EOF)
        if ('a' <= c && c <= 'z')
            putchar(c + 'A' - 'a');
        else
            putchar(c);
}
```

The statement

```
fp = fopen(argv[1], "r");
```

opens the file specified by the first command line argument for reading. The pointer fp can be thought of as pointing to this file. The while loop beginning with the line

```
while ((c = getc(fp)) != EOF)
```

will read characters from this file into c until the end of the file is reached. After this program has been compiled, it can be executed by the command

  a.out file

The output of the program will be written on stdout. The command

  a.out infile > outfile

will cause the output of the program to be redirected to *outfile*.

The next program will double space an input file and write to both `stdout` and an output file. For each newline character in the input file, a second one will be added. We have written the program to be much more robust than the previous example.

```
/*** double space the lines in a file ***/

#include    <stdio.h>

main(argc, argv)
int     argc;
char    *argv[];
{
      int     c;
      FILE    *myfile_in, *myfile_out, *fopen();

      if (argc != 3) {
          fprintf(stderr, "\nusage: %s infile outfile\n", *argv);
          exit(1);
      }
      if ((myfile_in = fopen(*++argv, "r")) == NULL) {
          fprintf(stderr, "\nmain:  cannot open %s\n", *argv);
          exit(1);
      }
      if ((myfile_out = fopen(*++argv, "w")) == NULL) {
          fprintf(stderr, "\nmain:  cannot open %s\n", *argv);
          exit(1);
      }
      while ((c = getc(myfile_in)) != EOF) {
          putc(c, myfile_out);
          putc(c, stdout);        /* echo to stdout also  */
          if (c == '\n') {        /* double space */
              putc(c, myfile_out);
              putc(c, stdout);
          }
      }
      fclose(myfile_in);
      fclose(myfile_out);
}
```

Suppose that this program has been compiled and that the executable code is in the file *double_space*. If the command line

   double_space file1

is typed, then `argc` will have value 2, which we consider to be abnormal. If `argc` has any value other than 3, the program writes an appropriate message to `stderr` and exits by invoking the system function `exit()`. Since the argument to `exit()` has a nonzero value, it is considered an abnormal exit. Now suppose that the command line

   double_space file1 file2

is typed. Since argc has the value 3, control passes to the next if statement. The expression

```
(myfile_in = fopen(*++argv, "r")) == NULL
```

is used to open the file specified by the first command line argument. Instead of *++argv we could have written argv[1]. Notice that the parentheses are necessary, because = has lower precedence than ==. If for some reason fopen() is unable to open the file, the pointer value NULL is returned, and in that case we exit the program with an appropriate message written to stderr.

11.5 THE MACROS IN *ctype.h*

The system provides a standard header file *ctype.h*, which contains a set of macros that are used to test or convert characters. They are made accessible by the preprocessor control line

```
#include   <ctype.h>
```

Those macros that only test a character return an int value that is nonzero (*true*) or 0 (*false*). Since they are implemented by table lookup, they are very efficient.

Macro	*Nonzero (true) is returned if:*
isalpha(c)	c is a letter
isupper(c)	c is an uppercase letter
islower(c)	c is a lowercase letter
isdigit(c)	c is a digit
isxdigit(c)	c is a hexadecimal digit
isspace(c)	c is a white space character
isalnum(c)	c is a letter or digit
ispunct(c)	c is a punctuation character
isprint(c)	c is a printable character
iscntrl(c)	c is a control character
isascii(c)	c is an ASCII code

Macro	*Effect*
toupper(c)	changes c from lowercase to uppercase
tolower(c)	changes c from uppercase to lowercase
toascii(c)	changes c to ASCII code

11.6 AN EXAMPLE: CRUNCH A C PROGRAM

We will use the macros in the standard header file *ctype.h* and file processing functions
in the standard library to write a program called *crunch* that removes some of the
extraneous white space and all comments from a file containing C code. It does not
remove all possible white space. To write such a program would be more difficult.
Disk space is often a limited resource. Our *crunch* program will typically reduce by
20% the space required to store the source code of a C program. As we shall see later,
the UNIX utility *cb*, the C beautifier, will reformat a crunched program (but not restore
any discarded comments).

The first function is used to remove comments.

```
#include    <stdio.h>

eat_comment(fp)
FILE    *fp;
{
    char    c1, c2;

    for ( ; ; )
        if ((c1 = getc(fp)) == '*')
            if ((c2 = getc(fp)) == '*')
                ungetc(c2, fp);
            else if (c2 == '/')
                return;
}
```

This function assumes that you are inside a comment and discards all characters
including the comment terminator */. Notice that ungetc() is necessary. If c2 was
tested for being equal to / and instead was equal to *, this second asterisk would be
discarded. Without the use of ungetc(), the code would not treat a string such as **/
as the end of a comment.

The next function is used to remove most of the excess white space. This function
places newline characters into the output file whenever they are encountered in the
input file. The first character that is not white space is pushed back into the file.

```
#include    <stdio.h>
#include    <ctype.h>

eat_white_space(ifp, ofp)
FILE    *ifp, *ofp;
{
    int    c;

    while (isspace(c = getc(ifp)))
        if (c == '\n')
            putc(c, ofp);
    ungetc(c, ifp);
}
```

There are special difficulties with strings. A string is bracketed by a pair of double quote characters. However, inside the string a double quote may appear preceded by a backslash character \. An escaped double quote does not terminate the string. Furthermore a double quote may occur in a character constant as '"' or '\"'. The functions out_string(), out_bslash(), and out_char() are intended to take care of these cases.

```c
#include    <stdio.h>

out_string(ifp, ofp)
FILE    *ifp, *ofp;
{
    char    c;

    putc('"', ofp);
    while ((c = getc(ifp)) != '"')
        if (c == '\\')
            out_bslash(ifp, ofp);
        else
            putc(c, ofp);
    putc(c, ofp);
}


out_bslash(ifp, ofp)
FILE    *ifp, *ofp;
{
    char    c;

    putc('\\', ofp);
    c = getc(ifp);
    putc(c, ofp);
}

out_char(ifp, ofp)
FILE    *ifp, *ofp;
{
    char    c;

    putc('\'', ofp);
    while ((c = getc(ifp)) != '\'')
        if (c == '\\')
            out_bslash(ifp, ofp);
        else
            putc(c, ofp);
    putc(c, ofp);
}
```

The majority of the work is done in crunch(), which uses a switch statement to handle the various cases. This construction makes it easily extensible to other cases.

```
#include    <stdio.h>

crunch(ifp, ofp )
FILE    *ifp, *ofp;
{
        int    c1, c2;

        while ((c1 = getc(ifp)) != EOF)
                switch (c1) {
                case '/':
                        if ((c2 = getc(ifp)) == '*') {
                                eat_comment(ifp);
                                putc(' ', ofp);
                        }
                        else {
                                putc('/', ofp);
                                ungetc(c2, ifp);
                        }
                        break;
                case ' ':
                case '\t':
                        putc(' ', ofp);
                        eat_white_space(ifp, ofp);
                        break;
                case '\\':        /*  backslash escape  */
                        out_bslash(ifp, ofp);
                        break;
                case '\'':        /*  quoted character  */
                        out_char(ifp, ofp);
                        break;
                case '"':
                        out_string(ifp, ofp);
                        break;
                default:
                        putc(c1, ofp);
                }

}
```

In the function `main()` we check that `argc` has the desired value. We have arranged for the program to read from `stdin` and write to `stdout`, but it would be easy to change `main()` so that an input and/or an output file is specified via `argv`. This would not require modification of the other functions in the program.

```
/***  crunch  c  code by removing comments and white space  ***/

#include   <stdio.h>

main(argc, argv)
int    argc;
char   *argv[];
{
    if (argc != 1) {
        fprintf(stderr,
            "\nusage:  %s  < infile > outfile\n\n", *argv);
        exit(1);
    }
    crunch(stdin, stdout);
    exit(0);
}
```

11.7 FILE DESCRIPTOR INPUT/OUTPUT

A *file descriptor* is a nonnegative integer associated with a file. In this section we describe a set of library functions that are used with file descriptors. Library functions using file descriptors need not be portable. Moreover, they require programmer specified buffers. In contrast, functions in the standard library making use of a pointer to FILE are usually buffered. We also discuss the standard library function `system()`, which is designed to communicate with the operating system.

Until this section, the functions in the standard library that we have described are available and standardized (within limits) on all full C systems. These functions are basically machine independent and portable. In sharp contrast to this are the low-level input/output functions that make use of file descriptors. File descriptors are a mechanism by which functions communicate with the UNIX operating system. The low-level library functions described in this section can be viewed as functional formats of corresponding machine language system calls. These functions are inherently machine dependent and nonportable. To increase portability, some non-UNIX C implementations attempt to provide analogous functions. However, in many non-UNIX operating systems, these functions are lacking.

The next table contains the file descriptors associated with the standard files. Following that table is a description of functions in the UNIX standard library that make use of file descriptors.

File name	*Associated file descriptor*
stdin	0
stdout	1
stderr	2

Some functions in the standard library to be used with file descriptors

creat(file_name, protection)

> file_name is a string. In UNIX, protection is defined by three-digit octal codes; on other systems different conventions may be used. creat() returns a file descriptor or −1 if it fails. If the named file already exists, it is truncated to length zero, otherwise a new file is created with the specified protection.

open(file_name, access)

> Returns a file descriptor or −1 for fail; access is 0 for read, 1 for write, or 2 for both. All further references to the file are via the file descriptor.

close(fd)

> fd is a file descriptor. If a file is closed, 0 is returned; otherwise −1 is returned for fail.

read(fd, buffer, n)

> An attempt is made to read from the file associated with the file descriptor fd into the location specified by buffer at most n bytes; typically buffer is a character array of sufficient size to hold n bytes. If fd is 0 (stdin), then at most one line will be read. The file is not read beyond EOF; read() returns the actual number of bytes read or −1 for fail.

write(fd, buffer, n)

> buffer is the address of n contiguous bytes of storage; the contents of buffer is written to the file associated with the file descriptor fd. The actual number of bytes written or −1 for fail is returned; if the value returned is not n, it should be regarded as an error.

lseek(fd, offset, place)

> offset is an integer: it can be negative, zero, or positive; place is an integer that can be 0, 1, or 2 corresponding to the current position in the file, the beginning of the file, or the end of the file, respectively. The current position in

the file associated with the file descriptor fd is moved to offset bytes from place and its value is returned as a long.

We will illustrate the use of file descriptors by writing a program that appends to the end of a file some systems information and one line of user-supplied text. The idea is that this information could be of use to the user at some later time; it can be viewed as a convenient way of keeping a diary. The following UNIX commands will be used.

Command	*What it does*
date	prints the current date and time
pwd	prints the working directory
whoami	prints the user's login name

The first function uses system() to append desired systems information to the file, whose name is passed in as a string.

```
#define    MAXLINE    81

sys_info(file_name)
char    *file_name;
{
       char    s[MAXLINE], *strcat(), *strcpy();

       strcpy(s, "date >> ");
       strcat(s, file_name);
       system(s);
       strcpy(s, "pwd >> ");
       strcat(s, file_name);
       system(s);
       strcpy(s, "whoami >> ");
       strcat(s, file_name);
       system(s);
}
```

Suppose that "myfile" is the string pointed to by file_name. Then strcpy() and strcat() are used to create in s the string

```
"date >> myfile"
```

The statement

```
system(s);
```

passes the string "date >> myfile" to the operating system to be used as a command line. The symbols >> mean that the output of the command is to be appended to the named file.

```
#define    BUFSIZE    81

main(argc, argv)
int    argc;
char    *argv[];
{
      char    mybuf[BUFSIZE];
      int     fd, n;
      long    lseek();

      if (argc != 2) {
          printf("\nusage:  %s  file\n\n", argv[0]);
          exit(1);
      }
      if ((fd = open(argv[1], 1)) == -1)
          fd = creat(argv[1], 0777);
      sys_info(argv[1]);
      lseek(fd, 0L, 2);
      printf("\ninput one line of information\n\n");
      n = read(1, mybuf, BUFSIZE);
      write(fd, mybuf, n);
}
```

In `main()`, the file named in `argv[1]` is opened if it exists; otherwise, it is created with protection mode `0777`. In a protection mode, each octal digit controls read, write, and execute privileges for the file. The first octal digit controls privileges for the user, the second octal digit controls privileges for the group, and the third octal digit controls privileges for all others.

Meaning of each octal digit in the protection mode

Mnemonic	Bit representation	Octal representation
r__	100	04
_w_	010	02
__x	001	01
rw_	110	06
r_x	101	05
_wx	011	03
rwx	111	07

Examples of protection modes

Mnemonic	Octal representation
rw_____	0600
rw____r__	0604
rwxr_xr_x	0755
rwxrwxrwx	0777

The statement

```
lseek(fd, 0L, 2);
```

is used to move the current position in the file associated with the file descriptor fd to the end of that file. The statement

```
n = read(1, mybuf, BUFSIZE);
```

causes at most BUFSIZE characters to be read from stdout and placed in mybuf. The statement

```
write(fd, mybuf, n);
```

causes n characters to be written from mybuf into the file associated with the file descriptor fd.

11.8 REDIRECTION AND PIPING IN UNIX

The UNIX operating system provides convenient mechanisms to reassign the standard input and output files. Ordinarily these are connected to the keyboard and screen, respectively. A UNIX command or C program expects these files to be available without special bookkeeping. The programmer need not create, open, close, or otherwise administer these files. The standard output may be reassigned by using the redirection symbol > as in

cmd > file

Thus compiling a program to the executable file *a.out* and invoking it as

a.out > out_file

causes any output from *a.out* written to stdout to be redirected to *out_file*. If *out_file* does not exist, it will be created. If it exists, it will be overwritten. The redirection symbols >> cause output written to stdout to be redirected to the end of the named file. If the file does not exist, it is created. If the file exists, the output of the command is appended to it.

In an analogous fashion stdin is redirected by using the symbol <. Thus

cmd < file

takes the named file as input to *cmd* in place of stdin. Of course, a command line can redirect both stdin and stdout:

cmd < in_file > out_file

Because it allows for flexibility, redirection is a powerful facility.

Another useful UNIX facility is a "pipe." The `stdout` of one command can be "piped" to the `stdin` of another command. The symbol | is used to designate a pipe. Thus the command line

cmd1 | cmd2

takes any output of *cmd1* written to `stdout` as the input of *cmd2*. For this to work, *cmd2* must read `stdin`. The UNIX command *wc* (for "word count") counts lines, words, and characters in one or more files and writes to `stdout`. If no files are specified on the command line, then *wc* reads `stdin`. The command *date*, on the other hand, writes to `stdout`, but does not accept input from any file. Thus

date | wc   will work, but   *wc | date*

will fail. Of course, pipes and redirection can both be used in the same command line.

date | wc > temp

The user can create sequences of piped commands and use them to sequentially process data. Such a sequence is called a pipeline. The UNIX software tool philosophy is to write small pieces of code to do one thing well. Then, with the use of pipes and redirection, the user can readily combine a sequence of simple commands to accomplish a more complicated action.

11.9 AN EXAMPLE: PRINTING A TABLE OF CONTENTS

We will write a program capable of producing a table of contents from a properly formatted text file. The program will read as input one or more files, or if no file is given, it will read `stdin`. It will write to `stdout`. Thus the program will be suitable to use with redirection or to use in a pipe.

We will adopt conventions from *troff*, a widely used text formatter in UNIX. In *troff*, formatting commands begin with a "." in column one. Lines beginning with .sh are printed as section headings. If *troff* were to be used to print this chapter, then the file it acted on would contain

```
.sh 1 "INPUT/OUTPUT AND THE UNIX ENVIRONMENT" 11
text
.sh 2 "THE OUTPUT FUNCTION printf()"
text
.sh 2 "THE INPUT FUNCTION scanf()"
etc
```

The general form of a section heading is

> . sh *M* "*heading*" $N_1 N_2 \ldots N_k$

with the .sh starting in column one. The integer *M* represents the "depth" of the section heading and the integers $N_1 , \ldots , N_k$ are optional and represent the section number. Thus a depth of 3 and the numbers 11 9 1 would print the section number 11.9.1 regardless of the previous numbering.

All the functions in our program will make use of the following header file:

In file ptoc.h:

```
#include    <ctype.h>
#include    <stdio.h>

#define   MAXLINE     1000
#define   MAXTITLE    100
#define   MAXSECNO    6

#define   ERROR(message, line)    {                        \
      fprintf(stderr, "\n%s%s\n%35s\n\n%s\n\n",            \
          "error:  ", message,                             \
          "the line in error follows:", line);             \
      exit(1);                                              \
      }

#define   SET(p)    {                  \
      while (!isspace(*(p)))            \
          ++p;                          \
      while (isspace(*(p)))             \
          ++p;                          \
      }
```

Our program will either take a file from stdin or take files named on the command line and produce a table of contents in stdout by extracting the section heading information. The function main() largely takes care of housekeeping, checking for errors in file openings.

```
/***  print a table of contents  ***/

#include   "ptoc.h"

main(argc, argv)
int    argc;
char   *argv[];
{
      int    i;
      FILE   *fp, *fopen();

      fprintf(stderr, "\n%s\n%s\n%s",
            "this program makes a table of contents.",
            "section headings are extracted from",
            "the following files:   ");
      fprintf(stderr, "%s\n",
            (argc == 1) ? "stdin" : argv[1]);
      for (i = 2; i < argc; ++i)
            fprintf(stderr, "%22s%s\n", "", argv[i]);
      fprintf(stderr, "\n\n");
      if (argc == 1)
            prn_headings(stdin);
      else
            for (i = 1; i < argc; ++i) {
                  if ((fp = fopen(argv[i], "r")) == NULL) {
                        fprintf(stderr, "%s: cannot open\n", argv[i]);
                        exit(1);
                  }
                  prn_headings(fp);
                  fclose(fp);
            }
}
```

The real work in main() is accomplished by calling prn_headings(). This function checks to see if a line of text begins with .sh starting in column one.

```
#include    "ptoc.h"

prn_headings(fp)
FILE    *fp;
{
    char    line[MAXLINE], title[MAXTITLE];
    int     i, nsec, secno[MAXSECNO];

    for (i = 0; i < MAXSECNO; ++i)    /* initialize to zero */
        secno[i] = 0;
    while (fgets(line, MAXLINE, fp) != NULL)
        if (strncmp(line, ".sh", 3) == 0) {
            get_head_info(line, secno, title, &nsec);
            for (i = 1; i < nsec; ++i)
                putc('\t', stdout);
            printf("%d", secno[0]);
            if (nsec == 1)
                putchar('.');
            else for (i = 1; i < nsec; ++i)
                printf(".%d", secno[i]);
            printf("%s%s\n", "   ", title);
        }
}
```

Any line that starts with .sh is passed to get_head_info(), which extracts a title and computes a current section number. The extracted information is printed using an indented format. Proper indenting is accomplished by outputting an appropriate number of tabs \t. The current section numbers are stored in the array secno[]. This is automatically incremented unless explicitly reset. Here is the function get_head_info.c.

```
#include    "ptoc.h"

get_head_info(line, secno, title, nsec_ptr)
char    *line, *title;
int     secno[];        /*  current values  */
int     *nsec_ptr;      /*  .sh nsec  */
{
    char    *p = line;
    int     i;

    check_head(line);
    SET(p);         /*  point at nsec  */
    sscanf(p, "%d", nsec_ptr);
    ++secno[*nsec_ptr - 1];
    SET(p);         /*  point at  "  */
    ++p;            /*  point at title  */
    for (i = 0; *p != '"'; )      /*  collect title  */
        title[i++] = *p++;
    title[i] = '\0';
    SET(p);         /*  point at section numbers  */
    for (i = 0; isdigit(*p); ++i) {
        sscanf(p, "%d", &secno[i]);
        SET(p);
    }
    for (i = *nsec_ptr; i < MAXSECNO; ++i)
        secno[i] = 0;
}
```

The function check_head() is called to check for errors. Then the extraction of the key information within line[] is accomplished. First, the number following the .sh is found. This number represents the "depth" of the section heading and its value is stored into *nsec_ptr. Next, the title is extracted. Finally, a search is made for optional section numbers. If these are present, then secno[] is reinitialized to their values, otherwise the old values are retained.

The function check_head() is designed to catch some obvious errors. It certainly will not catch them all.

```
#include    "ptoc.h"

check_head(line)
char    *line;
{
    char    *p = line;
    int     nsec;

    SET(p);
    if (!isdigit(*p))
        ERROR("depth number after .sh is missing", line);
    sscanf(p, "%d", &nsec);
    if (nsec > MAXSECNO)
        ERROR("section depth exceeds limit", line);
    SET(p);
    if (*p != '"')
        ERROR("title not where expected", line);
    ++p;
    while (*p != '"')       /*  find matching  "  */
        ++p;
    SET(p);
    while (isdigit(*p) || isspace(*p))
        ++p;
    if (*p != '\0')
        ERROR("an illegal character follows title", line);
}
```

11.10 THE *cc* COMPILER

The resident UNIX C compiler is invoked by the command *cc*. Like many other UNIX commands it has a host of useful options. We will describe some of the most important features of *cc*.

When a complete program is contained in a single file, say *pgm.c*, then the command

cc pgm.c

will translate the C code in *pgm.c* into executable object code and write it in the file *a.out*. The command *a.out* will execute the program. A simple option is the flag −*o*, used as follows:

cc −o pgm pgm.c

This will cause the executable code to be written into the file *pgm* rather than *a.out*. In effect this automatically renames *a.out*.

The *cc* compiler actually does its work in two stages, a compile phase and a load phase. If *file.c* contains one or more functions and the command

cc −c file.c

is given, then an object file named *file.o* is created. This *.o* file can now be compiled with other files, or by itself if it contains a main(), to produce an executable file. A program that exists in a number of files might be compiled as follows:

cc −o runrun main.c file1.c file2.c

Because more than one file is being compiled, the files *main.o*, *file1.o*, and *file2.o* containing object code, as well as the file *runrun* containing executable object code, will be produced. The *.o* extension designates files containing object code. These files can be considered to be compiled but not loaded. If later a change is made to *main.c*, the command

cc −o runrun main.c file1.o file2.o

will produce a new executable file. The compiler will allow a mix of *.c* and *.o* and *.s* files.

Some useful options to the cc command

−O   attempt code optimization.
−E   generate C code with the macros expanded and print on stdout.
−S   generate a *.s* file containing assembly language.
−D*name=def*   place the line #define *name def* into the C code.
−U*name*   remove any #define *name* line from the C code.
−c   produce a *.o* file but not *a.out*.
−p   add code to allow an execution profile post mortem.

Suppose the file *example.c* contains the following code:

```
main()
{
      int   i = 15, j;

      j = 7 * i;
}
```

With the command

    cc −S example.c

the resulting file *example.s* on our VAX will contain

```
LL0:
            .data
            .text
            .align   1
            .globl   _main
_main:
            .word    L12
            jbr      L14
L15:
            movl     $15,-4(fp)
            mull3    $7,-4(fp),r0
            movl     r0,-8(fp)
            ret
            .set     L12,0x0
L14:
            subl2    $8,sp
            jbr      L15
            .data
```

For those familiar with machine organization, this shows that the constant 15 is stored on the stack by the movl instruction. Then 7 and the value just stored are multiplied in register 0 by the mull3 instruction. Finally, register 0 is stored on the stack in the position that is equivalent to the source variable j, and control is returned to the calling environment by ret. We can create an executable *a.out* file with the command

    cc example.s

The −p option used with *cc* causes the compiler to produce code that counts the number of times each routine is called. If the compiler creates an executable file, then it is arranged so that the library function monitor() is automatically called upon execution, and a file *mon.out* is created. The file *mon.out* is then used by the *prof* command to generate an execution profile. As an example of how this all works, suppose that we want an execution profile of the *crunch* program written earlier in this chapter. We first compile the program with the −p option.

```
cc -p -o crunch        main_crunch.c        \
                       crunch.c             \
                       eat_comment.c        \
                       eat_white_space.c    \
                       out_bslash.c         \
                       out_char.c           \
                       out_string.c
```

A backslash at the end of a command line allows the command to continue to the next line. We are purposely compiling this program from a collection of files, each containing one function. We leave as an exercise the experiment of seeing what happens when all the functions exist in just one file, which is then compiled with the *−p* option. We next give the command

  cat ∗.c | crunch > temp

This concatenates all files ending in *.c* in the current directory and pipes them to *crunch*, which then writes to the file *temp*. The idea is to give *crunch* a real workout. Now, when we give the command

  prof crunch

the following is printed on the screen:

%time	cumsecs	#call	ms/call	name
47.7	0.52	1	516.83	_crunch
18.5	0.72	1291	0.15	_eat_white_space
10.8	0.83	1321	0.09	_ungetc
6.2	0.90	75	0.89	_out_string
6.2	0.97	15	4.45	_read
3.1	1.00	24	1.39	_eat_comment
3.1	1.03	2	16.67	_write
1.5	1.05	15	1.11	__filbuf
1.5	1.07	1	16.67	_main
1.5	1.08			mcount
0.0	1.08	3	0.00	__flsbuf
0.0	1.08	2	0.00	_fstat
0.0	1.08	1	0.00	_gtty
0.0	1.08	1	0.00	_ioctl
0.0	1.08	1	0.00	_isatty
0.0	1.08	104	0.00	_out_bslash
0.0	1.08	70	0.00	_out_char
0.0	1.08	1	0.00	_profil

Not all of the named functions are user defined; some such as _read are system routines. Such a profile can be very useful when working to improve execution time efficiency.

11.11 THE C VERIFIER *lint*

The command *lint* takes a file containing C code and issues a variety of messages aimed at improving program correctness, efficiency, and portability. For example, *lint* indicates if data or functions are declared but unused. It will also detect whether code is inadvertently unreachable. Generally speaking, one should always use *lint* before proceeding to actual compilation. Suppose that the file *lintex.c* contains the following code:

```
main()        /*  nonsense  */
{
      char          y = '1',  z;
      int           x = 'p';
      extern float  dbl();

      goto L1;
      while (1 != 0) {
L1:          x += (long)y;
             printf("nonsense: %d\n",x);
      }
      return (y);
}
```

The command

> *lint −hxa lintex.c*

gives the following suggestions:

```
lintex.c(8):  warning: constant in conditional context
lintex.c(8):  warning: loop not entered at top
lintex.c(9):  warning: long assignment may lose accuracy
lintex.c(12): warning: statement not reached
lintex.c(3):  warning: z unused in function main
dbl defined( ???(5) ), but never used
```

The reader should consult a UNIX manual to find the meaning of the options *−hxa*. There are other options as well.

11.12 THE C PRETTY PRINT COMMAND *cb*

The purpose of a "pretty print" program is to take as input a file containing source code and to produce as output the same code nicely formatted. UNIX provides the *cb* command, which stands for C beautifier, to "pretty print" C code. Throughout this book we have stayed with some standard indenting and spacing conventions when writing code. These conventions are meant to make code more readable and to display the program logic. The command *cb* reads from stdin and writes to stdout. If the input is redirected from a file containing C code, then that code will be "pretty printed" or "beautified" and then written on stdout. If *program.c* contains C code, then the command

> *cb < program.c*

will "pretty print" it on the screen and the command

    cb < program.c > pgm.c

will "pretty print" it and write it in the file *pgm.c*. Ideally, one should be in the habit of writing code that does not require further pretty printing.

11.13 THE *make* COMMAND

UNIX and C are well suited to developing modular programs. Particular programs can require a large number of files and display complicated dependencies on system library files and locally defined files. The *make* command requires all of these dependencies to be contained in a file whose default name is *makefile* or *Makefile*. The contents of such a file might be

    `runrun: run.o file1.o file2.o;  cc -o runrun run.o file1.o file2.o`

This means that the executable program *runrun* depends on three object files, which are to be compiled as

    cc -o runrun run.o file1.o file2.o

Suppose that *file1.c* has been rewritten. This requires that it be recompiled and linked to other object files that depend on it. The command *make,* when executed, tests to see if any file has been modified since its last invocation. When necessary, the command recompiles those files that have been modified, or depend on the modification, and produces a new executable program named *runrun.*

A *makefile* consists of a series of blank separated target files, then a colon, then a blank separated series of prerequisite files. The targets are dependent in some way on the named prerequisite files and must be updated when the prerequisite files are modified. The updating action, such as compilation, is specified after a semicolon or after a tab character at the start of a new line. As an example, here is the file that we used in the development of the *ptoc* program.

    In makefile:

```
#  ptoc: print a table of contents

ptoc:   ptoc_main.o  prn_headings.o  \
        get_head_info.o  check_head.o

        cc  -o ptoc  ptoc_main.o      \
                     prn_headings.o   \
                     get_head_info.o  \
                     check_head.o

ptoc_main.o  prn_headings.o  \
get_head_info.o  check_head.o:  ptoc.h
```

A comment occurs between a # character and a newline character. The backslash character is used to continue a line. The character that occurs just before the cc is a tab. The *make* routine knows that a *.o* file depends on a corresponding *.c* file. Notice that all the *.o* files depend on *ptoc.h*. Suppose that the file *ptoc.h* is changed and then the command *make* is given. The default updating action of recompilation of all the *.o* files (target files) then occurs.

The *make* command has many useful options. The reader should consult a UNIX manual and experiment with *make* to better understand its use. Indeed most of the material in this section, and to a lesser extent the other parts of this chapter, are best tested and used in conjunction with a UNIX manual to provide further detail and a description of any local variations.

11.14 THE FUTURE OF C: SOME FINAL COMMENTS

Today C is one of the most important programming languages available; tomorrow we expect it to be even more important. It is important because of its UNIX connection, its portability and size, and its elegance and power. We wish to say a few final words about C and suggest something about its prospects.

The UNIX world was at first only Bell Laboratories, and later a few disparate computer science departments. Today, UNIX is in widespread use on machines of all sizes. It is widely found on university campuses around the world, and it is the dominant low-end commercial time-sharing operating system. C is the language of UNIX, and its use and facilities are intimately intertwined in such a way that C is often the language of preference on a UNIX system.

C is easily portable. Writing a new C compiler takes a few man-months. Inexpensive C compilers are routinely advertised in the trade literature, several for under $100. The portability comes from omitting system dependent functions from the actual language. Thus each system can use utilities such as an input/output library that are written to conform to local constraints. The language is in many ways easily translated to machine code. Many of its features, such as representing *true* as a nonzero value or incrementing a variable by means of the ++ operator, closely parallel standard machine operations. Only "call by value" is needed for parameter passing, and all functions are on the same external level, so that the run-time environment is readily managed by a simple stack discipline. The language is small and unrestrictive. Thus not many constructs need to be translated and these constructs need not be artificially restrained.

The language is very powerful. It has an extensive set of operators that gives the programmer a strong command of the machine. Together with standard libraries, it is easily extensible. The data types interact in an orthogonal fashion. Structures, arrays, and enumeration types can be combined in any logical manner. The different storage classes provide both modularity and privacy. C is really a system that includes a librarian, a macro-preprocessor, a compiler, and a general loader. Moreover, facilities such as *lint*, *cb*, and *make* can be considered as extensions to the system.

Some problems exist. C requires a high degree of programmer discipline. The language allows a large variety of side effects and this can lead to overly tricky and obscure code. Certain semantic ambiguities exist, both explicitly and implicitly, that create nonportability problems and idiosyncratic bugs. The compiler may reorder expressions to accommodate efficient translation or evaluation. The order of evaluation of argument lists is unspecified. For example, on a VAX, argument lists are generally evaluated right to left. This conforms to the stacking discipline of last in first out. The syntax of C is ambiguous, especially in regard to allowing very complicated declarations. Apparently the syntax would allow a function definition that returns an array, but this is semantically illegal.

One suspects that the various standards committees will move toward an agreed upon formal syntax and to more explicit semantics. There is also the likelihood that C systems will be provided with portable standard libraries as is common on UNIX systems. To expand the language or to restrain the use of its constructs to conform to a particular discipline is not in the spirit of C. The merits of C lie in its elegant terseness. As a language, C is an evolutionary fixed point that, for the moment, is a natural balance among the various needs of programmer and system. We hope and expect that C will not change into D, as some have predicted. C is a natural starting point for building software, much as zero is a natural starting point for building the integers.

11.15 SUMMARY

1. C uses libraries that are not part of the language to perform input/output and to compute mathematical functions. The standard library has an extensive set of basic and high-level input/output routines.

2. The output function `printf()` and the input function `scanf()` use conversion specifications in a control string to deal with a variable length list of arguments.

3. A file is thought of as a stream of characters that are accessed or written sequentially. Three standard files are `stdin`, `stdout`, and `stderr`. The file `stdin` is usually connected to the keyboard and used by `scanf()`. The files `stdout` and `stderr` are usually connected to the screen and used by `printf()` and `fprintf(stderr, . . . )`, respectively. The file `stderr` is also used by the system to write error messages.

4. Programmers may declare files by including `<stdio.h>`, which contains the definition of the structure `FILE`, and then declaring a file pointer such as

    ```
    FILE    *my_file_ptr;
    ```

    The statement

    ```
    my_file_ptr = fopen("my_file", "r");
    ```

    will open the file *my_file* for reading. Similarly, one uses `"w"` for writing and `"a"` for appending. A file must be opened before it can be used.

5. A standard collection of functions exists to access a file through its file pointer. For example, `getc(file_pointer)` reads one character from the pointed at file.

6. The standard header file *ctype.h* provides a complete set of character test macros and conversion macros. A typical macro such as `isdigit(c)` is nonzero if the character c is a digit and zero otherwise.

7. A further set of input/output functions act on integer file descriptors. The file descriptors of `stdin`, `stdout`, and `stderr` are 0, 1, and 2, respectively. Unlike stream input/output, these routines require user-specified buffers. A typical function is `write(file_desc, buffer, nbytes)`, where `buffer` is a character array and `nbytes` is the number of bytes to be written to the designated file.

8. C was originally invented to write the UNIX operating system. Both have grown up together and are intimately connected. Most host systems have UNIX-like utilities that are accessible through C. The function `system(command)` takes a string named `command` and passes it to the host operating system for execution.

9. The output to `stdout` may be redirected as in the command *cmd > file*. The input from `stdin` may be redirected as in the command *cmd < file*.

10. UNIX was originally invented to provide a sophisticated and productive environment for the computer professional. As such, it has a multitude of extremely useful tools for software development. The C compiler *cc* is itself an elaborate program provided with numerous options. A most useful option is the $-p$ flag, which causes the program when executed to produce a *mon.out* file. This file can be examined by the *prof* command to obtain an execution profile of the original program.

11. Among the most useful UNIX programming aids are:

lint	the C verifier
cb	the C "pretty printer"
make	a general program file administrator

11.16 EXERCISES

1. Examine the contents of your local *stdio.h*, *ctype.h*, and *math.h* files. Compare them to the header files discussed in this book listing any major differences.

2. Write an elementary "run-off" program. Make up a list of at least five commands such as the following:

Command	Meaning
.sp n	skip n lines
.pp	start a new paragraph
.fi	print equal width lines in fill mode
.in n	indent n spaces
.sh "*heading*"	print a section heading

Each command begins in column one and is on a line by itself. The commands are to be interspersed in ordinary text. Your "run-off" program should read one or more text files and write the properly formatted text to stdout.

3. Write getstring() and putstring() routines. They should use getc() and putc() to read and write strings from a designated file.

4. The following is one definition of FILE:

```
extern  struct  _iobuf {
          int     _cnt;
          char    *_ptr;
          char    *_base;
          short   _flag;
          char    _file;
} _iob[_NFILE];

#define FILE    struct _iobuf
#define stdin   (&_iob[0])
#define stdout  (&_iob[1])
#define stderr  (&_iob[2])
```

What is the significance of the symbolic constant _NFILE? Create a file and use putc() and getc() to write and read from it. While doing this, experimentally determine the member values of the structure _iobuf and their significance.

5. Modify the *ptoc* program to also detect the prefix .uh in column one. A line of the form

.uh "*heading*"

should create an unnumbered heading. Collect these lines and print them indented, but not numbered, underneath the previous section heading.

6. Run the *crunch* program on a collection of your own .c files and see how much space is saved on average.

7. Create a profile of the *crunch* program by first putting all the functions in one file, say, *crunch.c*, and then giving the command line

    cc −p crunch.c; cat *.c | a.out > temp; prof a.out

    Compare the results with what you get when you compile the *crunch* program with the −*p* option from a collection of files, each containing one function.

8. Profile the routines of the *crunch* program as described in this chapter. Then see if you can recode the program so that it is at least 10% more efficient than before.

9. Modify the *crunch* program to eliminate excess newline characters from C source files, making sure to preserve any newline that affects the syntactic correctness of the code.

10. Rewrite the *crunch* program to write out to a second file all the removed space, listed by line number. Start the line number at 0 (of course) and increment by one for each newline character in the file.

11. The following series of exercises will show how to write a systems file utility program similar to the UNIX command *rm*. The basic program removes a file from the user's directory.

```
main(argc, argv)        /*  remove a file  */
int     argc;
char    *argv[];
{
      unlink(argv[1]);
}
```

    Modify this program to remove one or more files.

12. Modify the program in exercise 11 to accept redirected input as well as a list of file names. Make this program more robust by testing for any simple user mistakes such as incorrect arguments. Print error messages to stderr.

13. Modify the program in exercise 12 to allow for optional flags. The command

    rm −i file1 file2 . . .

    should interactively prompt the user with the name of each file and ask if it is to be removed. If a y is typed, the file is to be removed, otherwise not. The command

    rm −e file1 file2 . . .

    should echo the name of each file removed. The flags should be detectable in various combinations such as −*ie* or −*i* −*e*.

14. After the following program has been run, precisely which characters are in the file *temp*?

```
#include    <stdio.h>

main()
{
    FILE    *fp, *fopen();

    fp = fopen("temp", "w");
    fprintf(fp, "\n%s\n\n", "ABC");
}
```

If UNIX is available to you, read the on-line manual concerning the command *od* (for octal dump). Use the command first with no flag, then with the flag −*x*, and then with the flag −*c*, to investigate the contents of *temp*.

15. After three characters have been read from a file, can ungetc() be used to push three characters back onto the file? Write a program to test this.

Appendix
ASCII Character Codes

Left\Right Digits	ASCII *American Standard Code for Information Interchange*									
	0	1	2	3	4	5	6	7	8	9
0	nul	soh	stx	etx	eot	enq	ack	bel	bs	ht
1	nl	vt	np	cr	so	si	dle	dc1	dc2	dc3
2	dc4	nak	syn	etb	can	em	sub	esc	fs	gs
3	rs	us	sp	!	"	#	$	%	&	'
4	(	)	*	+	,	−	.	/	0	1
5	2	3	4	5	6	7	8	9	:	;
6	<	=	>	?	@	A	B	C	D	E
7	F	G	H	I	J	K	L	M	N	O
8	P	Q	R	S	T	U	V	W	X	Y
9	Z	[	\	]	^	−	`	a	b	c
10	d	e	f	g	h	i	j	k	l	m
11	n	o	p	q	r	s	t	u	v	w
12	x	y	z	{	|	}	~	del		

Some observations

1. Character codes 0–31 and 127 are nonprinting.
2. Character code 32 prints a single space.
3. Character codes for digits 0 through 9 are contiguous.
4. Character codes for letters A through Z are contiguous.
5. Character codes for letters a through z are contiguous.
6. The difference between a capital letter and the corresponding. lowercase letter is 32.

The meaning of some of the abbreviations

nul	null	nl	new line
ht	horizontal tab	esc	escape
cr	carriage return	bs	back space
bel	bell	vt	vertical tab

Index to Selected Programs and Functions

Chapter 0

a traditional first program - obscurely written   3

Chapter 1

the distance of a marathon in kilometers   9
measuring the pacific sea   12
computing sums   19
compute minimum, maximum, sum, and average   23
capitalize lowercase letters and double space   27
have a nice day   36
the best possible minmax algorithm - Pohl, 1972   51

Chapter 2

read in two integers and print their sum   57

Chapter 3

integer arithmetic   72
increment and decrement expressions   76
compute the size of the fundamental types   78
compute areas of triangles, squares, and circles   81
trigonometric tables   82
char and int input-output on ascii machines   84
decimal, hexadecimal, octal conversions   92
what is the effect when sin() is not declared?   94
print everything possible   95
compute powers of 2   96

Chapter 4

evaluation stops as soon as true/false is determined	108
count blanks, digits, letters, newlines, and others	114
a table of values for some boolean functions	118
a test that fails	121
print fibonacci numbers and quotients	123
print all primes less than LIMIT	125

Chapter 5

a function with a simple header and body	136
the sum of squares of integers from 1 to n	140
test sum of squares	140
the sum of kth powers of integers from 1 to n	141
m raised to the nth power	141
print a table of sums of kth powers	141
simple interactive statistics	146
a pseudo random number generator	153
create an array of pseudo random numbers	153
a family of pseudo random number generators	155

Chapter 6

print the bit representation of an int	172
pack 4 characters into an int	172
unpack an int into 4 characters	173
create employee data in a short int	173
compute the next day	176
compute the next day with casts	176
paper, rock, scissors: a game	178

Chapter 7

pointer arithmetic is not integer arithmetic	197
merge a[] and b[] into c[]	200
mergesort: use merge() to sort an array	201
arrays and pointers are different	204
count the number of words in a string	209
sort words lexicographically	212

Chapter 8

reverse the characters between s[j] and s[k] recursively	227
partition a[] with respect to pivot	230
find the kth rank order element in a[]	233
find a root of f() by bisection	236

Chapter 9

complex arithmetic	263
probability of flushing	274

Chapter 10

list creation by recursion	284
list creation by iteration	285
count a list recursively	287
print a list recursively	287
concatenate list a and b with a as head	288
inserting an element in a linked list	289
recursive deletion of a list	290
basic stack routines	292
reversing a string using a stack	293
stack evaluation of Polish	295
inorder binary tree traversal	297
preorder and postorder traversal	298
creating a binary tree	298
create a linked binary tree from an array	299
create a new node	301
preorder traversal of general trees	302
buildtree constructs a tree from an array of edges	303

Chapter 11

capitalize all the letters in a file	321
double space the lines in a file	322
crunch c code by removing comments and white space	327
print a table of contents	334

Index

ABC, 38, 348
ada, 61
address, 16, 188
Aho, Hopcroft, and Ullman, 308
ALGOL, 1, 58, 240, 248
algorithm, 52
alignment, 271
a.out, 5
append mode, 44
argc, 215
argument command line, 45, 215
argument count, 45
argument list, 14, 309
argument macro, 241
argument variable, 45
argv, 215
arithmetic types, 68
array, 33, 188
   argument, 197
   base address, 196
   declaration, 194, 209
   dimension, 193, 209, 210, 216
   indexing, 195
   initialization, 194, 204, 217
   lower bound, 194
   pointer relationship, 196
   ragged, 217
   size, 36, 194
   storage allocation, 209
   storage mapping function, 210
   string, 36
   upper bound, 194
ASCII, 27
asm, 61

assignment expression, 68
assignment statement, 9
assignment structure, 261
associativity, 73
auto, 149

B, 1
Backus-Naur Form (BNF), 58
BCD, 278
BCPL, 1
Bell Laboratories, 1
binary, 89
bisection, 235
bit, 71, 173, 271
bitwise operator, 167
block, 137
   inner, 147
   nested, 149
   outer, 147
   parallel, 149
break statement, 51, 163
bubble sort, 35, 199, 214
byte, 71, 91, 271

C, 1
%c, 15, 39, 310, 315
C beautifier, 341
C compiler, 5, 337
C speed of light, 239
C verifier lint, 340
call by reference, 160, 192, 193
call by value, 31, 142
calloc(), 302

capitalize(), 42
carriage return, 24, 84
case, 165
cast, 35, 87
cat, 340
cb, 341
cc, 5, 337
cc options, 239, 338
char, 24, 66, 83
character, 27
check_head(), 337
close(), 328
coercion (conversion), 86
comma expression, 119, 120
command line, 215
comment, 9, 57, 62
commutative operator, 93
compilation, 36, 56
complex add(), 264
complex conjugate(), 264
complex multiply(), 264
complexity, 50
computer, 5
concatenate(), 288
constant, 63, 88
    character, 63, 83, 88
    decimal, 71
    double, 88
    expression, 63, 89
    floating, 71
    hexadecimal, 71, 89
    integer, 64, 88
    long, 88
    octal, 91
    pointer, 41, 188, 196
    symbolic, 239
continue, 163
control string, 10, 14, 88, 309
control-c, 24
control-d, 21
conversion automatic, 86
conversion character (format), 10, 15, 16
conversion specifications, 10, 311, 315
cos(), 64
creat(), 328
crunch(), 326
crunch a C program, 324
crypt, 222

%d, 15, 310, 315
dangling else problem, 112, 125

data types, 66
date, 329, 332
declaration, 9, 66
default, 165
#define, 11, 239
delete_list(), 290
derived type, 253, 268
digit, 71
discriminant, 132
dissection
    ABC, 38
    capitalize, 27
    change_it, 204
    create_rand, 48
    letters, 46
    list_words, 43
    marathon, 9
    mergesort, 201
    nice_day, 36
    pacific_sea, 12
    partition, 231
    process, 30
    sea, 7
    sort_words, 212
    sum, 20
    sum, lexical level, 57
divide and conquer, 229
do statement, 120
documentation, 63, 137, 239, 253
double, 9
doubly linked list, 306
dynamic data structures, 280

%e, 13, 15, 310, 315
e (base of the natural logarithms), 134, 239
eat_comment(), 324
eat_white_space(), 324
EBCDIC, 83
echo, 215, 223
efficiency, 227, 229, 249, 340
else part, 112
encryption, 222
end-of-file, 20
end-of-string, 203
#endif, 242
enum, 174
enumeration syntax, 174
enumeration type, 162, 174
enumerator, 174
EOF, 21, 26, 239

epsilon, 97
equality expression, 103, 104
Eratosthenes, Sieve of, 278
error messages, 54
evaluate (), 295
exchange (), 160
exit (), 320
exp (), 82
exponential part, 79
expression, 10
    assignment, 68, 85
    bitwise, 167
    comma, 119, 120
    constant, 63, 89
    equality, 103, 104
    logical, 18, 104, 106, 107
    relational, 101
extern, 149
external storage class, 150

%f, 10, 15, 310, 315
factorial, 226
factorial (), 226
false, 18, 100, 239
fclose (), 318
fgetc (), 319
fgets (), 319
fibonacci (), 228
Fibonacci numbers, 122, 227
Fibonacci numbers, table, 228
field, 15, 269
field width, 15
file, 44, 317
    descriptor, 327, 328
    descriptor, input/output, 327
    mode, 44
    privileges, 330
    stderr, 317
    stdin, 317
    stdout, 317
FILE, 44
find_pivot (), 230
float, 9
floating constants, 10, 79
floating types, 10, 68, 78
flow of control, 17, 162
fopen (), 44, 318
for statement, 17, 116
formal parameter, 137

format, (conversion character), 10, 15, 16, 311, 315
    %c, 15, 39, 310, 315
    %d, 15, 310, 315
    %e, 13, 15, 310, 315
    %f, 10,15, 310, 315
    %g, 15, 310
    %lf, 16, 17
    %o, 92, 310, 315
    %s, 15, 310, 315
    %[*string*], 315
    %u, 310, 315
    %x, 92, 310, 315
fortran, 61
fprintf (), 47, 317
fput (), 319
fputs (), 319
fractional part, 79
free (), 290
fscanf (), 317
fseek (), 320
ftell (), 320
function, 28, 136
    argument list, 143, 144
    arguments structure, 259
    array arguments, 198
    body, 137
    call by reference, 160, 192, 193
    call by value, 142
    definition, 136
    formal parameter, 137
    functions as arguments, 234
    header, 136
    invocation, 142, 143
    mathematical, 82
    parameter, 137
    pointer parameter, 191
    recursion, 225
    type specifier, 138
fundamental data types, 67
future of C, 343

%g, 15, 310
game of paper, rock, scissors, 177
game, poker, 272
garbage, 145, 194
gcd (), 251
general linked list, 299
generic_recursion (), 288
getc (), 318
getchar (), 24, 319

get_head_info(), 336
gets(), 319
global, 137, 192
golden mean, 122
goto statement, 162

header file, 14
heap, 308
hexadecimal, 90
hexadecimal digit, 90
Hoare, C. Anthony R., 229
Horner's rule, 221

identifier, 8, 60
if statement, 17, 109
#if, 242
#ifdef, 242
#ifndef, 242
#include, 14, 238
incremental patchwork program, 163
index, 33
index(), 205
infinite loop, 115, 117, 126
infix expression, 293
initialization, 13, 217
    array, 194, 204, 217
    pointer, 189, 217
    string, 204, 217
    structure, 272
    variable, 13
inorder(), 297
input/output, 309
insert(), 289
int, 9, 70
integer, 8
integer overflow, 71
integer part, 79
integral types, 68, 77
Intel 8086, 77
Intel 8088, 77
invocation, 143
isalnum(), 323
isalpha(), 323
isascii(), 323
iscntrl(), 323
isdigit(), 323
islower(), 323
ispnct(), 323
isprint(), 323

isspace(), 323
isupper(), 323
isxdigit(), 323

jbr, 339
jump (goto), 162

kepler(), 238
Kepler, Johannes, 237
Kernighan, Brian, 1
keyword (reserved word), 9, 61
knight's tour, 251
Knuth, Donald Ervin, 47, 203

label, 162
labeled statement, 162
lexical level, 57
%lf, 16, 17
library, 156
#line, 244
linear linked list, 282
link, 280
lint, 5, 95, 144, 254, 340
list, 280
    counting, 287
    creation, 284
    deletion, 289
    insertion, 288
    operations, 283
    printing, 287
local, 137
log(), 82
logical expressions, 104
logical operators, 104
long, 67
lseek(), 328

machine accuracy, 97, 103
machine dependent, 71, 76, 87, 97
macro, 225, 241
macro arguments, 241
macros in *ctype.h*, 323
main(), 7, 215
make, 33, 342
makefile, 342
malloc(), 282
mask, 171
mathematical library, 82

member, 255
merge(), 200
mergesort(), 201
MIN() macro, 242
minmax(), 51
mode, 44
modular, 2
modulus operator %, 72
Monte Carlo simulation, 160
multi-dimensional arrays, 209
multiply(), 255
mv, 6

nested loops, 118, 125
newline \n, 7
nibble, 91, 279
nonprinting character, 7, 56
not operator !, 105
null character \0, 84
NULL pointer value, 188, 281

%o, 92, 310, 315
octal digit, 91
octal number, 91
one-dimensional array, 193
one's complement, 168
open(), 328
operating system, 5
operator, 57, 61
    addition +, 10, 72, 93
    address &, 16, 188, 189
    arithmetic, 72
    assignment =, 73, 85
    assignment operators *op=*, 85
    associativity, 73, 262
    bitwise, 167
    bitwise and &, 93, 167, 169
    bitwise exclusive or ^, 93, 167, 169
    bitwise inclusive or ¦, 93, 167, 169
    cast (*type*), 35, 87
    comma , , 119
    commutative, 93, 263
    conditional ?:, 166
    decrement --, 73, 75
    dereferencing (indirection) *, 41, 189
    division /, 10, 72
    equality, 99, 103
    equals ==, 20, 99, 103
    greater than >, 99
    greater than or equal to >=, 99

operator (cont.)
    increment ++, 18, 73, 75
    indirection (dereferencing) *, 41
    left shift <<, 167, 169
    less than <, 99
    less than or equal to <=, 18, 99
    logical, 99
    logical and &&, 28, 99
    logical negation !, 99
    logical or ¦ ¦, 99
    modulus %, 72
    multiplication *, 10, 72, 93
    not equals !=, 99, 103
    one's complement ~, 167, 168
    precedence, 73, 262
    relational, 99, 101
    right shift >>, 167, 170
    sizeof, 78
    structure member, 255
    structure pointer ->, 258
    subtraction -, 72, 93
    unary minus -, 72
order(), 193
order of evaluation, 92, 263
out_bslash(), 325
out_char(), 325
output, 6
out_string(), 325
overflow, 71

pack, 172
palindrome, 221, 222
paper, rock, scissors: a game, 135
parameter, 137
partition break size, 229
partition(), 230
Pascal, 1
pascal, 61
pi, 235, 239
pipe, 332, 239
pivot element, 229
Pohl, Ira, 50, 251, 252
Pohl-Warnsdorf rule, 252
pointer, 38, 188
    argument, 197
    arithmetic, 196
    array, 212
    array relationship, 196
    assignment, 188
    constant, 188, 196

pointer (cont.)
  declaration, 188
  indirection, 189
  initialization, 189, 217
  parameter, 191
poker, 272
Polish expression evaluator, 295
Polish (parenthesis-free) notation, 293
pop ( ), 292
portable, 2, 239, 253
positional notation, 89
postfix operator, 93
postorder ( ), 298
precedence, 73
precision, 80, 311
prefix operator, 93
preorder ( ), 298
preprocessor, 11, 238
preprocessor control lines, 238
pretty print, 341
prime number, 124
prime, Sieve of Eratosthenes, 278
printf ( ), 7, 14, 309
  control string / argument list, 309
  conversion characters, 310
  field, 311
  field width, 311
  precision, 311
  related functions, 317
printing a table of contents, 332
print_list ( ), 287
privacy, 153, 155
prn_headings ( ), 335
problem-solving process, 4
production (rewriting rule), 58
prof, 340
programming, 4
prompt, 34, 36
protection mode, 330
pseudo random number generator, 153
push ( ), 293
putc ( ), 319
putchar ( ), 24, 319
puts ( ), 319
pwd, 329

qsort ( ), 244
quicksort ( ), 229

ragged arrays, 216
rand ( ), 48, 233

random ( ), 48, 153, 155
random number generator, 47
range, 80
rank_order ( ), 233
read ( ), 328
read mode, 44
real number, 8
recursion, 225
redirection, 21, 28, 331, 332
redirection and piping in UNIX, 331
register, 149
relational expressions, 101
reserved word (keyword), 9, 61
return statement, 138
reverse ( ), 227, 293
rewind ( ), 320
rewriting rule (production), 58
Richards, Martin, 1
Riemann sum, 248
rindex ( ), 206
Ritchie, Dennis, 1
root ( ), 236
run-time, 6, 53

%s, 15, 310, 315
scalar dot_product ( ), 254
scanf ( ), 14, 16, 314
  assignment suppression, 315
  control string / argument list, 314
  conversion characters, 315
  related functions, 317
  special string, 315
scope, 147
sentinel, 37, 203
separator, 61
SET ( ), 333
short, 67
shuffle ( ), 273
side effect, 76, 152, 192
sign extension, 87
significant figures, 80
sin ( ), 64
sizeof, 78
sorting, 35
  bubble sort, 35, 199, 214
  efficiency, 50, 199, 203
  heapsort, 308
  internal, 229
  mergesort, 201
  quicksort, 229

sprintf(), 317
sqrt(), 64
sscanf(), 317
stack operations, 291
standard library, 7, 205, 318, 328
statement
   assignment, 9
   break, 51, 163
   compound, 18, 108
   continue, 163
   do, 120
   empty, 109
   for, 17, 116
   goto, 162
   if, 17, 109
   if-else, 17, 111
   labeled, 162
   return, 32, 138
   switch, 165
   while, 17, 114
static, 149
stdio.h, 25
storage allocation, dynamic, 282, 290, 302
storage allocation for unions, 268
storage class, 149
   auto, 149
   extern, 149, 150
   register, 149, 152
   static, 149, 153
   static external, 154
storage mapping function, 210, 211
strcat(), 206, 207, 329
strcmp(), 205
strcpy(), 39, 206, 329
string, 35, 203
   array of character, 203
   constant, 7, 203
   end-of-string character \0, 37, 203
   initialization, 204, 217
   palindrome, 221
   standard functions, 205
%[*string*], 315
string_to_list(), 284
strlen(), 205, 206
strncat(), 206
strncmp(), 205
strncpy(), 206
struct, 253
structure, 255
   assignment, 261

structure (cont.)
   declaration, 256
   initialization, 272
   member, 255
   member assignment, 255
   member operator, 255
   pointer access, 260
   pointer operator ->, 258
   self-referential, 280
   syntax, 256
stty cbreak, 25
subscript, 33
switch statement, 165
syntactic category, 58
syntactic sugar, 240
syntactic symbol, 59
syntax, 58
syntax error, 5, 129
sys_info(), 329
system(), 320, 329

tab character \t, 83, 95
tables and lists
   constants of type char and their values, 83, 84
   constants of various types, 88
   conversion character, 15, 16
   conversion in arithmetic expressions, 86, 87
   decimal binary hexadecimal and octal numbers, 91
   expression evaluation, 74, 77, 86, 101, 104, 106, 107, 120, 126, 128, 167, 168, 169, 170, 171, 190, 207, 208, 224, 259
   file modes, 44
   functions in the standard library, 318
   fundamental data types, 67
   hexadecimal digits, 90
   hexadecimal numbers and their decimal conversion, 90
   illegal pointer constructs, 191
   keywords, 61
   operator precedence and associativity: a final look, 262
   operator semantics, 101, 103, 105, 107, 169
   operators, 85, 99, 167
   precedence and associativity, 73, 100, 168, 262

tables and lists (cont.)
  printf() conversion characters, 310
  printf() fields, 312, 313, 314
  production symbols, 59
  scanf() conversion characters, 315
  string handling functions, 205
  switch semantics, 166
  useful options to the cc command, 338
tan(), 64
text editor, 5
Thompson, Ken, 1
time, 158
toascii(), 323
token, 56
tolower(), 323
top down, 136
toupper(), 323
tree, 296
  binary, 296
  creation, 298
  general, 300
  leaf, 296
  level, 308
  root, 296
  subtree, 296
  traversal, 297
troff, 332
true, 18, 100, 239
truth table, 133
twin prime, 135
two-dimensional arrays, 210
two's complement, 167, 168
type enum, 174
type int, 70
type specifier, 138
typedef, 253

%u, 310, 315
#undef, 242
underscore _, 60
ungetc(), 319, 324
union, 253, 268
UNIX, 1, 5, 309, 327
UNIX command
  a.out, 5
  cat, 340
  cb, 341
  cc, 5, 337

UNIX command (cont.)
  crypt, 222
  date, 329, 332
  echo, 215, 223
  lint, 5, 340
  make, 33, 342
  mv, 6
  prof, 340
  pwd, 329
  stty cbreak, 25
  time, 158
  troff, 332
  vi, 5
  wc, 332
  whoami, 329
UNIX command interpreter, 320
UNIX command redirection <, 21, 331
UNIX flags, 223, 243, 338, 341
UNIX redirection and piping, 331
UNIX software tool philosophy, 332
unlink(), 320
unpack, 172
unsigned, 67

variable, 8, 70
VAX, 71, 77, 78, 80, 94, 152, 170, 173,
    197, 227, 270, 279, 313
vi, 5
void, 144

Warnsdorf's rule, 251, 252
wc, 332
while statement, 17, 114
white space, 57
whoami, 329
word, 71
worst case, 22
write(), 328
write mode, 44

%x format, 310

you_won(), 181

zero, 1, 100, 344